Ohio's Criminal Justice System

Carolina Academic Press

State-Specific Criminal Justice Series

Arkansas's Criminal Justice System
Edward Powers and Janet K. Wilson

California's Criminal Justice System
Second Edition
Christine L. Gardiner and Pamela Fiber-Ostrow, eds.

Florida's Criminal Justice System
William G. Doerner

Georgia's Criminal Justice System
Deborah Mitchell Robinson

Illinois's Criminal Justice System
Jill Joline Myers and Todd Lough, eds.

Missouri's Criminal Justice System
Frances P. Reddington, ed.

North Carolina's Criminal Justice System
Second Edition
Paul E. Knepper and Mark Jones

Ohio's Criminal Justice System
Joshua B. Hill, Nancy E. Marion, Kevin M. Cashen,
R. James Orr, III, and Kendra J. Kec

Pennsylvania's Criminal Justice System
Mary P. Brewster and Harry R. Dammer, eds.

West Virginia's Criminal Justice System
Kimberly A. DeTardo-Bora, Dhruba J. Bora, and Samuel L. Dameron

Ohio's Criminal Justice System

Joshua B. Hill

Nancy E. Marion

Kevin M. Cashen

R. James Orr, III

Kendra J. Kec

CAROLINA ACADEMIC PRESS

Durham, North Carolina

Library of Congress Cataloging-in-Publication Data

Hill, Joshua B.
  Ohio's criminal justice system / by Joshua Hill, Nancy E. Marion, Kevin
Cashen, Robert Orr, Kendra Kec.
      pages cm. -- (State-specific criminal justice series)
  Includes bibliographical references and index.
  ISBN 978-1-61163-450-1 (alk. paper)
  1. Criminal justice, Administration of--Ohio. 2. Law enforcement--Ohio. I.
Title.

  HV9955.O3H55 2015
  364.9771--dc23

                            2015000198

                  CAROLINA ACADEMIC PRESS
                          700 Kent Street
                 Durham, North Carolina 27701
                   Telephone (919) 489-7486
                      Fax (919) 493-5668
                      www.cap-press.com

Printed in Canada

Contents

Series Note

Carolina Academic Press' state-specific criminal justice series fills a gap in the field of criminal justice education. One drawback with many current introduction to criminal justice texts is that they pertain to the essentially non-existent "American" criminal justice system and ignore the local landscape. Each state has its unique legislature, executive branch, law enforcement system, court and appellate review system, state supreme court, correctional system, and juvenile justice apparatus. Since many criminal justice students embark upon careers in their home states, they are better served by being exposed to their own states' criminal justice systems. Texts in this series are designed to be used as primary texts or as supplements to more general introductory criminal justice texts.

Ohio's Criminal Justice System

Chapter 1

Introduction and Ohio's Place in the Nation

Learning Objectives

After reading this chapter, students will be able to:

- Describe why a state-level approach is important.
- Outline the basic role of the U.S. Constitution on the state level.
- Describe the federalization of law enforcement.
- Understand the complexity of the justice system.
- Outline the history of the criminal justice system in Ohio.
- Name and explain major court cases originating from Ohio.
- Explain the significance of the Governor, legislature, and interest groups in state-level criminal justice development.

Introduction

This book, *Ohio's Criminal Justice System*, is being produced as part of the state-specific criminal justice series published by Carolina Academic Press. As such, it has a unique focus among criminal justice textbooks. Rather than examining the theoretical criminal justice system presented in most introductory books, this book focuses on the actual crime in and criminal justice system of the state of Ohio. This not only provides concrete elements to apply the theoretical system to, but it can also serve as a way for the material to hit closer to home, so to speak.

As most undergraduate criminal justice programs present the introductory material in the same fashion (usually crime, police, courts, and corrections), this book holds to that same pattern, but rather than simply presenting the abstract elements that are normally focused upon, it presents them as they play out within the state of Ohio. This emphasis on application also means that there are a number of specific elements somewhat unique to Ohio that are covered. Of particular interest to many students will be the discussion of the death penalty in the state as well as the elements pertaining to juvenile justice which make Ohio's system different from other states.

This book also attempts to contextualize Ohio's criminal justice system by frequent comparisons to other states. This is meant to allow the reader to understand not just how the system operates in one state's context, but to allow for broader understanding of *why* the system in Ohio operates as it does. Through understanding where Ohio stands in each of its criminal justice elements, it is possible for the reader to examine questions of how the criminal justice system in Ohio can improve over time.

Each chapter, therefore, provides comparisons of the system that has developed in Ohio with the larger criminal justice system in the United States. Unsurprisingly, there are significant differences in the specific application of the general principals usually taught in the context of introductory criminal justice textbooks.

In short, the book attempts, like the others in this series, to fill an important gap. It addresses a state-specific criminal justice system to allow for application of the theoretical models presented of the "American system" in introductory criminal justice classes. Through comparisons to other states, the direct explanation of unique elements in Ohio's criminal justice system, and by providing a complete context in which to understand it, this book will hopefully provide the real-world context for introductory criminal justice courses.

Why the State Level?

Though federal crime control policy receives extensive media attention, the vast majority of both legislation and executive action take place at the state or local levels of government (Marion and Oliver, 2011). Unsurprisingly, the amount of state-level action to combat crime, or treat related issues like drug addiction, also far exceed the amount of programs provided by the federal government. Yet most people remain unaware of this fact, and tend to focus their attention on the most visible parts of government—the President and Congress (Lyons and Scheingold, 2000). Therefore, any analysis of the criminal justice system should first start with the state level.

Though often overlooked, the fact is that most crimes are violations of state law, rather than federal law (Federal Judicial Center, 2014). The Constitution of the United States enumerates the powers at the federal level, but anything not directly addressed by the text of the Constitution (or incorporated by the

Federal Courts), is "reserved" for the states—meaning they address the rules at their level. Crime control is not an enumerated power, and therefore states are free to make their own laws (within the confines of the Constitution) regarding crime and its control (Marion and Oliver, 2011).

This fact, that the states can make their own crime policy, though seemingly straightforward, is more difficult in application. There is a great deal of complexity even at the state level, as politics frequently play into elements like budgeting. The constitutional issues themselves are not simple. In addition to the enumerated and reserved powers, there are also concurrent powers, or those areas over which states and the federal government have joint control. One example of this is the court system, wherein there is correspondence between the federal level and state level, and sometimes cases move from one into the other. Moreover, since the 1960s the federal government has been more active in crime control policy, and has used the Constitution's "elastic clause" (which allows Congress to "make all laws which shall be necessary and proper") to justify this expansion, in an act which some have termed the "federalization of crime" (Oliver, 2003).

Despite this expansion however, the majority of crime is still defined within the state and addressed by state and local agencies, though there has been increasing reliance on the federal government for funds, especially as Homeland Security has become more important (Oliver, Marion, and Hill, 2014). The full impact of these changes have yet to be felt, but there is reason to believe that the criminal justice system in Ohio, as well as in other states, is becoming increasingly complex. Much of this complexity will be clear in the chapters examining Law Enforcement in Ohio and the Court System in Ohio, as these are the areas which have become increasingly influenced by federal-level policies and funding issues.

Politics and Criminal Justice

While people generally like to think of the criminal justice process as a strict following of a given set of rules resulting in a just outcome, the reality is that the process is largely political. This stems from the fact that at each stage of the process there are politics at play. For instance, the development of criminal justice policies are (usually) based around legislative agendas, rather than solid research (Marion and Oliver, 2011). Budgets too, are often political, with debates about emphasis on treatment and rehabilitation pitted against those who take a more retributive approach to criminal justice.

This politization does not stop at policy development, however, as politics plays a clear role in the election of a variety of criminal justice system agents, like Sheriffs, prosecutors, and judges. The fact that these individuals have to run for office, most affiliated with a specific party, means that politics has a significant impact on the development and implementation of all aspects of the criminal justice system in Ohio. This section examines the impact of two political elements on the criminal justice system in Ohio. The first is the Governor's office, which represents the chief executive of Ohio. The second is the legislature, which develops the laws executed by the executive branch of state government.

Ohio Governors and Criminal Justice

As the primary executive authority in the state the Governor has a large impact on executive actions within it, though he (or she) is not the only person with a say in the process (Lamis and Usher, 2007). In terms of the criminal justice process the Governor serves several specific function, all of which can have a profound impact on the way the state handles crime and criminal justice. First, the Governor is responsible for setting the agenda (Unah and Coggins, 2013). In practice, that means the Governor is responsible for shaping the approach to criminal justice issues faced by the state. For instance, he may want to focus on a program combatting narcotics use, or on police reform. One way he can further his agenda is by appealing to the public, using the "power of the bully pulpit."

Another way the Governor can influence the criminal justice process is through the power of appointment (National Governors Association, 2014). By appointing individuals to various boards or commissions, even as heads of executive departments, the Governor can ensure that her agenda is carried forward—at least within the executive branch of state government. Through appointing individuals with a similar ideology or approach, the impact on the criminal justice system can be significant. Moreover, through the creation of new agencies, the Governor can actually develop new areas of criminal justice practice within the state.

Another power the Governor can use that has a direct relation to the criminal justice process is the power to grant clemency (Associated Press, 2014). The power to pardon is one that is less frequently used today than in the past, and one that has perhaps been abused in prior decades (Kobil, 1991). However, the process is generally well-considered, with recommendations from the Ohio Adult Parole Authority.

Finally, the Governor has the power to influence legislation. He can do this through suggesting potential legislation to the Ohio state legislature, persuading people to support specific policies of the Governor's administration, or through the veto.

Different Governors have had different criminal justice priorities, with many focusing on law enforcement and corrections, and more recently, on Homeland Security. As new Governors are elected, these priorities will continue to change, directly and indirectly influencing the way the criminal justice system in Ohio works. However, as important to the system as the Governor is, they are not the only actors with the ability to influence criminal justice policy and practice. In the next section, the other major state-level actor is dealt with— the legislature.

Ohio Legislature

While the Governor is responsible for signing bills into law and execution of the laws passed, the laws themselves are developed by the Ohio General Assembly. This group, comprised of the Ohio House of Representatives and the Ohio Senate, are responsible for creating new criminal offenses, changing prior legislation to reflect changing interests, or adjusting punishments. There are ninety-nine members of the House and thirty-three members of the Senate (Ohio State Legislature, 2014).

While the Ohio State Constitution incorporates the General Assembly, the House and the Senate each create their own operational rules and choose their own leadership. As part of these developments, committees have been established in both parts of the Legislature. These committees were developed to assist the General Assembly with its large workflow. Specifically, committees, and their attendant subcommittees, are responsible for most of the writing and editing of bills.

There are three primary types of committees. The first, a standing committee, is a committee that has a permanent presence in the legislature. The second type is an ad hoc committee, which are formed to look at a specific bill on a non-permanent basis. Finally, there is a joint committee, to which both members of the House and Senate belong. There are also other types of committees, such as select committees, which are created to look at a specific issue or complete a specific task. Among the committees established include two House standing committees that are specifically relevant to the operation of the criminal justice system, and two Senate standing committees.

The two House standing committees that are responsible for examining issues dealing with criminal justice are the House Committee on the Judiciary, and the House Committee on Transportation, Public Safety and Homeland

Security. There are other committees that have more or less indirect impacts on the criminal justice system as well. In particular, committees controlling financial elements can have a large impact on how well the system is able to operate. Committees like Ways and Means and the Finance and Appropriations Committee are very important to the entire legislative process—criminal justice notwithstanding.

The Senate, like the House, has two important criminal justice related committees. The Senate Committee on Criminal Justice primarily focuses on policies and issues that directly impact criminal law. The other major Senate committee that has jurisdiction over criminal justice activities, is the Senate Committee on Public Safety, Local Government, and Veterans Affairs, though like the House, there are several Senate committees that have an indirect impact through budgeting, etc.

In fiscal year 2014, Ohio's legislature appropriated over $1.5 billion in justice and public protection dollars. It comprised over 5% of Ohio's budget at the state level (see Figure 1.1 for complete amounts). This is just short of the amount spent on higher education in Ohio, and though the amount has decreased slightly in recent years, criminal justice remains one of more expensive elements at the state level.

Interest Groups

Though legislators themselves are responsible for making the laws that the Governor signs, many individuals and organizations have input into those bills. Those who are seeking to influence the legislative process from outside are known as interest groups (Marion and Oliver, 2011). These groups usually have a specific agenda or constituency whose views they are trying to protect through the formation of laws. Criminal justice legislation is no different than any other legislation in this regard. For instance, one of the major interest groups in Ohio regarding criminal justice issues are crime victims, represented by organizations like the Ohio Alliance to End Sexual Violence (OAESV), the Ohio Domestic Violence Network (ODVN), and Parents of Murdered Children. These groups have an obvious interest in influencing the legislative process in order to further their organization's goals.

Victims are not, however, the only people who comprise interest groups. One of the most important, though infrequently mentioned, interest groups in Ohio are law enforcement officers (Sheldon, 2011). Prior to the 1980s law enforcement employees in Ohio were prohibited from collective bargaining. Thanks to the work of interest groups like the Fraternal Order of Police of

Figure 1.1: Ohio FY 2014–2015 Budget

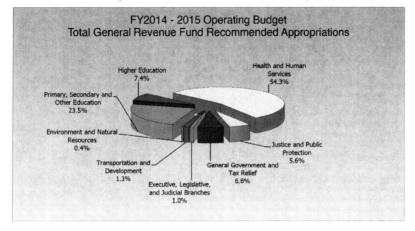

GRF Appropriations (dollars in millions)

Function	FY 2013 Estimate	FY 2014	% Change	FY 2015	% Change
Primary, Secondary and Other Education	$ 6,923.0	$ 7,320.0	5.7%	$ 7,540.4	3.0%
Higher Education	$ 2,308.0	$ 2,323.0	0.6%	$ 2,376.1	2.3%
Health and Human Services	$ 13,912.3	$ 16,293.5	17.1%	$ 18,013.0	10.6%
Justice and Public Protection	$ 1,732.7	$ 1,760.2	1.6%	$ 1,753.9	-0.4%
General Government and Other	$ 1,998.2	$ 2,049.3	2.6%	$ 2,123.5	3.6%
Executive, Legislative, and Judicial Branches	$ 301.9	$ 308.8	2.3%	$ 311.0	0.7%
Transportation and Development	$ 381.5	$ 400.8	5.1%	$ 423.9	5.8%
Environment and Natural Resources	$ 97.9	$ 116.6	19.1%	$ 120.1	2.9%
Total	$ 27,655.6	$ 30,572.2	10.5%	$ 32,662.0	6.8%

Note: Numbers may not add to total due to rounding
Source: Ohio Office of Budget and Management, February 2013

Ohio and other law enforcement interest groups, Ohio law provided for the unionization of sworn officers and the ability to engage in collective bargaining beginning in the 1980s. Today, most law enforcement officers in Ohio belong to a union, pay a fair share fee, and are covered by a collective bargaining agreement. Collective bargaining has had a significant impact regarding the conditions of employment for both the officer and the employer. Under collective bargaining the union may negotiate all matters pertaining to wages, hours, or terms and other conditions of employment and the continuation, modification, or deletion of an existing provision of a collective bargaining agreement (48 Ohio Rev. Code 2014).

The legislative process in Ohio is similar to that in many other states. However, because each state has developed in unique ways, understanding the process in Ohio is key to understanding how policies have developed in the state. Additionally, without knowing how laws are made, policies developed, and budgets created, it is difficult to anticipate what will happen in the coming years in the context of the criminal justice system.

Ohio's National Impact on Law Enforcement Criminal Procedure

While the primary focus of this book is how the system of criminal justice in the United States interacts with Ohio's criminal justice system, it is worth noting that Ohio has had a significant impact on several elements in American system of criminal justice. In areas as diverse as death penalty administration to police training, Ohio has been at the forefront of criminal justice. One area in which Ohio has had a particularly strong impact on the overall system is through U.S. Supreme Court cases originating from the state.

Ohio's criminal justice system has contributed several significant elements through U.S. Supreme Court landmark decisions regarding criminal procedure and the U.S. Constitution. In particular, there are three famous cases that still have an important impact. These are *Mapp v. Ohio* (1961), *Terry v. Ohio* (1968), and *Ohio v. Robinette* (1996).

Mapp v. Ohio (1961) was a search and seizure case testing the limits of the Fourth Amendment to the U.S. Constitution. Officers of the Cleveland, Ohio Police Department suspected Dollree Mapp of "hiding a person in her home who was wanted for questioning in connection of a recent bombing, and there was a large amount of gambling paraphernalia being hidden in the home" (*Mapp v. Ohio*, 1961). Three Cleveland police officers knocked on Mapp's door and demanded entrance. Mapp, after calling her lawyer, refused to let them in without a search warrant (Samaha, 2015, p. 386). The case continued,

> The officers again sought entrance some three hours later when four or more additional officers arrived on the scene. When Miss Mapp did not come to the door immediately, at least one of the several doors to the house was forcibly opened. (A police officer testified that 'we did pry the screen door to gain entrance'; the attorney on the scene testified that a policeman 'tried to kick in the door' and then 'broke the glass in the door and somebody reached in and opened the door and let them in'; the appellant testified that 'The back door was broken.')
> Meanwhile Miss Mapp's attorney arrived, but the officers, having secured their own entry, and continuing in their defiance of the law, would permit him neither to see Miss Mapp nor to enter the house. It appears that Miss Mapp was halfway down the stairs from the upper

floor to the front door when the officers, in this high-handed manner, broke into the hall. She demanded to see the search warrant. A paper, claimed to be a warrant, was held up by one of the officers. She grabbed the "warrant" and placed it in her bosom. A struggle ensued in which the officers recovered the piece of paper and as a result of which they handcuffed appellant because she had been "belligerent" in resisting their official rescue of the "warrant" from her person.

Running roughshod over Mapp, a policeman "grabbed" her, "twisted (her) hand," and she "yelled (and) pleaded with him" because "it was hurting." Mapp, in handcuffs, was then forcibly taken upstairs to her bedroom where the officers searched a dresser, a chest of drawers, a closet, and some suitcases. They also looked into a photo album and through personal papers belonging to Mapp. The search spread to the rest of the second floor including the child's bedroom, the living room, the kitchen, and a dinette. The basement of the building and a trunk found were also searched. The obscene materials for possession of which she was ultimately convicted were discovered in the course of that widespread search (*Mapp v. Ohio*, 1961, pp. 644–45).

Ignoring an apparent First Amendment issue of freedom of speech (possessing obscene materials), the U.S. Supreme Court declared that "all evidence obtained by searches and seizures in violation of the Constitution is, by [the Fourth Amendment], inadmissible in a state court" (Ibid.). "Mapp had been convicted on the basis of illegally obtained evidence. This was an historic—and controversial—decision. It placed the requirement of excluding illegally obtained evidence from court at all levels of the government" (Oyez Project, 2014).

Terry v. Ohio (1968) is a landmark case involving the Fourth Amendment issue of law enforcement stop and frisk. The court decision provides the current standard for law enforcement officers stopping and frisking citizens based on articulable facts in order to provide safety to the officer and citizens during a reasonable encounter (*Terry v. Ohio*, 1968). Stop-and-frisk law grew out of the practical problems police officers face in preventing and investigating crime on the streets and other public places in our largest cities (Samaha, 2015, p. 106).

John Terry and two other men were observed by a plain clothes policeman in what the officer believed to be "casing a job, a stick-up." The officer stopped and frisked the three men, and found weapons on two of them. Terry was convicted of carrying a concealed weapon and sentenced to three years in jail.

The United States Supreme Court held that the search undertaken by the officer was reasonable under the Fourth Amendment and that the weapons seized could be introduced into evidence against Terry. Attempting to focus narrowly on the facts of this particular case, the Court found that the officer acted on more than a "hunch" and that "a reasonably prudent man would have been warranted in believing [Terry] was armed and thus presented a threat to the officer's safety while he was investigating his suspicious behavior." The Court found that the searches undertaken were limited in scope and designed to protect the officer's safety incident to the investigation (Oyez Project, *Terry v. Ohio*, 2014).

As a result, a Terry stop has become synonymous with an investigative stop— "a short detention that must be justified by an objective manifestation that the person is or is not about to be involved in criminal activity" (Walker & Hemmens, 2011, p. 29).

Ohio v. Robinette (1996) tested the voluntariness of a Fourth Amendment consent search. Robert Robinette was stopped for speeding by a Montgomery County Sheriff's Deputy. The deputy issued a warning "and asked him if he had any illegal contraband, weapons, or drugs in his car. Robinette answered "no" but after agreeing to have his car searched, the officer found some marijuana and a pill that later proved to be a powerful drug" (Oyez Project, *Ohio v. Robinette*, 1996). The United State Supreme Court held that when looking at the totality of the circumstances it may be reasonably concluded that if a defendant consents to be searched, even if not first advised that he is "free to go," the ensuing search will be recognized as voluntary. The Court also added that Robinette's arrest on drug possession charges was lawful, even though the arresting officer did not stop him on an initial suspicion of drug possession nor intend to even issue him a speeding ticket (*Ohio v. Robinette*, 1996).

These cases are still widely cited, and significantly affect the action of the criminal justice system (in particular, the police) today. In particular, *Terry* is one of the most important police procedure cases ever to come before the Supreme Court. It is also established one of the most frequently utilized types of searches by police nation-wide, the so-called "Terry stop."

Summary

While many criminal justice texts focus on the national system of criminal justice, it is clear that the system they describe is largely fictional. The state system, on the other hand, because of the specific context it provides, is essential to understand for those attempting to enter the criminal justice professions, or those who are simply interested in the topic. However, in order to understand the state and local systems in Ohio, it is important to get a complete picture of the context that the system is operating in. To that end, understanding Ohio's economic situation, educational levels, and the development of the criminal justice system within the state are important for a complete understanding.

Moreover, the fact that Ohio has contributed nationally in the development of important criminal justice cases, specifically police procedure, suggests exactly why the context of states is important. Without understanding how the policing (or really any of the elements of the system) system works in Ohio, the understanding of those impacts on the federal system cannot be easily understood.

Key Terms

Ad Hoc Committee
Clemency
Collective Bargaining
Elastic Clause
Enumerated Powers
Federalization of Crime
Joint Committee
Mapp v. Ohio

Reserved Powers
Standing Committee
Terry Stop
Terry v. Ohio
Union
Veto
Ways and Means

Resources

Ohio Alliance to End Sexual Violence
    http://www.oaesv.org/
Ohio Association of Chiefs of Police
    http://www.oacp.org/
Ohio Domestic Violence Network
    http://www.odvn.org/
Ohio Governor's Office
    http://www.governor.ohio.gov/
Ohio State Legislature
    http://www.legislature.state.oh.us/

Review Questions

1. Why is a state-level approach to the study of criminal justice important?
2. How has Ohio impacted police procedure at the national level?
3. How does the U.S. Constitution impact criminal justice on the state level?
4. From what governmental level do most of the court cases and other issues stem?
5. How has state and local law enforcement been "federalized" in recent years.
6. What was the main point of *Mapp v. Ohio*?
7. What is the role of the Governor when it comes to the criminal justice system in Ohio?
8. Who makes criminal law in Ohio, and what parties go into making those laws?

References

48 Ohio Rev. Code §4117.08 (2014), available at http://codes.ohio.gov/orc/4117.

Associated Press. (April 30, 2014). *John Kasich, Ohio Governor, grants clemency to condemned inmate.* Retrieved from http://www.huffingtonpost.com/2014/04/30/arthur-tyler_n_5243126.html.

Federal Judicial Center (2014). What the Federal Courts Do. Retrieved from http://www.fjc.gov/federal/courts.nsf/autoframe!openform&nav=menu1&page=/federal/courts.nsf/page/152.

Kobil, D.T. (1991). Do the paperwork or die: Clemency, Ohio style? *Ohio State Law Journal, 52,* 655.

Lamis, A.P., and Usher, B. (Eds). (2007). *Ohio politics.* Kent, OH: Kent State University Press.

Lyons, W. and Scheingold, S. (2000). *The politics of crime and punishment* in *Criminal Justice 2000: The Nature of Crime: Continuity and Change.* U.S. Department of Justice. Retrieved from http://www.ncjrs.org/criminal_justice2000/vol_1/02c.pdf.

Mapp v. Ohio, 367 U.S. 643 (1961).

Marion, N. and Oliver, W.M. (2011). *Public policy of crime and criminal justice.* Upper Saddle River, NJ: Prentice Hall.

McBride, J.T., and Taddeo, R.J. (2009). *History of law enforcement, Lake County, Ohio.* Brunswick, OH: Crown Custom Publishing.

Mersch, C. (2007). *Cincinnati Police History.* Mount Pleasant, SC: Arcadia.

National Governors Association. (2014). *Governors' powers and authority.* Retrieved from http://www.nga.org/cms/home/management-resources/governors-powers-and-authority.html#appointment.

Ohio State Highway Patrol. (2008). 75 Years of Excellence A History of the Ohio State Highway Patrol 1933–2008. Columbus, OH: Ohio State Highway Patrol.

Ohio State Legislature. (2014). Organizational chart of Ohio's state government. Retrieved from http://www.legislature.state.oh.us/organizational.cfm.

Ohio v. Robinette, 519 U.S. 33 (1996).

Oliver, W.M. (2003). Law and order presidency. Upper Saddle River, NJ: Prentice Hall.

Oliver, W.M., Marion, N.E., and Hill, J.B. (2014). Introduction to homeland security: Policy, organization, and administration. Burlington, MA: Jones and Bartlett.

Oyez Project. (2014). Mapp v. Ohio. Retrieved from http://www.oyez.org/cases/1960-1969/1960/1960_236.

Samaha, J. (2015). Criminal procedure. Boston, MA: Cengage.

Shelden, R.G. (2011). Interest groups and criminal justice policy. Center on Juvenile and Criminal Justice Research Brief. Retrieved from http://www.cjcj.org/uploads/cjcj/documents/interest_groups_and_criminal_justice_policy.pdf

Shough, J.G. (1945). History of the police department, Columbus, Ohio, 1821–1945. Columbus, OH: Heer.

Terry v. Ohio, 392 U.S. 1 (1968).

Unah, I., and Coggins, E. (2013). When governors speak up for justice: Punishment politics and mass incarceration in the American states. Journal of Political Science and Public Affairs, 1, 1–12.

Walker, J.T. and Hemmens, C. (2011). Legal guide for police: Constitutional issues (9th ed.). Cambridge, MA: Elsevier.

Chapter 2

Crime in Ohio

Learning Objectives

After reading this chapter, students will be able to:

- Identify Ohio's place in the nation in regards to criminal behavior.
- Identify and explain crime trends in Ohio.
- Explain the Ohio Criminal Justice Statistics Office.
- Examine the issues surrounding the "dark figure of crime" and explain how it affects official statistics.
- Critique official statistics at both the state and national level.
- Explain the purpose of the Uniform Crime Report and where those statistics come from.
- Explain the National Crime Victimization Survey, and how it relates to criminal justice statistics.
- The importance of drug crime in understanding the overall criminal activity in Ohio.
- Compare the rates of Ohio's crime to the rest of the country.
- Explain factors that may influence criminal activity in Ohio.

Introduction

As in all states, the problem of crime in Ohio has been a difficult one to address. Though generally having relatively low rates of violent crime, Ohio has consistently has higher-than-average rates of property crime. This chapter is an attempt at placing crime in Ohio in a larger context, that of crime in the United States. The goal is to provide the reader with both an understanding of the "crime picture" in Ohio as well as some warnings and suggestions about how to interpret crime data in general. Throughout the chapter, there are tables and figures to help the reader understand where Ohio fits in with the overall

Table 2.1: Characteristics of UCR and NCVS Compared

UCR	NCVS
Based on police records	Based on victimization survey
Uses index crimes as primary measure	Covers a wide range of incidents
Voluntary reports from 18,000 police agencies	Nationally representative survey of households
Run continuously since 1929	Run continuously since 1973

Source: FBI's Crime in the United States, 2004

crime rates in the United States, as well as definitions to assist in understanding exactly what crimes fall into different categories.

Much of the data that we use to talk about crime comes from two primary sources, the Uniform Crime Report (UCR), produced by the Federal Bureau of Investigation (FBI), and the National Crime Victimization Survey (NCVS). Though they measure different parts of the overall crime picture, the two work together to help us understand what crime looks like in any given state as well as the country as a whole (Federal Bureau of Investigation, 2014). More complete information about the UCR and NCVS are given in Table 2.1, below.

A Cautionary Note

One of the interesting issues with the study of crime and criminal justice is the problematic nature of crime data. The UCR relies on the collection of records based on felony incidents reported to the police. This seems like a good measurement at first blush, but when one considers the number of steps required before a report is ready to be sent to the FBI, it is easy to see where there are pitfalls. The steps in reporting are as follows:

- Discovery of crime
- Call to the authorities
- Dispatch
- Report filed
- Report Sent to FBI

At each of these points, the process can be broken and the crime may never make it to the UCR. This lack of complete information is usually referred to as "the dark figure of crime" (Skogan, 1977). It suggests that there is more crime happening than actually gets reported in official statistics like the UCR.

In fact, the NCVS was developed, in part, to help estimate the dark figure of crime, and help with calculating a more accurate rate of crime by understanding rates of victimization (Bureau of Justice Statistics, 2014).

In addition to the lack of reporting, there are also issues with the crimes that are not counted in the UCR. For instance, until 2012, according to the UCR's definition of forcible rape (discussed more below), only women could be raped (Federal Bureau of Investigation, 2012). This has thereby under-counted rapes in general, and eliminated an entire category of people (men) from being counted as victims. Fortunately, the NCVS, because of its survey approach, attempts to correct for this problem by including a broader defini-tion of sexual assault.

Importantly, the statistics generally used from the UCR are from what are termed "index crimes," or serious crimes, though the UCR does have addi-tional data on less serious crimes as well. A complete list of index crimes is found in Table 2.2, below.

Complicating the data issues further, the UCR uses what is called the "hi-erarchy rule." That is, only the crime at the highest level (e.g., murder vs. rob-bery) is counted in the report (Federal Bureau of Investigation, 2004). This means that a case where someone is robbed, then shot, is counted as a single incident in the UCR, with the event represented as a homicide (or aggravated assault) rather than a robbery. This contributes to the problem of under-counting crime across the United States, and Ohio is no different, though with the development and use of the National Incident Based Reporting System (NIBRS), described in Figure 2.1, it is hoped that many of these problems will be addressed.

Figure 2.1: NIBRS

National Incident Based Reporting System (NIBRS)
NIBRS is the FBI's response to law enforcement's need for additional, usable data. While originally piloted in 1987, NIBRS has been slow to develop more completely, in part because of the resource limitations frequent in criminal justice endeavours. NIBRS, as of 2012, collections information from about 6,115 agencies, or about a third of agencies who report to the UCR.
NIBRS differentiates itself from the UCR primarily because of the depth of informa-tion captured by the system. Rather than only incident data, NIBRS captures the race, age, and sex of victims and arrestees, as well as information on the location, time of day and types of weapons/force involved in the incident. Moreover, NIBRS features additional categories and crime types.

Source: National Incident Based Reporting System (FBI)

Table 2.2: Index Crimes

Offense	Definition
Criminal Homicide	a.) Murder and nonnegligent manslaughter: the willful (nonnegligent) killing of one human being by another. Deaths caused by negligence, attempts to kill, assaults to kill, suicides, and accidental deaths are excluded. The program classifies justifiable homicides separately and limits the definition to: (1) the killing of a felon by a law enforcement officer in the line of duty; or (2) the killing of a felon, during the commission of a felony, by a private citizen. b.) Manslaughter by negligence: the killing of another person through gross negligence. Deaths of persons due to their own negligence, accidental deaths not resulting from gross negligence, and traffic fatalities are not included in the category Manslaughter by Negligence.
Forcible Rape	Penetration, no matter how slight, of the vagina or anus with any body part or object, or oral penetration by a sex organ of another person, without the consent of the victim. (New definition, with data reflecting the change beginning in 2013)
Robbery	The taking or attempting to take anything of value from the care, custody, or control of a person or persons by force or threat of force or violence and/or by putting the victim in fear.
Aggravated Assault	An unlawful attack by one person upon another for the purpose of inflicting severe or aggravated bodily injury. This type of assault usually is accompanied by the use of a weapon or by means likely to produce death or great bodily harm. Simple assaults are excluded.
Burglary	The unlawful entry of a structure to commit a felony or a theft. Attempted forcible entry is included.
Larceny-theft	The unlawful taking, carrying, leading, or riding away of property from the possession or constructive possession of another. Examples are thefts of bicycles, motor vehicle parts and accessories, shoplifting, pocketpicking, or the stealing of any property or article that is not taken by force and violence or by fraud. Attempted larcenies are included. Embezzlement, confidence games, forgery, check fraud, etc., are excluded.
Motor Vehicle Theft	The theft or attempted theft of a motor vehicle. A motor vehicle is self-propelled and runs on land surface and not on rails. Motorboats, construction equipment, airplanes, and farming equipment are specifically excluded from this category.
Arson	Any willful or malicious burning or attempt to burn, with or without intent to defraud, a dwelling house, public building, motor vehicle or aircraft, personal property of another, etc. Arson statistics are not included in this table-building tool.

Source: Uniform Crime Report

Though NIBRS offers a solution to many of the issues related to the UCR, the delay in its adoption, coupled with its voluntary nature, have made it less widely used. In the future, with its increasing adoption by police agencies around the U.S., it will prove to be a significant improvement on our current data collection.

Triangulation and Context

In order to accurately assess crime in Ohio, or anywhere for that matter, it is therefore essential that multiple sources be used. Both the NCVS and the UCR have strengths and weaknesses, but by using them together, one can gain a reasonably good idea of what crime looks like throughout the U.S. One of the facts that is revealed through triangulation of the two datasets is that crime has dropped dramatically since the mid 1990s, nationwide (Blumstein and Wallman, 2005). Ohio is no different, with overall rates of crime falling in that period from all-time highs to lower and more consistent levels. In the sections below, a snapshot of the most recent data available for Ohio's crime rates are given. It relies primarily on UCR data, as NCVS data cannot be generalized down to the state level because of their sampling methodology. This snapshot is useful when considering the role of the criminal justice system in Ohio, and where Ohio stands in comparison to the rest of the nation.

Ohio's Crime Problem

Violent Crime and Murder

While states like Tennessee, Florida, and California tend to have very high rates of both violent and property crimes, Ohio remained below the national average for violent crime. There were 435 murders recorded in 2012, with the three largest cities in Ohio, Cincinnati, Cleveland, and Columbus, accounting for 51% of the homicides. The state ranked 27th in terms of the homicide rate in 2012.[1] A comparison between Ohio's and the national average of homicide can be seen below, in Figure 2.2.

---

1. One has to be careful when ranking states in terms of crime. Because states are quite different in terms of population make-up and density, a ranking hides some significant factors when looking at crimes between states. Rankings are only as useful as the person making them is careful. Here the raking is used just to give overall context.

Figure 2.2: Homicides in the U.S. and Ohio, 1979–2012

Along with the category of "homicide and non-negligent manslaughter" (what we normally think of as murder), the Uniform Crime Report (UCR) includes three other crimes under the rubric of violent crime: forcible rape, robbery, and aggravated assault. These are explored in the sections below.

Forcible Rape

In terms of forcible rape, while Ohio has seen a decline in the past 5 years to approximately 3,658, it still remains higher than the national average, with 32 per 100,000 population (Ohio Bureau of Public Safety, 2013; Federal Bureau of Investigation, 2013). As sexual crimes are among the most inconsistently reported crimes to the police, it is unclear how accurate these counts are, at least according to the UCR (Bachman, 1998).

The NCVS takes a different approach to measuring rape, specifically asking respondents for their victimization information rather than relying on police reports. An additional, and important, difference between the UCR's measure of forcible rape and the NCVS's is that crimes against men have been included in the NCVS for a longer period of time. Those reports had been excluded from the UCR based on their definition of forcible rape. Because the NCVS uses a nationally representative sample, rather than complete reports, a specific report on the sexual assaults in Ohio is not possible to compile. However, in Figure 2.3, below, a general comparison at the national level between the UCR and NCVS, in terms of sexual assault, is provided.

Another important thing to keep in mind when examining rape data is that an increase in reporting is not necessarily a bad thing. While it appears as if rape has gone up, it may be that more women are willing to report the crime than

Figure 2.3: Comparison between NCVS and UCR on rape

	2004	2012
—●— NCVS Overall Number	134,860	170,400
⋯◈⋯ UCR Overall Number	95,089	84,376

Year

Source: Crime in America, 2013; NCVS Criminal Victimization, 2013

have been in the past. While this tends to make numbers appear inflated, and seemingly points to an increase in crime, it may actual be a sign that the American society is taking rape as a crime much more seriously.

Robbery

The last crime categorized as violent by the UCR is robbery. While often conflated with the non-violent crime of burglary, robbery involves the force, or threat of force or violence, or the use of fear to gain property. Ohio's rate of robbery, though the lowest in a decade, is still above the national average with 132 per 100,000 population as of 2012 (Federal Bureau of Investigation, 2013). Robberies were most often committed with a firearm, though other weapons were frequently used. They were most often committed on the street.

Property Crime

The story of property crime in Ohio is quite different from violent crime, with Ohio exceeding the national average in 2010. Though larceny-theft has decreased over the past 10 years, Ohio has remained consistently above the national average according to the Uniform Crime Report. In fact, though the overall property crime rate of the United States is down, particularly since the mid-1990s, Ohio's property crime rate has remained fairly consistent for the past 10 years, each year remaining above the nation's average of property crime.

Burglary

Burglary is one of the few crimes that has seen an increase in recent years. As of 2010, the burglary rate was nearly 1,000 per 100,000 in population (112,000 in total). This is higher than the national average. Most of these burglaries occurred during the day in residential locations, or at night in commercial locations. The estimated loss in property from burglary in 2009 alone was $101 million.

Larceny-Theft

Larceny-theft, which includes a variety of types of crime, has decreased in recent years, though the most current rates put the amount at 2,052 thefts per 100,000 in population. This is, again, higher than the national average. Larceny cost the state over $150 million in 2009.

Motor Vehicle Theft

Motor vehicle theft is the least common of the property crimes captured by the UCR (other than Arson). In this category, there were a total of 19,512 reported vehicle thefts in Ohio in 2012, and the rate is 169 per 100,000 population as of 2012, the most current data available. Of the vehicles stolen in the U.S. in 2010 (data for Ohio is not available), 73% were automobiles, 17% were larger vehicles such as trucks, and other vehicles accounted for 11% of the total number of vehicles stolen.

Summary

Overall, the current crime rate in Ohio places the state squarely in the middle of the pack in comparison to the rest of the country. While the rates of violent crime are generally lower, as of 2011, than the rest of the U.S., the rates of property crime are generally higher. This is driven by relatively high numbers of burglaries and larceny-thefts. The low rates of violent crime comport with historical data, that suggests that Ohio is simply not that violent—at least in terms of the crimes that the UCR tracks.

Crime Trends

Through the cross-sectional (a more formal name for the snapshots in time given above) approach to crime data taken above is useful for understanding how much crime is being committed at a certain point it time, it is also use-

Figure 2.4: Crime Drop in the U.S.

Reason	
Mass Incarceration	One theory is that as we put more people into prisons who commit crime, there are simply fewer crime-prone individuals to engage in criminal activity.
Social Programs	Social programs may provide enough support to re-entering offenders, offenders with drug problems or other issues that we are seeing an impact in overall crime.
Welfare	The amount of mean-tested welfare has increased dramatically over the past 30 years, it may be that we've reached a point where the relative amount of welfare is sufficient to prevent some kinds of crime.
Policing	Policing has become more pro-active and community-centered, which may help contribute to a decline in the crime rate.
Demographics	America is getting older. With nearly half the population 50 years old or older, it's possible that because older people commit fewer crimes, we are simply seeing the results of the aging population.
Lead	Lead is known to contribute to several factors associated with criminal activity. With lead standards put in place in the mid to late 1970s we would expect those coming of age in the mid 1990s to commit less crime because of the smaller amount of lead.

ful to examine crime trends, or rates of crime over time. This can give one a much better understanding of how crime is progressing, or regressing, in an area. Additionally, it can assist in pointing towards other elements, like employment, education, or health that may be having a significant impact on crime and criminal behavior. In the sections below, crime trends for the state of Ohio are examined and compared to the overall state of crime in the United States.

One thing to keep in mind is that the United States as a whole, and Ohio is no exception, has experienced a dramatic decline in nearly all forms of crime since the early 1990s. Why this has happened is not totally clear, though many theories have been advanced including those seen in Figure 2.4, above.

The fact that crime has declined in the past three decades does not mean that it is not still a significant problem. In particular, though the rates are low for this half the decade, they remain at a high level, when considering the low levels of crime in the early part of the 20th century. While this is no doubt attributable, in part, to better reporting, there remains the question of whether the crime rate has found a new, relatively stable level, or whether crimes may increase again.

Violent Crime Trends

When examining violent crime in the context of crime trends, Ohio follows the general pattern of the U.S. in regards to violent crimes. As is easily seen in Figure 2.5, violent crime increased dramatically during the 1970s, through the 1980s, and began to drop in the early 1990s. However, in the mid 2000s, Ohio's violent crime rate rose slightly, and though down some, has remained relatively stable over the course of the decade.

Figure 2.5: Violent Crime in the U.S. and Ohio, 1960–2010

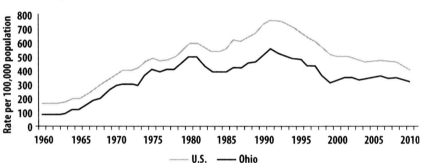

Retrieved from http://www.publicsafety.ohio.gov/links/ocjs_Statistics.pdf.

When the violent crime rate is broken into its constituent parts within the state of Ohio, seen in Figure 2.6, it is easy to see that much of this drop has been in aggravated assaults. Robberies, on the other hand, have seen a recent resurgence, particularly in the past 10 years, though it has fallen to a recent low as of 2012. This fluctuation is not really reflected in either murder or forcible rape, both of which have remained relatively constant over the past 30 years in terms of raw numbers, though the rates have tended to fluctuate over time, particularly in terms of rape.

Property Crime Trends

As seen in Figure 2.6, property crime in the U.S., and Ohio, has followed the same trajectory as crime in general. There was a steep increase in property

Figure 2.6: Violent Crime in Ohio

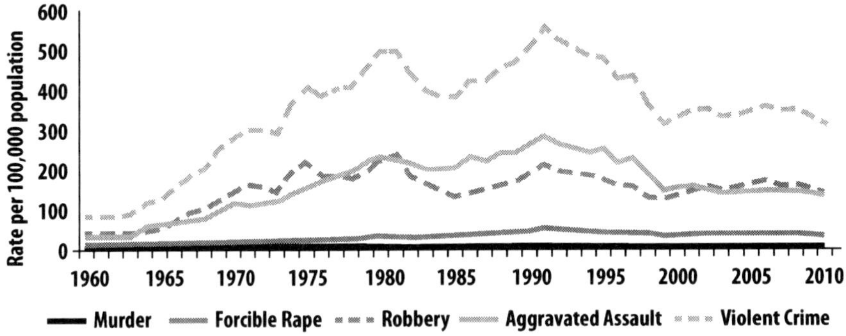

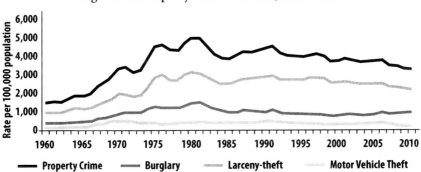

Retrieved from http://www.publicsafety.ohio.gov/links/ocjs_Statistics.pdf.

crimes throughout the 70s and 80s, but since the early 1990s there has been a
steady decline. Unlike violent crime however, with the exception of burglary,
all of the property crimes measured have generally stayed low. Figure 2.7, gives
a complete picture of property crime trends in Ohio, by crime type, since the
1960s.

Figure 2.7: Property Crime in Ohio, 1960–2010

Retrieved from http://www.publicsafety.ohio.gov/links/ocjs_Statistics.pdf.

Where Crime Happens

Rather than simply examining the question of *what* crime looks like, it is also
important to examine *where* crime happens in order to help gain a complete

understanding of crime. Like most activities, crime is not evenly distributed in terms of geography. For a variety of reasons, like population density, much crime is concentrated in the cities. In Ohio, the total number of violent crimes committed was 17,243. Of these, 13,040, or about 76%, were committed in metropolitan areas of the state—in other words, cities. Similarly, over 60% of property crimes were committed in cities in 2011 (Ohio Department of Public Safety, 2012).

In terms of the locations with the highest crime rates in Ohio, it is unsurprisingly Ohio's largest cities. Columbus, Cleveland, Cincinnati and Toledo account for the majority of the crime in the state (Ohio Department of Public Safety, 2011). The largest six cities accounted for over 45% of the crimes committed in Ohio in 2011. When considering that there are over 360 cities in Ohio, the imbalance is noteworthy.

However, just because crime is prevalent primarily in cities does not mean that rural counties are unaffected. Some of the highest *rates* of crime are in Ohio's rural counties, because of the relatively low numbers in terms of population in comparison to the number of crimes committed. In particular, property crime rates tend to be high in rural counties. Interpret these rates with caution, however, as even a single murder in a small enough town would cause it to rank as high as some major cities in terms of violent crimes (Ohio Department of Public Safety, 2011).

Ohio's Drug Problem

One area in which Ohio faces a unique, and very serious, problem in terms of crimes is drugs. In particular, Ohio has had a significant issue with both prescription drug abuse, and opioid abuse more generally. In 2008, for instance, accidental drug overdose accounted for 4.3 deaths per day, on average (Ohio Department of Justice Services, 2013). This represented a 319% increase when compared to only 9 years prior. Nearly all of these accidental deaths were caused by illegal opioids, like heroin, and prescription opioids, like oxycodone or hydrocodone.

Unlike much of the violent crime and property crime, drug use is state wide, and especially prevalent in the southern part of Ohio. The map below, in Figure 2.8, gives a more complete picture of the amount of drug use in Ohio, gaging by accidental overdoses. While not a perfect measure of drug crime, which is hard to get an accurate count of because of the clandestine nature of drug abuse, it gives a relatively good idea of where the problem is most prevalent.

Figure 2.8: Narcotics and other poisoning death rates, 2000–2007.

Retrieved from http://www.publicsafety.ohio.gov/links/2013_Ohio_Drug_Task_Force_ Report.pdf.

Another way to gauge drug crimes in Ohio is by examining the number of arrests. The Ohio Multi-Jurisdictional Task Force is focused on combatting Ohio's drug problem. In 2013, they had 9,481 cases they examined, 5,332 of which resulted in indictments for "street drugs," (either dealing or use) a list of which can be seen in Table 2.3, below. The majority of indictments for most drugs were for trafficking, with the exception of methamphetamine and where the indictments were primarily for possession.

Table 2.3: Street Drugs Removed

Type of Drug	Amount Removed	Estimated Value
Cocaine	189,481 grams	$100/gram
Crack	12,244 grams	$100/gram
Heroin	80,139 grams 221 UD 540 hits	$150/gram
Marijuana (processed)	20,648 pounds	$1,407/pound
Marijuana (plants)	13,079 plants	$1,000/plant
LSD	2,814 UD	$10/UD
Ecstasy	12,012 UD	$15/UD
Methamphetamine	38,233 grams	$100/gram
Psilocybin mushrooms	231,352 grams	$15/gram
Bath salts	71,679 grams	$40/gram
Synthetic hallucinogens (K2, Spice, etc.)	433,518 grams	$15/gram $75/packet

Source: http://www.publicsafety.ohio.gov/links/2013_Ohio_Drug_Task_Force_Report.pdf.

In terms of pharmaceutical drugs, there were 1,201 investigations resulting in 672 indictments. The majority of the drugs seized were anti-depressants or opioids. The most commonly seized drugs were Alprozolam (Xanax) and Hydrocodone. Complete figures for the amount of drugs seized and diverted can be seen in Table 2.4.

Summary

Crime rates, while not perfect, allow us to get a picture of crime at a given point, or over time. The UCR, with its shortcomings, is the primary source for our crime rates, with the NCVS in a supporting role. Within the state of Ohio, there has been an increasing emphasis on the use of the NIBRS system, but as the data system is not yet complete, the reliance on the UCR remains.

While not comparable to states like California and Florida, Ohio's crime problem remains serious, especially in regards to property crime. Like the rest

Table 2.4: Prescription Drugs Removed

Type of Drug	Amount seized
Alprazolam (Xanax)	2,487 (26)
Amphetamine mixture (Adderall)	800 (12)
Buprenorphine (Subutex, Suboxone)	953(29)
Butorphanol Tartrate (Stadol NS)	0
Carisoprodol (Soma)	130 (2)
Clonazepam (Klonopin)	335 (12)
Dextroamphetamine	6 (1)
Codeine (Tylenol #3, Tylenol #4, cough syrup)	191 (3)
Diazapam (Valium)	847 (13)
Fentanyl	116 (8)
Hydrocodone (Vicodin, Lortab, Lorcet)	13,709 (25)
Hydromorphone (Dilaudid)	389 (8)
Lorazepam (Ativan)	176 (5)
Meperidine (Demerol)	0
Methadone (liquid/wafers/pills)	185 (8)
Methylphenidate (Ritalin)	57 (4)
Morphine (MS Contin, EMBEDA, Kadian)	305 (15)
Oxycodone-ER (Oxycontin)	2,909 (17)
Oxycodone-IR (Percocet, Percodan, etc.)	11,824 (33)
Oxymorphone (Opana)	258 (9)
Pheneratamine (Adipex-P, Fastin, Ionamin)	109 (2)
Tramadol (Ultram, Ultracet)	314 (10)
Zolpidem Tartrate (Ambien)	36 (2)

Source: Ohio Multi-Jurisdictional Task Force Report, 2013.

of the United States however, Ohio has experienced a drop in crime over the past 20 years, with violent crime dropping below, and remaining, below the national average.

Key Terms

Arson
Burglary
Crime Rate
Forcible Rape
Hierarchy Rule
Index Crime
Larceny-Theft
Motor Vehicle Theft
Murder
National Crime Victimization Survey

National Incident Based Reporting
   System
Prescription Drugs
Property Crime
Rank
Robbery
Street Drugs
Trend
Uniform Crime Report
Violent Crime

Resources

Bureau of Justice Statistics
    http://www.bjs.gov/
FBI Uniform Crime Report
    http://www.fbi.gov/about-us/cjis/ucr/ucr
Ohio Department of Criminal Justice Services
    http://www.ocjs.ohio.gov/
Ohio Narcotics Association Regional Coordinating Officers
    http://www.ohionarco.org/about-us/ohios-drug-task-forces/

Review Questions

1. What are the main sources of data for crime statistics in the United States?
2. What are the primary differences in the UCR and the NCVS?
3. What was the change in the UCR's definition of forcible rape and why was it important?
4. What are some of the potential causes for the crime drop in the U.S.?
5. How does Ohio compare in terms of property and violent crime to the U.S. as a whole?
6. What crime problems are unique to Ohio?
7. What is one way we can tell how bad drug use is in Ohio?
8. What are the strengths of looking at crime trends?

References

Bachman, R. (1998). The factors related to rape reporting behavior and arrest: New evidence from the National Crime Victimization Survey. *Criminal Justice and Behavior, 25*, 8–29.

Blumstein, A., and Wallman, J. (2005). *The crime drop in America.* New York, NY: Cambridge University Press.

Bureau of Justice Statistics. (2014). NCVS Redesign. Retrieved from http://www.bjs.gov/index.cfm?ty=tp&tid=91.

Federal Bureau of Investigation. (2004a). *Crime in the United States—Appendix IV: The nation's two crime measures.* Retrieved from https://www2.fbi.gov/ucr/cius_04/appendices/appendix_04.html.

Federal Bureau of Investigation. (2004b). General Information. Retrieved from http://www2.fbi.gov/ucr/ucr_general.html.

Federal Bureau of Investigation. (2012). Attorney General Eric Holder announces revisions to the Uniform Crime Report's definition of rape. Retrieved from http://www.fbi.gov/news/pressrel/press-releases/attorney-general-eric-holder-announces-revisions-to-the-uniform-crime-reports-definition-of-rape.

Ohio Department of Public Safety. (2010). *Crime in Ohio.* Retrieved from http://www.publicsafety.ohio.gov/links/ocjs_Statistics.pdf.

Ohio Department of Public Safety. (2013). *Ohio multi-jurisdictional task force report.* Retrieved from http://www.publicsafety.ohio.gov/links/2013_Ohio_Drug_Task_Force_Report.pdf.

Ohio Department of Public Safety. (2014). *OCJS Special Report: Crime in the United States 2013.* Retrieved from http://www.publicsafety.ohio.gov/links/ocjs_crime_in_us2013.pdf.

Skogan, W.G. (1977). Dimensions of the dark figure of unreported crime. *Crime and Delinquency, 23*, 41–50.

Chapter 3

Local, State, and Federal Law Enforcement in Ohio

Learning Objectives

After reading this chapter, students will be able to:

- Provide a historical sketch of Ohio law enforcement.
- Outline federal, state, and local law enforcement agencies having jurisdiction within the State of Ohio.
- Examine the role of municipal, county, and special jurisdiction agencies in Ohio.
- Explain the role of the Bureau of Criminal Identification and Investigation.
- Describe the role of the Ohio Department of Public Safety.
- Define the mission of each federal, state, and local law enforcement agency having jurisdiction within the State of Ohio.
- Describe the role of homeland security as it pertains to State of Ohio law enforcement.
- Identify minimum standards for employment as a State of Ohio law enforcement officer.

Introduction

Ohio law enforcement is bound to enforce the law of Ohio, maintain peace and public order, protect property, and provide necessary services as necessary in the execution of an officer's duties. What is fascinating is the scope that encompasses the duties of Ohio's law enforcement officers. No other government entity, private sector agency or private citizen has the broad authority to arrest, detain and recommend the prosecution of criminal charges regarding citizen violations of law. Ohio local law enforcement agencies and the Ohio State Highway patrol execute their law enforcement duties twenty-four hours a day, seven days a week, and 365 days a year. No other government entity provides this level of citizen access to services.

The elements underlining officer commitment is outlined in the oath of office each Ohio certified law enforcement officer must swear to at the beginning of their career.

> I do solemnly swear that I will support the Constitution of the United States of America, and the Constitution and laws of the State of Ohio, and the laws and ordinances of the jurisdiction, and the rules and regulations of the department and jurisdiction of my political entity, and that I will well and faithfully discharge the duties of the office of police officer, to which I have been appointed according to law and to the best of my ability.[1]

The law enforcement oath of office provides the foundation for the execution of duties and ethical guidance. An officer is bound to support the Constitution of the United States, the State of Ohio, and laws and ordinances of the jurisdiction. The breadth of this simple charge requires education, training, and experience to master the enforcement of law and the provision of service. Part of this chapter will outline these requirements.

Ohio's Policing History

Ohio was granted statehood by the United States in 1803. Prior to this, the area was considered frontier territory to be wrestled from the Native Americans and settled. Frontier justice consisted of local militia, citizens forming an armed posse, or vigilantism by an individual or family. A sheriff was appointed by the Colonial Governor to maintain order. The first sheriff was Colonel Ebenezer Sproat, who was appointed in 1788. His jurisdiction was what was then Washington County, which was all of eastern Ohio from the Ohio River to Lake Erie. When Ohio became a state, the position of sheriff became an elected position. William Skinner was the first sheriff to be elected by the voters.

Police agencies across the state developed first in major cities, and each city saw a different path to organized law enforcement. In Cincinnati, officials as early as 1803 established the night watch, a group comprised of male citizens

---

1. The oath is based on the standard oath by an officer candidate during a swearing in ceremony. Oaths may vary slightly by jurisdiction but are based on Ohio law and the precepts dictated by the Ohio Peace Officer Training Commission. This particular wording is a modified version of the Columbus, Ohio Police Department Oath. (Columbus, 2014)

who patrolled the streets at night in an attempt to prevent criminal activity. They were not paid for their services but volunteered their time in order to keep the city and its residents safe. As the city grew larger, officials decided to compensate the members of the night watch by paying them $1 per night. In time, the night watch system evolved into a small police department. The police department became even more stable during the Civil War when the agency was mobilized to fight off rebels who invaded the city.

At the end of the war, the agency continued to thrive and began to rely more on the technology of the time. They added call boxes in 1870 as a way for citizens to contact officers if they needed help. These were converted to telephone boxes thirteen years later. Additionally, in 1881, Cincinnati became the second city in the US to use patrol wagons to transfer offenders to local jails.

The police department in Cincinnati hired officers who were more diverse than in other cities. They hired their first black officer in 1884, but it was not until after World War II when females were hired. The first policewomen on the force were assigned to work in the juvenile bureau (Mersch, 2007).

The police department in Columbus evolved differently. City officials there chose Samual King as their first Marshall, or police authority, to oversee the city's safety. Knowing that King would need help, Columbus officials sought to create a night watch similar to the one in Cincinnati. They did so in 1821 when the Columbus Borough Council passed an ordinance stating, "whereas many evil disposed persons create disturbances at night with impunity when good citizens are at rest; therefore let it be resolved that a watch be established to commence their routes at 10 of the clock p.m. and to continue until 5 of the clock a.m. of each night in the week" (Shough, 1945, p. 17). Not long after, in 1850, the position of Marshal became an elected position with a term of one year. But in 1851, a new position called the "captain of the watch" was created. So there were both elected and appointed leadership positions in the Columbus department. The officers, however, were not always happy with the agency and the workplace. Their disagreements over wages and conditions led to a strike in 1873. They were out of work for six hours when they agreed to return to work after being promised increased wages. Their return was also prompted by riots that occurred in the unpoliced city.

The police department in Cleveland was established differently from those in Cincinnati or Columbus. It was established in 1866 when the Ohio legislature passed the Metropolitan Police Act. Thirty-six officers were hired and the agency was formed (McBride and Taddeo, 2009).

In the 1920s and 1930s, members of the Ohio legislature debated the necessity of a state-wide law enforcement agency to augment the city-wide agencies. The debate revolved around the need for a full or partial state-wide agency, and the potential use of such an agency to settle labor disputes. Those opposed to a state-wide agency were powerful and convincing, and they were able to defeat the proposal many times. However, in 1933 this changed when the legislature passed a bill that created the Ohio State Highway Patrol (OSHP). According to the bill, "the highway patrol would enforce: state laws relating to registration and licensing of motor vehicles; laws relating to motor vehicle use and operation on the highways; and all laws for the protection of highways" (Ohio State Highway Patrol, 2008, p. 7). However, the OSHP was not granted full law enforcement powers in the legislation. One provision specifically prohibited the OSHP from being involved in labor disputes and strikes—a political concession for passage.

The newest OSHP officers did not have good working conditions. They were required to work six days a week and be on call 24 hours a day. They were authorized and trained on motorcycles instead of cars because it was thought that motorcycles were more economical. The working environment improved in 1941 after the Ohio legislature provided for a state pension system and increased the officers' salaries. They also "gave the Patrol jurisdiction over all rural roads, and included the power to make felony arrests" (Ohio State Highway Patrol, 2008, p. 21). The number of patrolmen rose to 300 after these changes were made. More changes came in 1947 when OSHP was given the responsibility of "enforcing aviation offenses and investigating all aircraft crashed" (Ohio State Highway Patrol, 2008, p. 28).

OSHP made the decision to hire a diverse group of officers to patrol the state. The first black officer to complete OSHP basic training and become a patrolman occurred in 1955. An interesting aspect of OSHP history is that women were prohibited from being hired by the state patrol until 1976. It was at this time that the first woman graduated from the OSHP basic academy. This was due in part to OSHP compliance with the Equal Employment Opportunity Commission's Conciliation Agreement (Ohio State Highway Patrol, 2008). As a result of these changes, the term "patrolman" was changed to "trooper."

In the major cities and smaller towns across Ohio, police eventually progressed from foot patrol to horse patrol and then to cars; from call boxes to telephones and radios and computers. They developed sophisticated crime scene investigations, crime lab analysis, and use computers. Today, law enforcement agencies across Ohio differ in terms of their organization and jurisdiction. These are described below.

Overview of Agencies

"As a result of the fear of a strong central government that existed at the time of the nation's founding, the U.S. Constitution has no provision for a national police force with broad enforcement powers" (Albanese, 2013, p. 131). Similar to other states, Ohio has tiered law enforcement; meaning local, state, and federal law enforcement throughout state geographic boundaries. Each agency is limited in its enforcement action due to legal jurisdiction as defined by law. Jurisdiction may be defined by geographic location, types of law enforced, and level of government. In total, Ohio has 978 state and local law enforcement agencies operating within its boundaries (Ohio Attorney General's Office, 2012).

In the last 35 years Ohio law enforcement agencies have had the opportunity to meet the Commission on Accreditation for Law Enforcement Agencies (CALEA) standards for accreditation. The purpose of CALEA "is to improve the delivery of public safety services, primarily by: maintaining a body of standards, developed by public safety practitioners, covering a wide range of up-to-date public safety initiatives; establishing and administering an accreditation process; and recognizing professional excellence" (CALEA, 2014). CALEA standards address six major law enforcement areas:

1. role, responsibilities, and relationships with other agencies;
2. organization, management, and administration;
3. personnel administration;
4. law enforcement operations, operational support, and traffic law enforcement;
5. detainee and court-related services; and
6. auxiliary and technical services (CALEA, 2014).

Currently there are 58 accredited Ohio law enforcement agencies and 17 Ohio agencies are in the process of earning accreditation (CALEA, 2014). In fact, in 2013 the Genoa Township Police Department and The Ohio State University Department of Public Safety earned CALEA accreditation status.

Local Agencies

As mentioned before, the most common type of law enforcement agency in Ohio is local rather than state or federal. Local law enforcement consists of county sheriff's offices, municipal police departments, township police departments, constables, and agencies with special jurisdiction. Local law enforcement is tasked with ensuring state law and local ordinance compliance. Typical duties range from enforcement of law, traffic concerns, criminal investigations, public relations, and other services as deemed necessary. In 2012 there were 33,592 local law enforcement officers in Ohio (Ohio Attorney General's Office, 2012).

County Sheriff's Offices

There are eighty-eight counties in Ohio, and each has an independent sheriff's office. The Sheriff is the chief law enforcement officer in the county and provides a wide array of law enforcement services. For instance, the primary duty of a Sheriff includes providing court services (common pleas); corrections (county jail); protection of unincorporated county land; protection within all municipalities, townships, and villages (with joint jurisdiction in those that have their own police forces). Further, they are responsible for providing line officer services (patrol and investigation), 911 dispatch services, court security services and more (Ohio Buckeye Sheriff's Association, 2014).

Ohio sheriffs and the operation of their offices are governed by Chapter 311 of the Ohio Revised Code (ORC). An Ohio Sheriff is elected by popular vote to a four-year term and may be re-elected an unlimited number of times, with many sheriff's being elected to multiple terms. A candidate for Sheriff must be a U.S. citizen, a county resident for at least one year, follow election laws, have a high school education or general equivalency diploma, free of felony or first-degree misdemeanor criminal convictions, been fingerprinted for a criminal record check, provided a residence and employment history for the six years leading up to the election, has been awarded an Ohio peace officer training certificate, been employed full-time as a law enforcement officer within four years of election, has two years of law enforcement supervisory experience or has completed two years of post-secondary education (Ohio Revised Code, ORC Chapter 311.01 Election and qualifications of sheriff, 2014). A newly elected sheriff must successfully complete a two-week basic training course approved by the Ohio peace officer training commission to learn the duties and requirements for the office of Sheriff. In addition, for every year in office, the Sheriff must attend sixteen hours of continuous education (Ohio Revised Code, ORC Chapter 311.01 Election and qualifications of sheriff, 2014).

The sheriff's office must be located within the county of jurisdiction. The sheriff may appoint deputies, special deputies, correctional workers, dispatchers, and other staff as needed. The selection process of employees can vary by county. The sheriff's budget is set by the elected county commissioners. The budget serves as a control measure by the county commissioners regarding the number of employees that can be employed, services provided, jail operations, and the purchase and maintenance of necessary law enforcement equipment.

At times, the relationship between the sheriff and county commissioners can be strained due to competing interests regarding funding.

All county sheriffs operate a county jail. The jail houses inmates who are charged with a crime awaiting judiciary review, inmates who are sentenced to jail by a court of competent jurisdiction upon conviction of a misdemeanor or low level felony, and probation or parole violators. Jail time must not exceed a year. In June of each year the sheriff must provide to the county commissioners a proposed jail operation budget for the following fiscal year.

Two other important services Ohio sheriffs are required to provide to county residents are sex offender registration and firearm concealed carry (CCW) permit registration. Ohio sheriffs make public sex offender registration including what crime the offender was convicted of, the offender's age, address, personal identifiers, and a photo. Regarding concealed carry registration, a criminal record check for all applicants must be completed by the sheriff's office and some sheriff's departments provide the necessary training to obtain a CCW permit.

Ohio sheriffs work collaboratively with other law enforcement agencies and participate in a variety of task forces or shared services. Examples of task forces would be a drug enforcement task force or a child predator task force. Examples of shared services would be a county wide dispatch center or special response team. On occasion there can be jurisdictional conflict between the sheriff and another law enforcement agency however the conflict is typically short-lived due to the overriding law enforcement need for collaboration and the fact that the sheriff is an elected official and must face re-election every four years.[2]

Municipal Police Departments

The majority of law enforcement agencies in Ohio are municipal police departments. In fact, in 2010 there were 788 municipal police departments in Ohio (Ohio Office of Criminal Justice Services, 2011). The size of a municipal police department varies greatly due to geographic jurisdiction, population density, community wealth, and rate of crime. Typically police departments are categorized as small (1–10 police officers), medium (11–60 police officers), and large (over 60 police officers). The majority of departments throughout Ohio fall under the small police departments category, due to the rural nature of most of the state.

---

2. ORC Chapter 311 outlines additional requirements of the Sheriff and not all requirements are covered in this brief outline. Please refer to ORC 311 for additional requirements.

According to Ohio law, municipal police departments fall under the local department of public safety. How this is operationalized can vary but the two primary chain of command structures are the designated director of public safety or the city manager. The department itself is comprised of the Chief of Police at the top of the chain of command, and whatever other command elements are required by the agency (Ohio Revised Code, 737.05 Composition and control of police department, 2014). Under the purview of the Director of Public Safety, Police Chiefs have complete control over their agencies, with few exceptions. (Ohio Revised Code, 737.06 Chief of police, 2014). Ohio law also provides for the general duties of the police, which include preserving the peace, protecting persons and property, and enforcement of all ordinances criminal laws of the state and the United States, and enforcing warrants from other states. (Ohio Revised Code, 737.11 General duties of police and fire departments, 2014).[3] What is interesting regarding Ohio's general duties for police is the absence of providing needed enforcement related services, the largest category of job duties is requests by citizens. Municipal police departments provide a wide range of services that are only remotely related to the enforcement of law. For example, establishing and maintaining positive public relations through community involvement or acts of kindness.

Ohio municipal police departments employ the most law enforcement officers in Ohio, and typically have a large local budget, respond to the majority of Ohio crimes, and have the closest relationship to local citizens. There are significant differences between urban, suburban, and rural municipal police departments. These differences are guided by available money, the number of police officers, and crime rates. With this being said, all municipal police officers have the same powers as provided by being an Ohio-certified peace officer. Municipal police officers have full law enforcement power within their jurisdiction and felony arrest power outside of their jurisdiction. It is important to note that local policy and procedure will govern actions taken within and outside the municipal jurisdiction.

Township Police Departments

Ohio township police departments provide the same services and are structured similarly to municipal police departments. In fact, operationally a citizen would not notice a difference between township and municipal police departments. However, despite these many similarities, a difference does exist, based in the legal origin of township police departments.

---

3. ORC Chapter 737 outlines additional law regarding municipal public safety. Please refer to ORC737 for additional requirements.

Elected township trustees, the governing body of the township (similar duties as county commissioners), may authorize the creation of a township police district pursuant to ORC 505.48 (2014). The township police district will incorporate all or the majority of the township. The township trustees may levy a tax to support the operation of the township police department. The trustees determine the qualification for the chief of police, patrol officers, and other members that make up the township police department. The chief of police answers to the trustees for the operation of the police department.[4]

Another township office is that of township constables, though the position is infrequently used. They duplicate the services performed by several other municipal agencies, such as the sheriff, municipal and township police (hence the infrequent use).[5]

Agencies with Special Jurisdiction

Ohio agencies with special jurisdiction are considered law enforcement agencies, however their jurisdiction is limited in some capacity and they serve only a specific need in Ohio law enforcement. Agencies with special jurisdiction include port authority police, transit police, metropolitan housing authority police, park rangers and officers, and campus police.

State Agencies

State law enforcement agencies differ from local law enforcement agencies due to the enforcement of state criminal law with no power to enforce local ordinances or law. State criminal law includes crimes at the misdemeanor and felony levels. State law enforcement agencies typically have specialized jurisdiction over particular topic areas and are considered to have expertise in those areas.

Ohio Department of Public Safety

The Ohio Department of Public Safety (ODPS) is headed by a Director of Public Safety, part of the Governor's cabinet. "ODPS strives to fulfill its mission to save lives, reduce injuries and economic loss, to administer Ohio motor

---

4. ORC Chapter 505 outlines additional law regarding township trustees creating a police district and the operation of a township police department.

5. The township office of constable was primarily utilized in the 19th and 20th centuries but is not commonly found in the 21st century.

vehicle laws, and to preserve the safety and well-being of all citizens with the most cost effective and service oriented methods available" (Ohio Department of Public Safety, 2014). The Ohio Department of Public safety includes the following divisions:

1. Ohio State Highway Patrol
2. Ohio Homeland Security
3. Ohio Investigative Unit
4. Ohio Criminal Justice Services
5. Bureau of Motor Vehicles
6. Emergency Management Agency
7. Emergency Medical Services
8. ODPS Administration

Though each of the above divisions are important, the most common are covered in additional detail. These are the Ohio State Highway Patrol, Ohio Homeland Security, Ohio Investigative Unit, and Ohio Criminal Justice Services.[6]

Ohio State Highway Patrol (OSHP)

The Ohio State Highway Patrol is an internationally accredited agency whose mission is to protect life and property, promote traffic safety and provide professional public safety services with respect, compassion, and unbiased professionalism (Ohio State Highway Patrol, OSHP Duties, 2014). The ranking officer of the OSHP holds the rank of Colonel and is referred to as the Superintendent of the patrol. The Patrol provides:

- Statewide traffic services to keep our roadways safe;
- Statewide emergency response services and support services to the public and the criminal justice community;
- Investigation of criminal activities on state-owned and leased property throughout Ohio; and
- Security for the Governor and other dignitaries (Ohio State Highway Patrol, OSHP Duties, 2014).

The Patrol maintains a uniformed complement of about 1,600 officers. In addition, about 1,000 support personnel, including load limit inspectors, motor vehicle inspectors, motor carrier enforcement inspectors, dispatchers, elec-

---

6. It is important to note all the agencies under the Ohio Department of Public Safety support each other in the execution of their duties. The agencies chosen for description all have law enforcement as a primary duty.

tronics technicians, and civilian specialists complete the Patrol's personnel strength (Ohio State Highway Patrol, OSHP Duties, 2014). In addition, OSHP operates a volunteer, unpaid patrol auxiliary whose members donate hours to supplement and assist on-duty patrol officers and other OSHP initiatives. OSHP's headquarters is located in Columbus with the state subdivided into eight districts that consist of 59 patrol posts. District headquarters are located in or near the cities of Bucyrus, Cambridge, Cleveland, Columbus, Findlay, Jackson, Piqua, and Wilmington. OSHP operates its own training academy and follows the standards for law enforcement officer training as designated by law and the Ohio Peace Officer Training Commission. Local law enforcement officers may attend the OSHP training academy and this has proven to be a valuable networking tool for OSHP.

There are trained specialized law enforcement positions within OSHP. Among these are: plainclothes investigators; traffic and drug interdiction teams and canine officers; commercial enforcement coordinators, inspectors, a special response team and crash re-constructionists (Ohio State Highway Patrol, OSHP Duties, 2014). Routine operations are conducted almost exclusively from automobiles, however, OSHP also utilizes SUV's, fixed-wing aircraft, and helicopters in the course of its duties (Ohio State Highway Patrol, OSHP Duties, 2014).

OSHP provides law enforcement services on the Ohio Turnpike and is responsible for providing security and patrol on all state property to include the Ohio Capitol campus consisting of the Ohio Statehouse, Vern Riffe Government Center, Rhodes State Office Tower, as well as the Ohio Judicial Center, which houses the Ohio Supreme Court. OSHP works closely with Columbus PD regarding crowd control on or near the Ohio Capitol building. OSHP is responsible for investigating aircraft crashes and crimes committed with the Ohio prison system. They respond to major prison riots and have provided needed response during three major prison riots through the years. OSHP sponsors a number of programs conducive to their mission including Sobriety Checkpoints, Share the Road Safely, and the Blue Max auto larceny enforcement program.

An extremely important facet of OSHP operations is the oversight and operation of the Law Enforcement Automated Data System (LEADS), a statewide criminal justice communications network for law enforcement agencies and court systems. Qualified and trained users can inquire about information regarding driving records, vehicle ownership, outstanding warrants, criminal histories, and operator license images (Ohio State Highway Patrol, Offices and Units within the Patrol, 2014). LEADS serves as the gateway to the National Crime Information Center (NCIC). Through NCIC, LEADS users have access to the same information on a national and international level.

Table 3.1: OSHP 2013 Annual Statistics

YTD Activity	2013
Enforcement Stops	272,381
Non-Enforcement Activity	424,395
Warnings	193,604
Motorist Assists	130,090
Crashes Investigated	27,217
OVI Enforcement	10,627
Driving Under Suspension Enforcement	14,432
Seat Belt Enforcement	46,654
Commercial Vehicle Enforcement	19,622
Case Investigations Initiated	4,467
Felony Arrests	1,660
Felony Warrants Served	508
Misdemeanor Summons Issued	5,045
Misdemeanor Warrants Served	2,518
Drug Violations	4,389
Identity Theft Enforcements	90
Resisting Arrest Violations	329
Weapons Violations	265

Source: Ohio State Highway Patrol, 2014

Ohio Homeland Security

"Ohio Homeland Security (OHS) analyzes and shares information, increases awareness, reduces vulnerabilities, and develops strategies to prevent, prepare for, and protect against terrorism and other threats to public safety." This division of the Ohio Department of Public Safety is established by ORC Chapter 5502.03 which also defines the duties of OHS (Ohio Department of Public Safety, 2013 ODPS Annual Report, 2014, p. 29). OHS has established a broad scope of organizational goals, including investigating terrorism, collaborating with OHS partners for homeland security planning, providing training and educational opportunities, maintaining intelligence analysis production,

Figure 3.1: Terrorism Plots in Ohio

There has been significant terrorism in Ohio over the past several years.

Cleveland Bomb Plot—five men were arrested in April 2012 and accused of plotting to blow up a bridge near Cleveland.

Ahmed Hussein Mahamud—Ahmed Hussein Mahamud, a 26-year-old American citizen from Columbus, was charged in an indictment, unsealed in June 2011, with providing material support to Al Shabaab.

Hor & Amera Akl—Hor and Amera Akl, a married couple residing in Toledo, were arrested in 2010 and charged with providing material support to the designated terrorist organization Hizballah. In May 2011, the Akls pled guilty to conspiracy to provide material support to a foreign terrorist organization.

Jerry & Joe Kane—Jerry and Joe Kane, father and son anti-government extremists from Forest, Ohio, were killed in a shoot-out with Arkansas law enforcement after they fatally shot two West Memphis police officers during a traffic stop on May 20, 2010 (Ohio Homeland Security, 2014).

strengthening critical infrastructure and key resource (CIKR) protection, conducting outreach and measuring the effectiveness of the homeland security enterprise in Ohio (Ohio Homeland Security, 2014). OHS is also responsible for promulgating the State of Ohio Homeland Security Strategic plan with the latest version being 2011.

Another important function of OHS is to operate Ohio's statewide intelligence fusion center—Strategic Analysis Information Center (SAIC). SAIC is part of the National Fusion Center Network with a mission "to develop and support a statewide information sharing environment that is engaged with local, state and federal agencies from across Ohio in an effort to increase homeland security and support the national intelligence community" (Ohio Homeland Security, 2014). The SAIC supports Ohio law enforcement by providing information analysis resulting in the dissemination of intelligence to assist law enforcement in the investigation of homeland security threats and crime. Staffing the SAIC is a multijurisdictional partnership.

Ohio has not been immune to terrorism. As seen in Figure 3.1, Ohio has experienced several instances of terrorism—many of them related to international terrorism. Underlining the importance of OHS, the Southern Poverty Law Center, an organization dedicated to fighting hate and bigotry, lists 31 hate groups within the state. Examples of the hate groups are Fraternal White Knights of the Ku Klux Klan, Nation of Islam (a black nationalist group), Red October, and the Creativity Movement (Southern Poverty Law Center, 2014). In Figure 3.2, the organizational structure developed by Ohio Homeland Security to combat those threats is shown.

Figure 3.2: Ohio Homeland Security Organizational Chart

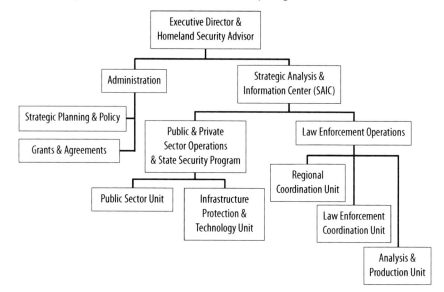

Source: Ohio Homeland Security, Homeland Security Organizational Chart, 2014

Ohio Investigative Unit

The Ohio Investigative Unit division of the Ohio Department of Public Safety is established by ORC Chapter 5502.13. "The Ohio Investigative Unit is committed to providing quality enforcement of state, federal and local laws with emphasis on liquor, food stamp and tobacco offenses, further offering educational guidance and professional assistance to law enforcement agencies and to the general public" (Ohio Investigative Unit, 2014). The Ohio Investigative Unit is the sole agency in the state of Ohio contracted by the U.S. Department of Agriculture — Food & Nutrition Service to investigate food stamp trafficking (Ohio Investigative Unit, 2014). The Ohio Investigative Unit works closely with the Ohio State Highway Patrol and local law enforcement when investigating cases within the agency's jurisdiction.

Ohio Criminal Justice Services

For law enforcement purposes, OCJS receives application for and distributes federal and grant funding including the Edward Byrne Memorial Justice Assistance Grant Law Enforcement (JAG LE) and Project Safe Neighborhoods Grant Program Anti-Gang Initiative (PSN Anti-Gang). Another significant area of focus for OCJS is the development and operation of the Ohio Incident-Based Reporting System (OIBRS), Ohio's version of the National Incident Based Reporting System (NIBRS), discussed in Chapter 2 (Ohio Criminal Justice Services, 2014).

As a support for local law enforcement, OCJS offers the Law Enforcement Officer's Toolkit, a state sponsored software solution for a low cost law enforcement records management system that integrates with OIBRS. "The Law Enforcement Officer's Toolkit effectively manages information on offense reports, arrests, citations, crash reports, property room items and investigator notes, as well as provides a master name index and other search capabilities. It is easily accessed on laptops in the field; allowing law enforcement to enter reports and maintain their presence on the road or in the community" (Ohio Criminal Justice Services, 2014). Over 335 law enforcement agencies in Ohio use the software (Ohio Criminal Justice Services, 2014).

Ohio Bureau of Criminal Identification and Investigation

The Ohio Bureau of Criminal Identification and Investigation (BCI) is a bureau under the Ohio Attorney General's Office. BCI has three divisions; identification, investigation, and laboratory. BCI is accredited through CALEA and offers their expertise to assist state law enforcement in the execution of their duties.

Identification Division

"The Identification Division provides up to date records and state of the art technology to law enforcement and other criminal justice agencies throughout Ohio. The Division serves as the central repository for all records for the State of Ohio and maintains fingerprints, palm prints, photographs, and other information related to arrests within the state" (BCI, BCI Identification Division, 2014). The Identification Division is responsible for maintaining and operating Ohio's Automated Fingerprint Identification System (AFIS). All state required background checks by law run through the division.

Investigation Division

The Investigation Division provides expert investigative services to Ohio law enforcement agencies. Many times small to medium law enforcement agencies do not have the resources available to develop expertise in certain areas of law enforcement. The Investigative Division fills this service niche.

The Investigations-Operations Division consists of the following units:

- The Crime Scene Unit helps local law enforcement process felony crime scenes for physical evidence and provides experts to testify in court. BCI's crime scene agents are among the most highly trained and best equipped in the nation and can contribute the latest crime scene processing techniques and forensic equipment to local investigations, ensuring the best opportunity for identifying and prosecuting criminals.
- The Crimes Against Children Initiative helps local authorities investigate and prosecute those who commit crimes against children. The investigative team at BCI has expertise in undercover online chat, peer-to-peer file sharing, forensic analysis of computers and other technology, and sex offender warrant enforcement. BCI staff also serve on the initiative's Rapid Response Team, which is available around the clock to jump-start investigations and assist victims.
- The Cyber Crimes Unit helps local officials deal with the increasingly complex technical and legal issues involved in computer crime investigations and prosecutions.
- The Environmental Enforcement Unit assists the Ohio Environmental Protection Agency, other state and federal agencies, and local law enforcement in investigating criminal environmental activity. Such activity includes hazardous, solid, and infectious waste dumping as well as water and air pollution.
- The newly formed Forensic Dive Team is available 24/7 to help Ohio law enforcement agencies recover criminal evidence in water, such as human remains, weapons, clothing, or tools. When asked for assistance by an Ohio law enforcement agency, BCI's Forensic Dive Team members will search the water, identify and document evidence, and properly recover the evidence. Recovered items will be sent to the BCI Laboratory for analysis. The team also will work closely with the Ohio Environmental Protection Agency to assist in its investigations of crimes, such as illegal underwater tire or barrel dumps.
- The Heroin Unit was established to assist Ohio communities with law enforcement, legal, and outreach assistance to combat the state's opiate epidemic. Drawing from both new and existing resources, the Heroin Initiative includes: (1) BCI investigative and laboratory services; (2) Ohio Organized Crime Investigations Commission assistance; (3) Prosecution support; and (4) Outreach and education services.
- The Narcotics Unit works with local law enforcement to combat illicit drug activity that ranges from street-level drug trafficking to complex,

multi-jurisdictional conspiracies. Agents can bring the latest technological tools to an investigation, including photo and video equipment, pen registers to track phone and internet activity, thermal imagery, body wires, vehicle tracking devices, and ground sensors. The Narcotics Unit also offers K-9 services, making four highly trained dogs and their BCI agent handlers available around the clock to aid in drug searches throughout the state.

- The Special Investigations Unit conducts probes that fall outside the scope of BCI's other investigative units. Typical cases include serial crimes, unsolved homicides, fugitive apprehension, police-involved shootings, public corruption investigations, and dignitary protection (BCI, BCI Investigation Division, 2014).

The Investigations-Investigative Services Division consists of the following units:

- The Criminal Intelligence Unit (CIU) collects, processes, analyzes, and disseminates criminal intelligence to law enforcement agencies throughout Ohio. The unit focuses on organized crime, major crimes, criminal gangs, fugitive apprehension, and organized drug trafficking operations.
- The Missing Persons Unit assists local law enforcement and families in locating and recovering missing children and adults. The unit issues Missing Child Alerts, Missing Adult Alerts, and AMBER Alerts in coordination with local law enforcement.
- Polygraph Unit: Uses computerized polygraph instruments to monitor a person's physiological responses to questions and help determine truthfulness. Polygraph tests can aid law enforcement in criminal cases and can be administered to suspects and witnesses.
- The Clandestine Drug Lab and Marijuana Eradication Unit focuses on methamphetamine and marijuana growing operations across the state. Drug lab agents can respond with vehicles equipped with breathing apparatuses, personal protective equipment, portable decontamination equipment, sampling gear, generators, and other tools to assess, process, and dismantle labs.
- The Technical Operations Unit provides direct field support for law enforcement agencies through the installation and use of technology. This includes audio and video recording devices, wiretaps, GPS tracking devices, and other technology needed for specific cases.
- Interpol Liaison: BCI is the state of Ohio's official liaison to Interpol, the world's largest international police organization. All three BCI divisions work with Interpol to field a variety of international requests including

locating individuals, conducting interviews, taking statements, and aiding in surveillance, photography, and research.
- LINK: Short for "Linking Individuals Not Known," LINK helps match unidentified remains with DNA submitted by relatives of missing individuals. Identifying such remains helps bring closure to families whose loved ones have been missing for several years.
- The Ohio Law Enforcement Gateway (OHLEG), a secure, electronic criminal justice information network, is an easy way for Ohio law enforcement agencies to share information to help solve and prevent crimes (BCI, BCI Investigation Division, 2014).

Laboratory Division

The Laboratory Division provides expertise laboratory services to Ohio law enforcement for the investigation and prosecution of crimes or identification of people. "Collectively processing more than 160,000 pieces of evidence a year, BCI's Laboratory Division employs the highest standards of care and most advanced forensic testing technologies to provide Ohio law enforcement with accurate, timely analysis of evidence. The laboratory's forensic scientists examine evidence and analyze and log suspect and convicted offender DNA. Staff members also provide expert testimony on their findings. BCI laboratories in London, Richfield, and Bowling Green received international accreditation from the American Society of Crime Laboratory Directors/Laboratory Accreditation Board (ASCLD/LAB) in the spring 2013, which assures the highest standard of quality within forensic laboratories" (BCI, Laboratory Division, 2014). Again, many times small to medium law enforcement agencies do not have the resources available to develop this expertise or provide the service themselves.

Ohio Department of Natural Resources

The Ohio Department of Natural Resources (ODNR) owns (State of Ohio) and manages more than 590,000 acres of land including 75 state parks, 21 state forests, 134 state nature preserves, and 138 wildlife areas (Ohio Department of Natural Resources, 2014). The department also has jurisdiction over more than 120,000 acres of inland waters; 7,000 miles of streams; 481 miles of Ohio River; and 2.25 million acres of Lake Erie (Ohio Department of Natural Resources, 2014). ODNR's mission statement is "Mission Statement: To ensure a balance between wise use and protection of our natural resources for the benefit of all" (Ohio Department of Natural Resources, 2014). In addition, ODNR licenses all hunting, fishing, and watercraft in the state. ODNR employs four different special jurisdiction law enforcement officers — Forest Officers (ORC 1503.29), Park Officers (ORC 1541.10), Watercraft Enforcement Officers (ORC 1547.521), Wildlife Officers (ORC 1531.13). These officers have full law enforcement powers within their special jurisdiction. For example, Wildlife Officers enforce "shall enforce all laws pertaining to the taking, possession, protection, preservation, management, and propagation of wild animals and all division rules. They shall enforce all laws against hunting without permission of the owner or authorized agent of the land on which the hunting is done. They may arrest on view and without issuance of a warrant" (Ohio Revised Code, 1531.13 Wildlife officers, 2014).[7]

Federal Agencies

Federal law enforcement agencies are well represented in Ohio, especially in the metropolitan areas. Federal law enforcement agencies cannot enforce Ohio or local law and are relegated to federal statutes that pertain to their niche within the federal law enforcement system. Federal law enforcement agencies tend to be investigative rather than primarily patrol-driven. Typically, state and local law enforcement support federal investigations and initiatives and on an infrequent basis, federal law enforcement supports state and local initiatives. Task forces combining federal, state, and local personnel and resources as collaborative partners are present in Ohio. For example, the Federal Bureau of Investigation (FBI) is responsible for the operation of Joint Terrorism Task Forces (JTTF) in Ohio. JTTFs take action against terrorism or suspected terrorism.

Federal Bureau of Investigation

The FBI has two division field offices in Ohio — Cincinnati and Cleveland. Agents may be assigned to smaller field offices within their respective division. Each division field office participates in partnership initiatives like a JTTF and Violent Gang Task Forces. Primarily the FBI investigates terrorism, counter-

---

7. The Ohio Department of Natural Resources is an often overlooked law enforcement agency and has direct contact with many Ohio citizens who hunt or visit Ohio's state parks.

intelligence, cyber-crime, public corruption, civil rights violations, organized crime, white-collar crime, violent crime and major thefts (Federal Bureau of Investigation, FBI, 2014). The FBI is responsible for the collection and analysis of local and state law enforcement data for the Uniform Crime Report (UCR) although the UCR is being replaced by the Nation Incident Based Reporting System (NIBRS). NIBRS is designed to correct data collection deficiencies. As noted before, OIBRS is Ohio's state and local version of NIBRS. OIBRS transfers crime data to NIBRS.

United States Customs and Border Protection

The U.S. Customs and Border Patrol (CBP) is "charged with keeping terrorists and their weapons out of the U.S. while facilitating lawful international travel and trade" (U.S. Customs and Border Patrol, 2014). CBP takes a comprehensive approach to border management and control, combining customs, immigration, border security, and agricultural protection into one coordinated and supportive activity (U.S. Customs and Border Patrol, 2014). CBP has recently expanded its presence in Ohio due to the Northern Border Initiative (NBI).

The State of Ohio shares a 158-mile border with Canada that cuts across Lake Erie. Ohio's northern border has international/domestic shipping routes, commercial fishing, land based utility facilities that include major oil refineries, power plants, water treatment plants, and recreational areas. CBP opened a port of entry for Toledo-Sandusky-Port Clinton in the late 2000s. CBP provides partnership services with state and local law enforcement agencies along Ohio's northern border.[8]

Additional federal agencies with a law enforcement mission are listed in Table 3.2.

---

8. The Ohio Department of Public Safety and its division of Homeland Security implemented the Northern Border Initiative that supports the CBP mission.

Table 3.2: Other federal agencies in Ohio

U.S. Agency	Mission	Ohio Application
Alcohol, Tobacco, and Firearms	ATF is a unique law enforcement agency in the United State Department of Justice that protects our communities from violent criminals, criminal organizations, the illegal use and trafficking of firearms, the illegal use and storage of explosives, acts of arson and bombings, acts of terrorism, and the illegal diversion of alcohol and tobacco products. We partner with communities, industries, law enforcement, and public safety agencies to safeguard the public we serve through information sharing, training, research and use of technology (U.S. Alcohol, Tobacco, and Firearms, 2014).	Better known as ATF, ATF officers provide investigative, laboratory and expertise to state and local law enforcement agencies regarding federal alcohol, tobacco, and firearms violations of law. ATF partners with state and local law enforcement agencies in regional task forces.
Coast Guard	The USCG is considered a military, multi-mission, and maritime agency. There are 11 mission areas, each with its own mission statement (U.S. Coast Guard, 2014).	Better known as USCG, USCG provides maritime and federal law enforcement services on Ohio's waterways. USCG has a strong drug interdiction and waterway rescue mission.
Drug Enforcement Agency	The mission of the Drug Enforcement Administration (DEA) is to enforce the controlled substances laws and regulations of the United States and bring to the criminal and civil justice system of the United States, or any other competent jurisdiction, those organizations and principal members of organizations, involved in the growing, manufacture, or distribution of controlled substances appearing in or destined for illicit traffic in the United States; and to recommend and support	Better known as DEA officers provide investigative, laboratory and expertise to state and local law enforcement agencies regarding drug violations of law. DEA partners with state and local law enforcement agencies in regional task forces.

Table 3.2: Other federal agencies in Ohio (cont.)

U.S. Agency	Mission	Ohio Application
Drug Enforcement Agency (cont.)	Non-enforcement programs aimed at reducing the availability of illicit controlled substances on the domestic and international markets (U.S. Drug Enforcement Agency, 2014).	
Marshals Service	To defend, protect, and enforce the American justice system (U.S. Marshals Service, 2012, p. 3).	The U.S. Marshals Service provides U.S. court security, federal warrant service, federal prisoner transport, witness protection, seizing and managing assets/forfeitures, and the execution of federal court orders. The U.S. Marshals Service partners on fugitive task forces.
Parole Commission	The mission of the U.S. Parole Commission is to promote Public Safety and strive for justice and fairness in the exercise of its authority to release, revoke and supervise offenders under its jurisdiction (U.S. Parole Commission, 2014).	U.S. Parole Officers supervise federal post release prisoners and work closely with state and local law enforcement in providing this supervision.
Probation and Pretrial Services	To assist the federal courts in the fair administration of justice. To protect the community. To bring about long-term positive change in individuals under supervision (U.S. Probation and Pretrial Services, 2014).	U.S. Probation Officers supervise offenders on pre-trial release, conduct pre-sentence investigations, and supervise offenders sentenced to federal probation. U.S. Probation Officers work closely with state and local law enforcement in the execution of their duties.
Secret Service	The mission of the United States Secret Service is to safeguard the nation's financial infrastructure and payment systems to preserve the integrity of the economy, and to protect national leaders, visiting heads of state and government, designated sites and National Special Security Events (U.S. Secret Service, 2014).	The U.S. Secret Service investigates financial crimes and provides foreign dignitary and federal public official protection services. The U.S. Secret Service works closely with state and local law enforcement in the execution of their investigative and protection duties.

Minimum Standards for
Ohio Law Enforcement Officers

Under Ohio's Attorney General, the Ohio Peace Officer Training Commission will:

> Oversee training requirements and curriculum for peace officers, private security, local corrections, jail personnel, K-9 units, and humane agents, in addition to firearms programs for public defender investigators, bailiffs, probation officers, and parole officers. They also oversee certification standards of peace officers. Academy staff provides instruction in basic, advanced, and technical subjects for the Ohio law enforcement community using the latest research and recommended professional practices (Ohio Attorney General, 2014).

Also under the Ohio Attorney General is the operation of the Ohio Peace Officer Training Academy (OPOTA). OPOTA provides necessary training for law enforcement officers in Ohio, oversees the delivery of basic academy curriculum, and tracks officer continuing education for compliance.

Training for Law Enforcement Officers in Ohio

According to Ohio law, all law enforcement officers must complete the peace officer basic training for certification as a peace officer prior to an original appointment on a permanent basis (Ohio Revised Code, 109.77 Certificate of completion of basic training program necessary for appointment, 2014). In addition, a law enforcement officer in Ohio must be free of felony conviction.

Every year an Ohio law enforcement officer is required to pass the firearms qualification course as designated by OPOTA (Ohio Revised Code, 109.801 Annual firearms requalification program, 2014). Also on an annual basis, Ohio law enforcement officers must complete up to twenty-four hours of continuing education training as proscribed by the Ohio Peace Officer Training Commission (Ohio Revised Code, 109.803 Continuing professional training for peace officers and troopers, 2014). Meeting the continuing education requirement can consist of a number of topics germane to law enforcement and may be delivered by the state or other trainers as approved by the individual agency administrator. Documentation of attendance and completion of the training is essential in meeting the state requirement.

Ohio Peace Officer Basic Academy

Ohio Peace Officer Basic Academy is offered in various locations through-out the state. All academies are required to follow the training curriculum set forth and approved by the Ohio Peace Officer Training Commission. In 2011 a law enforcement officer job task analysis was conducted to provide data for updating basic academy curriculum. In 2014 the basic academy training curriculum consisted of 605 training hours in thirteen topic areas as listed below (Ohio Peace Officer Training Commission, 2014).[9]

Graduating candidates must pass a final comprehensive exam with a 70% or above and successfully meet physical fitness standards.[10]

Summary

In essence, law enforcement in Ohio consists of local, state and federal agencies dedicated to the execution of their duties within their specific jurisdictions. Ohio law enforcement officers are well trained and due to their training requirements, strive to provide professional service to citizens. The many different law enforcement agencies work in partnership with each other to keep Ohio safe and secure. While an occasional disagreement may occur between agencies, the desire to practice their craft in order to ensure public safety quickly leads to a continued collaboration of effort.

Key Terms

Agencies with Special Jurisdiction
Bureau of Criminal Identification and Investigation
Commission on Accreditation for Law Enforcement
County Sheriff's Office

Federal Law Enforcement
Local Law Enforcement
Municipal Police Departments
Ohio Attorney General
Ohio Criminal Justice Services
Ohio Department of Natural Resources

---

9. California and Ohio are considered national leaders in law enforcement basic training due to training standards and requirements.

10. Many Ohio local law enforcement agencies have adopted OPOTA's physical fitness standards for entry-level testing. It is not unusual for multiple candidates to fail these standards during an entry-level test, even though the standards are well publicized.

Ohio Department of Public Safety
Ohio Homeland Security
Ohio Investigative Unit
Ohio Metropolitan Police Act
Ohio Peace Officer Training Academy
Ohio Peace Officer Training
  Commission

Ohio Revised Code
Ohio State Highway Patrol
State Law Enforcement
Township Constable
Township Police Department
U.S. Customs and Border Patrol

Resources

Bureau of Criminal Identification and Investigation
    http://www.ohioattorneygeneral.gov/Law-Enforcement/Bureau-of-
    Criminal-Investigation
Commission on Accreditation for Law Enforcement
    http://www.calea.org
Ohio Buckeye Sheriff's Association
    http://buckeyesheriffs.org
Ohio Department of Natural Resources
    http://ohiodnr.gov
Ohio Department of Public Safety
    http://publicsafety.ohio.gov
Ohio Homeland Security
    http://homelandsecurity.ohio.gov
Ohio Investigative Unit
    http://investigativeunit.ohio.gov
Ohio Peace Officer Training Academy
    http://www.ohioattorneygeneral.gov/Law-Enforcement/Ohio-Peace-
    Officer-Training-Academy
Ohio State Highway Patrol
    http://statepatrol.ohio.gov

Review Questions

1. Provide a historical sketch of Ohio law enforcement. What events do you
    consider as being historically significant in the development of Ohio law
    enforcement? Why?

2. Identify federal, state, and local law enforcement agencies having jurisdiction within the State of Ohio. What category of law enforcement agencies provides the most direct service to Ohio citizens?
3. Describe specific local, state, and federal law enforcement agency missions.
4. What are the different types of jurisdiction and how does agency jurisdiction help form the agency mission?
5. Describe the role of homeland security as it pertains to State of Ohio law enforcement. Why do you think homeland security is part of the overall law enforcement mission?
6. Identify minimum standards for employment as a State of Ohio law enforcement officer. List curriculum requirements for the Ohio peace officer basic training.
7. How does the Ohio Revised Code impact Ohio law enforcement?

References

Albanese, J. (2013). *Criminal Justice, 5th ed.* Upper Saddle River, NJ: Pearson Education, Inc.

BCI. (2014, June 18). *BCI Identification Division.* Retrieved from Ohio Attorney General: http://www.ohioattorneygeneral.gov/Law-Enforcement/ Bureau-of-Criminal-Investigation/Identification-Division.aspx.

BCI. (2014, June 18). *BCI Investigation Division.* Retrieved from Ohio Attorney General: http://www.ohioattorneygeneral.gov/Law-Enforcement/ Bureau-of-Criminal-Investigation/Investigation-Division.aspx.

BCI. (2014, June 18). *Laboratory Division.* Retrieved from Ohio Attorney General: http://www.ohioattorneygeneral.gov/Law-Enforcement/Bureau-of- Criminal-Investigation/Laboratory-Division.aspx.

CALEA. (2014, June 17). *The Commission.* Retrieved from Commission on Accreditation for Law Enforcement: http://www.calea.org/content/commission.

Columbus, O. P. (2014, June 2). *Official Oath.* Retrieved from columbuspolice.org: http://www.columbuspolice.org/FormsPublications/Directives/ Directives/oath.pdf.

Federal Bureau of Investigation. (2014, June 12). *Crime in the United States 2012 Table 77.* Retrieved from Unform Crime Report: http://www.fbi.gov/ about-us/cjis/ucr/crime-in-the-u.s/2012/crime-in-the-u.s.-2012/tables/ 77tabledatadecpdf/table_77_full_time_law_enforcement_employess_ by_state_2012.xls.

Federal Bureau of Investigation. (2014, June 19). *FBI—Homepage*. Retrieved from Federal Bureau of Investigation: http://www.fbi.gov/.

Mapp v. Ohio, 367 U.S. 643 (United States Supreme Court 1961).

McBride, J. T., & Taddeo, R. J. (2009). *History of Law Enforcement Lake County, Ohio 1849–2008*. Brunswick, OH: Crown Custom Publishing.

Mersch, C. (2007). *Cincinnati Police History*. Charleston, SC: Arcadia Publishing.

Officer Down Memorial. (2014, June 2). *ODMP Remembers*. Retrieved from Officer Down Memorial Page: http://www.odmp.org/officer/16637-constable-jacob-dearduff-sr.

Officer Down Memorial. (2014, June 19). *Ohio Line of Duty Deaths*. Retrieved from Officer Down Memorial: http://www.odmp.org/search/browse?state=OH.

Ohio Attorney General. (2014, June 19). *Ohio Peace Officer Training Academy*. Retrieved from Ohio Attorney General: http://www.ohioattorneygeneral.gov/Law-Enforcement/Ohio-Peace-Officer-Training-Academy.

Ohio Attorney General's Office. (2012). *Ohio Peace Officer Training Commission and Academy Annual Report*. Columbus: State of Ohio.

Ohio Buckeye Sheriff's Association. (2014, June 10). *History of Ohio Sheriffs*. Retrieved from Ohio Buckeye Sheriff's Association: http://buckeyesheriffs.org/history.htm.

Ohio Criminal Justice Services. (2014, June 18). *Law Enforcement Officer's Toolkit*. Retrieved from Ohio Criminal Justice Services: http://ocjs.ohio.gov/leot/.

Ohio Criminal Justice Services. (2014, June 18). *Ohio Incident-Based Reporting System*. Retrieved from Ohio Criminal Justice Services: http://ocjs.ohio.gov/oibrs/.

Ohio Department of Natural Resources. (2014, June 18). *History and Purpose of the Department of Natural Resources*. Retrieved from Ohio Department of Natural Resources: http://ohiodnr.gov/home/history-purpose.

Ohio Department of Public Safety. (2014). *2013 ODPS Annual Report*. Columbus, OH: Ohio Department of Public Safety.

Ohio Department of Public Safety. (2014, June 18). *Home*. Retrieved from Ohio Department of Public Safety: http://publicsafety.ohio.gov/index.stm.

Ohio Homeland Security. (2011). *State of Ohio Homeland Security Strategic Plan*. Columbus, OH: Ohio Homeland Security.

Ohio Homeland Security. (2014, June 18). *Homeland Security Fusion Center*. Retrieved from Ohio Homeland Security: http://homelandsecurity.ohio.gov/saic.stm.

Ohio Homeland Security. (2014, June 18). *Homeland Security Goals*. Retrieved from Ohio Homeland Security: http://homelandsecurity.ohio.gov/goals.stm.

Ohio Homeland Security. (2014, June 18). *Homeland Security Organizational Chart.* Retrieved from Ohio Homeland Security: http://homeland security.ohio.gov/goals.stm.

Ohio Homeland Security. (2014, June 18). *Welcome to Ohio Homeland Security.* Retrieved from Ohio Homeland Security: http://homelandsecurity.ohio.gov/index.stm.

Ohio Investigative Unit. (2014, June 18). *Welcome to the Ohio Investigative Unit.* Retrieved from Ohio Investigative Unit: http://investigativeunit.ohio.gov/index.stm.

Ohio Office of Criminal Justice Services. (2011). *Ohio Criminal Justice Statistics.* Columbus: State of Ohio.

Ohio Peace Officer Training Commission. (2014, July 1). Peace Officer Basic Training Audit Sheet. *Ohio Peace Officer Basic Training Curriculum.* London, OH, U.S.: Ohio Peace Officer Training Academy.

Ohio Revised Code. (2014, June 12). *ORC Chapter 311.01 Election and qualifications of sheriff.* Retrieved from Ohio Revised Code: http://codes.ohio.gov/orc/311.

Ohio Revised Code. (2014, June 12). *ORC Chapter 311.01 Election and qualifications of sheriff.* Retrieved from Ohio Revised Code: http://codes.ohio.gov/orc/311.

Ohio Revised Code. (2014, June 13). *4117.08 Matters subject to collective bargaining.* Retrieved from Ohio Revised Code: http://codes.ohio.gov/orc/4117.08.

Ohio Revised Code. (2014, June 16). *737.05 Composition and control of police department.* Retrieved from Ohio Revised Code: http://codes.ohio.gov/orc/737.05.

Ohio Revised Code. (2014, June 16). *737.06 Chief of police.* Retrieved from Ohio Revised Code: http://codes.ohio.gov/orc/737.06.

Ohio Revised Code. (2014, June 16). *737.11 General duties of police and fire departments.* Retrieved from Ohio Revised Code: http://codes.ohio.gov/orc/737.11.

Ohio Revised Code. (2014, June 18). *1531.13 Wildlife officers.* Retrieved from Ohio Revised Code: http://codes.ohio.gov/orc/1531.13.

Ohio Revised Code. (2014, June 18). *311.07 General powers and duties of sheriff.* Retrieved from Ohio Revised Code: http://codes.ohio.gov/orc/311.07.

Ohio Revised Code. (2014, June 19). *109.77 Certificate of completion of basic training program necessary for appointment.* Retrieved from Ohio Revised Code: http://codes.ohio.gov/orc/109.77.

Ohio Revised Code. (2014, June 19). *109.801 Annual firearms requalification program.* Retrieved from Ohio Revised Code: http://codes.ohio.gov/orc/109.801.

Ohio Revised Code. (2014, June 19). *109.803 Continuing professional training for peace officers and troopers.* Retrieved from Ohio Revised Code: http://codes.ohio.gov/orc/109.803.

Ohio Revised Code. (2014, June 19). *311.16. Annual report of sheriff.* Retrieved from Ohio Revised Code: http://codes.ohio.gov/orc/Search/311.16.

Ohio Revised Code. (2014, June 19). *311.20 Allowance for prisoners.* Retrieved from Oho Revised Code: http://codes.ohio.gov/orc/311.20.

Ohio Revised Code. (2014, June 19). *509.01 Designation of police constables.* Retrieved from Ohio Revised Code: http://codes.ohio.gov/orc/509.01.

Ohio Revised Code. (2014, June 19). *509.05 Powers and duties of police constables.* Retrieved from Ohio Revised Code: http://codes.ohio.gov/orc/509.05.

Ohio Revised Code. (2014, June 19). *509.10 Arrest on view or warrant—keep the peace.* Retrieved from Ohio Revised Code: http://codes.ohio.gov/orc/509.10.

Ohio v. Robinette, 117 S.Ct. 417 (United States Supreme Court 1996).

Ohio State Highway Patrol. (2008). *75 Years of Excellence A History of the Ohio State Highway Patrol 1933–2008.* Columbus, OH: Ohio State Highway Patrol.

Ohio State Highway Patrol. (2014, June 15). *Offices and Units within the Patrol.* Retrieved from Ohio State Highway Patrol: http://statepatrol.ohio.gov/units.stm.

Ohio State Highway Patrol. (2014, June 18). *OSHP Duties.* Retrieved from Ohio State Highway Patrol: http://statepatrol.ohio.gov/duties.stm.

Oyez Project. (1996). *Ohio v. Robinette.* Retrieved from The Oyez Project at IIT Chicago-Kent College of Law: http://www.oyez.org/cases/1990-1999/1996/1996_95_891.

Oyez Project. (2014, June 3). *Mapp v. Ohio.* Retrieved from The Oyez Project at IIT Chicago-Kent College of Law: http://www.oyez.org/cases/1960-1969/1960/1960_236.

Oyez Project. (2014, June 3). *Terry v. Ohio.* Retrieved from The Oyez Project at IIT Chicago-Kent College of Law: http://www.oyez.org/cases/1960-1969/1967/1967_67.

Samaha, J. (2015). *Criminal Procedure, 9th ed.* Stamford, CT: Cengage Learning.

Shough, J. G. (1945). *The History of the Columbus Police Department.* Columbus, OH: Heer Printing Company.

Southern Poverty Law Center. (2014, June 18). *Hate Map—Ohio.* Retrieved from Southern Poverty Law Center: http://www.splcenter.org/get-informed/hate-map#s=OH.

Terry v. Ohio, 392 U.S. 1 (United States Supreme Court 1968).

U.S. Alcohol, Tobacco, and Firearms. (2014, June 19). *About ATF*. Retrieved from U.S. Alcohol, Tobacco, and Firearms: http://www.atf.gov/content/About.

U.S. Coast Guard. (2014, June 19). *Missions*. Retrieved from U.S. Coast Guard: http://www.uscg.mil/top/missions/.

U.S. Customs and Border Patrol. (2014, June 19). *About CBP*. Retrieved from U.S. Customs and Border Patrol: http://www.cbp.gov/about.

U.S. Drug Enforcement Agency. (2014, June 19). *DEA Mission Statement*. Retrieved from U.S. Drug Enforcement Agency: http://www.justice.gov/dea/about/mission.shtml.

U.S. Marshalls Service. (2012). *Strategic Plan 2012–2016*. Washington, D.C.: U.S. Government.

U.S. Parole Commission. (2014, June 19). *United States Parole Commission Home*. Retrieved from U.S. Parole Commission: http://www.justice.gov/uspc/.

U.S. Probation and Pretrial Services. (2014, June 19). *Probation and Pretrial Services—Mission*. Retrieved from U.S. Probation and Pretrial Services: http://www.uscourts.gov/FederalCourts/ProbationPretrialServices/Mission.aspx.

U.S. Secret Service. (2014, June 19). *U.S. Secret Service Mission*. Retrieved from U.S. Secret Service: http://www.secretservice.gov/mission.shtml.

Walker, J. T., & Hemmens, C. (2011). *Legal Guide for Police Constitutional Issues, 9th ed*. Burlington, MA: Anderson Publishing.

Chapter 4

Ohio's Court System and Structure

Learning Objectives

After reading this chapter, students will be able to:

- Explain the structure of the courts in Ohio.
- Explain the relationship between the courts in Ohio and those in the federal system.
- Explain the role of Ohio's constitution in the structure of the court system.
- Explain the role of Ohio's Supreme Court in relation to the other courts in Ohio.
- Explain the function of Ohio's municipal courts.
- Understand the difference between courts of original and appellate jurisdiction.
- Understand the purpose of courts with special jurisdiction.

Introduction

As with most states, Ohio's government is divided along the same lines as the federal government—into three coequal branches (legislative, executive, and judicial), each with distinct areas of responsibility. These are established under the Ohio Constitution, in Articles II, III, and IV, respectively. Art I of the state Constitution contains Ohio's Bill of Rights which guarantees, among others, freedom of speech and assembly, freedom from unreasonable searches and seizures, the right to a trial, to be represented by counsel, to reasonable bail, and to other specific protections of what Ohio defines as "Inalienable Rights"— the rights of "enjoying and defending life and liberty, acquiring, possessing, and protecting property, and seeking and obtaining happiness and safety"

(Ohio Constitution, Art I, sec. 1). And, as will be described below, the court system in Ohio plays a significant role in protecting these rights.

As in other states, the primary function of the judicial branch is to fairly and impartially settle disputes according to the law. Ohio has, through its Constitution and by acts of the General Assembly, established a hierarchy of courts as well as a number of Commissions and other administrative bodies to accomplish this function. Responsibility for oversight and administration of these bodies and of the judicial branch, is placed with the Supreme Court and the Chief Justice.

History of the Ohio Court System

The First Ohio Constitution established the Supreme Court and court of common pleas in 1802. The three-judge Supreme court was appointed by Congress and was required to hold court in each county every year, "riding the circuit" by horseback across the state. By 1834, Ohio Supreme Court judges covered 72 counties and rode over 2,000 miles on horseback annually.

In 1807, the case of *Rutherford v. M'Faddon*, established the authority of judicial review, allowing the court to decide constitutionality of laws. In this case Calvin Pease, a judge of the Court of Common Pleas for the Third Circuit, had declared a section of an Ohio law in violation of the Ohio Constitution of 1803. The Ohio law permitted justices of the peace to oversee legal disputes involving property or money in excess of twenty dollars. Pease declared that the Constitution promised trial by jury and that the Ohio law was a clear violation of that guarantee. State Supreme Court Justices Samuel Huntington and George Tod sustained Pease's argument in the case *Rutherford v. M'Faddon*. Though there were efforts to impeach the justices as a result of this ruling, that effort failed and the doctrine became precedent.

In 1851 the Revised Constitution was adopted, increasing the size of the Supreme Court to five judges and declaring that Supreme Court judges would be elected. In 1857 the Ohio Supreme Court moved into the Ohio Statehouse, occupying the space that is now the Speaker's office. It remained there until 1901, when the court moved into the Ohio Statehouse's new Judiciary Annex.

In 1912 the state Constitution was again amended to increase the size of the Court, setting the number of Supreme Court judges to its present number of seven. This Constitution also created the position of chief justice and set each judicial term at six years.

Over the next several decades, the Court would see several "firsts": In 1915 Justice Edward S. Matthias began what would become a 38-year term, still the longest ever on Ohio Supreme Court. In 1922, Florence Allen was elected to the Supreme Court, making her the first female state Supreme Court justice in the nation. In 1969, Robert Duncan became the first African-American on the Supreme Court. Finally, in 1979, TV news cameras were allowed in Ohio courtrooms for trials and hearings.

The Supreme Court moves into its former home in the James A. Rhodes State Office Tower in 1974 and in 1977 the Office of Disciplinary Counsel was created to assist the Court in its oversight role by investigating allegations of professional misconduct by attorneys and judges.

In 1987 the Court launched an off-site court program intended to bring a greater public awareness to the work of the judicial system. Through this program, the Court travels to towns across the state twice a year to hear and vote on actual cases (Ohio Supreme Court, 2014; Martinez, 2014).

In 2001, construction began on the renovation of the new Ohio Judicial Center (formerly the Ohio Departments Building) located at 65 South Front Street in Columbus. Three years later, on February 17th 2004, the Supreme Court moved into the Ohio Judicial Center. This move marked the first time in Ohio's 200-year history that the judiciary was housed separately from the other two branches of state government, a move intended to emphasize its independence.

Organization of the Ohio Court System

Ohio operates with a Supreme Court, a number of Courts of Appeals, Courts of Common Pleas, and a number of specialized and lower courts. The diagram in Figure 4.1, shows the basic structure of the Judicial System in Ohio. We'll discuss each of these in turn.

The Supreme Court of Ohio

Article IV, Section 1, of the Ohio Constitution, establishes The Supreme Court of Ohio (as well as the other components of the court system), stating that "the judicial power of the state is vested in a Supreme Court, Courts of Appeals, Courts of Common Pleas and divisions thereof, and such other courts inferior to the Supreme Court as may from time to time be established by law." The home of the Supreme Court is the newly restored Thomas J. Moyer Ohio Judicial Center, formerly the Ohio Departments Building, located at 65 South Front Street. The courtroom is located on the first floor, the Clerk's Office is on the eighth floor, and the entrance to the Law Library is on the 11th floor with the library stacks spaced throughout the remainder of the 11th through 15th floors.

Figure 4.1: Ohio Judicial System structure

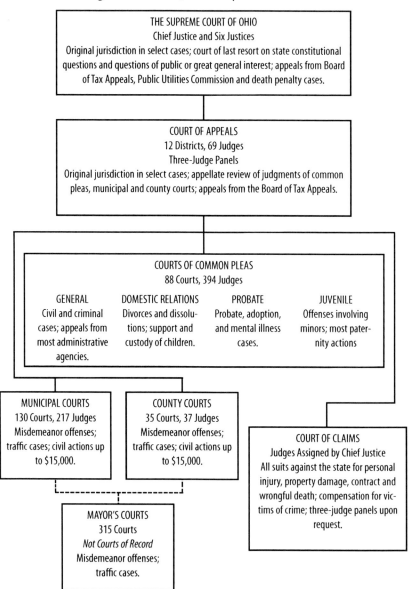

THE SUPREME COURT OF OHIO
Chief Justice and Six Justices
Original jurisdiction in select cases; court of last resort on state constitutional
questions and questions of public or great general interest; appeals from Board
of Tax Appeals, Public Utilities Commission and death penalty cases.

COURT OF APPEALS
12 Districts, 69 Judges
Three-Judge Panels
Original jurisdiction in select cases; appellate review of judgments of common
pleas, municipal and county courts; appeals from the Board of Tax Appeals.

COURTS OF COMMON PLEAS
88 Courts, 394 Judges

GENERAL	DOMESTIC RELATIONS	PROBATE	JUVENILE
Civil and criminal cases; appeals from most administrative agencies.	Divorces and dissolutions; support and custody of children.	Probate, adoption, and mental illness cases.	Offenses involving minors; most paternity actions

MUNICIPAL COURTS
130 Courts, 217 Judges
Misdemeanor offenses;
traffic cases; civil actions up
to $15,000.

COUNTY COURTS
35 Courts, 37 Judges
Misdemeanor offenses;
traffic cases; civil actions up
to $15,000.

COURT OF CLAIMS
Judges Assigned by Chief Justice
All suits against the state for personal
injury, property damage, contract and
wrongful death; compensation for victims of crime; three-judge panels upon
request.

MAYOR'S COURTS
315 Courts
Not Courts of Record
Misdemeanor offenses;
traffic cases.

Source: Ohio Courts Statistical Summary, 2012

While the Supreme Court was originally established with only three members, Article IV, Section 2, of the 1851 Constitution sets the size of the Court at seven— a Chief Justice and six Justices—and outlines the jurisdiction of the Court.

The Court has original jurisdiction for certain extraordinary remedies, including writs of habeas corpus (involving the release of persons allegedly unlawfully imprisoned or committed), writs of mandamus and procedendo (ordering a public official to do a required act), writs of prohibition (ordering a lower court to cease an unlawful act), and writs of quo warranto (against a person or corporation for usurpation, misuse or abuse of public office or corporate office or franchise).

Most of the business of the Supreme Court, however, comes from the exercise of its appellate jurisdiction, hearing appeals from the 12 district courts of appeals. The Court may grant leave to appeal criminal cases from the courts of appeals and may direct any court of appeals to certify its record on civil cases that are found to be "cases of public or great general interest." The Court must accept appeals of cases that originated in the courts of appeals; cases involving the death penalty; cases involving questions arising under the U.S. Constitution or the Ohio Constitution; and cases in which there have been conflicting opinions from two or more courts of appeals. The Court must also accept appeals from such administrative bodies as the Board of Tax Appeals and the Public Utilities Commission. Finally, the Court may also grant leave to appeal a case involving a contested election. This type of a case is unique because it is the only type of discretionary appeal that permits a case to be taken directly from the court of common pleas to the Supreme Court, bypassing the court of appeals. The Supreme Court is the court of last resort in Ohio.

The Supreme Court also has oversight responsibility for the judicial processes throughout the state. The Court establishes rules governing practice and procedure in Ohio's courts, such as the Rules of Evidence, the Rules of Civil Procedure, and the Rules of Criminal Procedure. These procedural rules adopted by the Supreme Court are submitted to the General Assembly but become effective on the Court's authority alone, unless both houses of the General Assembly adopt a concurrent resolution of disapproval. The Supreme Court also exercises a level of general oversight over all state courts through its rule-making authority. The "rules of superintendence" by which this is done set minimum standards for court administration statewide. Rules of superintendence do not have to be submitted to the General Assembly to become effective, unlike the procedural rules mentioned above. Finally, the Court also has oversight authority over all attorneys who practice in the state and before its courts. It has the authority to set rules for and provide oversight of the admission of attorneys to the practice of law in Ohio and it may discipline attorneys admitted to practice in the State who violate the rules governing the practice of law. Article IV, Section 5 of the Constitution grants rule making and other authority to the Court.

Ohio selects its judges through elections, a matter which will be discussed in more detail later. The Chief Justice and six Justices are elected to six-year terms on a nonpartisan ballot. Two Justices are chosen at the general election in even-numbered years. In the year when the Chief Justice is on the ballot, voters elect three members of the Court. A person must be an attorney with at least six years of experience in the practice of law to be elected or appointed to the Court. Appointments are made by the governor for vacancies that occur between elections.

The Supreme Court's Oversight Authority

The Ohio Constitution grants the Supreme Court the exclusive authority to regulate admission to the practice of law, over the discipline of attorneys admitted to practice, and over all other matters relating to the practice of law. In connection with this grant of authority, the Supreme Court has promulgated the Supreme Court Rules for the Government of the Bar of Ohio. These Rules address topics such as admission to practice, attorney discipline, attorney registration, continuing legal education, and the unauthorized practice of law.

The Constitution also gives the Supreme Court authority to prescribe rules governing practice and procedure in all courts of the state and to exercise general superintendence over all state courts. Procedural rules promulgated by the Supreme Court become effective unless both houses of the General Assembly adopt a concurrent resolution of disapproval. Rules of superintendence over state courts set minimum standards for court administration. Unlike procedural rules, rules of superintendence do not have to be submitted to the General Assembly to become effective.

In connection with all of the rules for which it has responsibility, the Supreme Court generally solicits public comment before adopting new rules or amendments in final form. The Court first publishes its rules and amendments in proposed form. These proposals appear in both the *Ohio State Bar Association Reports* and the *Ohio Official Advance Sheets* and indicate the period open for comment and the staff member to whom comments should be directed. The Court reviews all comments submitted before it decides whether to adopt or amend a rule.

Pursuant to the Constitution, the Chief Justice or a Justice designated by the Chief Justice is responsible for ruling on the disqualification of appellate and common pleas court judges. The procedure for obtaining review of a claim of disqualification against an appellate or common pleas judge is commenced by the filing of an affidavit of disqualification with the Clerk of the Supreme

Court. The Revised Code contains specific requirements governing the filing of affidavits of disqualification.

Subordinate Courts in Ohio

Courts of Appeals

The courts of appeals are established by Article IV, Section 1, of the Ohio Constitution and their jurisdiction is outlined in Article IV, Section 3. As the intermediate level appellate courts, the primary function of the Courts of Appeals is to hear appeals from the common pleas, municipal, and county courts. Each case is heard and decided by a three-judge panel.

The state is divided into 12 appellate districts, each of which is served by a court of appeals. The number of judges in each district depends on a variety of factors, including the district's population and the court's caseload. Each district has a minimum of four appellate judges. Appeals court judges are elected to six-year terms in even-numbered years. They must have been admitted to the practice of law in Ohio six years preceding commencement of the term.

Like the Supreme Court, the courts of appeals are assigned original jurisdiction over some matters by the state Constitution in addition to their appellate jurisdiction. The courts of appeals have original jurisdiction to hear applications for writs of habeas corpus, mandamus, procedendo, prohibition and quo warranto. Additionally, the 10th District Court of Appeals in Franklin County hears appeals from the Ohio Court of Claims.

As of 2012, there were 69 court of appeals judges. Court of appeals judges are elected in even-numbered years to six-year terms on a nonpartisan ballot and are required to be attorneys with at least six years of experience in the practice of law in order to serve. The Governor makes appointments to fill vacancies in courts of appeals that occur between elections.

The Court Of Claims

The Court of Claims has original jurisdiction to hear and determine all civil actions filed against the state of Ohio and its agencies. The court also hears appeals from decisions made by the attorney general on claims allowed under the Victims of Crime Act.

The Court of Claims decides civil claims typically involving contract disputes, property damage, personal injury, immunity of state officers and employees, discrimination and wrongful imprisonment. The Chief Justice assigns

Figure 4.2: Basic Ohio Court of Appeals information

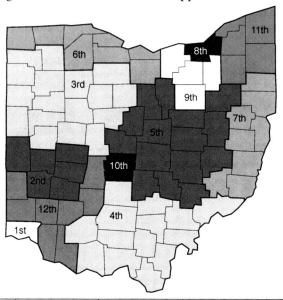

District	Number of Judges	Number of Counties	Population (2010)	Population per Judge
1st	6	1	802,374	113,729
2nd	5	6	1,030,621	206,124
3rd	4	17	787,269	196,817
4th	4	14	633,838	158,460
5th	6	15	1,484,932	247,489
6th	5	8	886,720	177,344
7th	4	8	560,760	140,190
8th	12	1	1,280,122	106,677
9th	5	4	1,129,989	225,998
10th	8	1	1,163,414	145,427
11th	5	5	796,658	159,332
12th	5	8	979,807	195,961
Total	69	88	11,536,504	2,073,548

Source: Compiled from the Court of Appeals Website at http://www.sconet.state.oh.us/Jud
System/districtCourts/default.asp.

judges to hear such cases. In almost every instance, a single judge will hear a case, but the Chief Justice may assign a panel of three judges to a civil action that presents novel or complex issues of law and fact.

Civil complaints filed for $2,500 or less are decided on the contents of the case file or "administratively" by the clerk or a deputy clerk of the court. Appeals from those decisions ("administrative determinations") may be taken to a judge of the court upon motion for court review. The court's judgment in these cases is not subject to further appeal.

Appeals filed by crime victims are heard and determined by a panel of three commissioners who are appointed by the Supreme Court for a term of six years. A further and final appeal from the panel's decision may be taken to a judge of the court. Like administrative determinations, the judge's decision is final.

Structural changes to the Court of Claims of Ohio that took effect in 2014 included the elimination of commissioners. The changes will save money and improve efficiency. Previously, a panel of three commissioners, appointed by the Supreme Court for six-year terms, heard and determined compensation appeals from crime victims. Appeals will now be handled by magistrates. Other changes as outlined in H.B. 261 (the law which adopted these changes) would lower the pay rate for Court of Claims judges, add a provision to give the Chief Justice of the state Supreme Court authority to decide if a Court of Claims judge should be disqualified, and re-establishes the Supreme Court's authority to reimburse local courts for the cost of using an acting judge. The amendment also gives the Supreme Court greater oversight of the use of acting judges.

According to the court's 2012 annual report the Court of Claims eliminated backlogs and cut costs by more than half a million dollars in 2012. In September of that year the court for the first time launched a pilot program for streaming select cases on the Internet in an effort to increase transparency and public understanding of its proceedings. In February, the Ohio Association for Justice recognized Reed and Chief Justice O'Connor for the reduced time it takes the Court of Claims to decide cases and other efficiencies.

Courts of Common Pleas

The court of common pleas, the only trial court created by the Ohio Constitution, is established by Article IV, Section 1, of the Constitution, and its duties are outlined in Article IV, Section 4. Each of the 88 counties in the state has its own court of common pleas. As with the upper courts, common pleas judges are elected to six-year terms on a nonpartisan ballot, and a person must be an attorney with at least six years of experience in the practice of law to be elected or appointed to the court.

Figure 4.3: Courts of Common Pleas, Basic Information

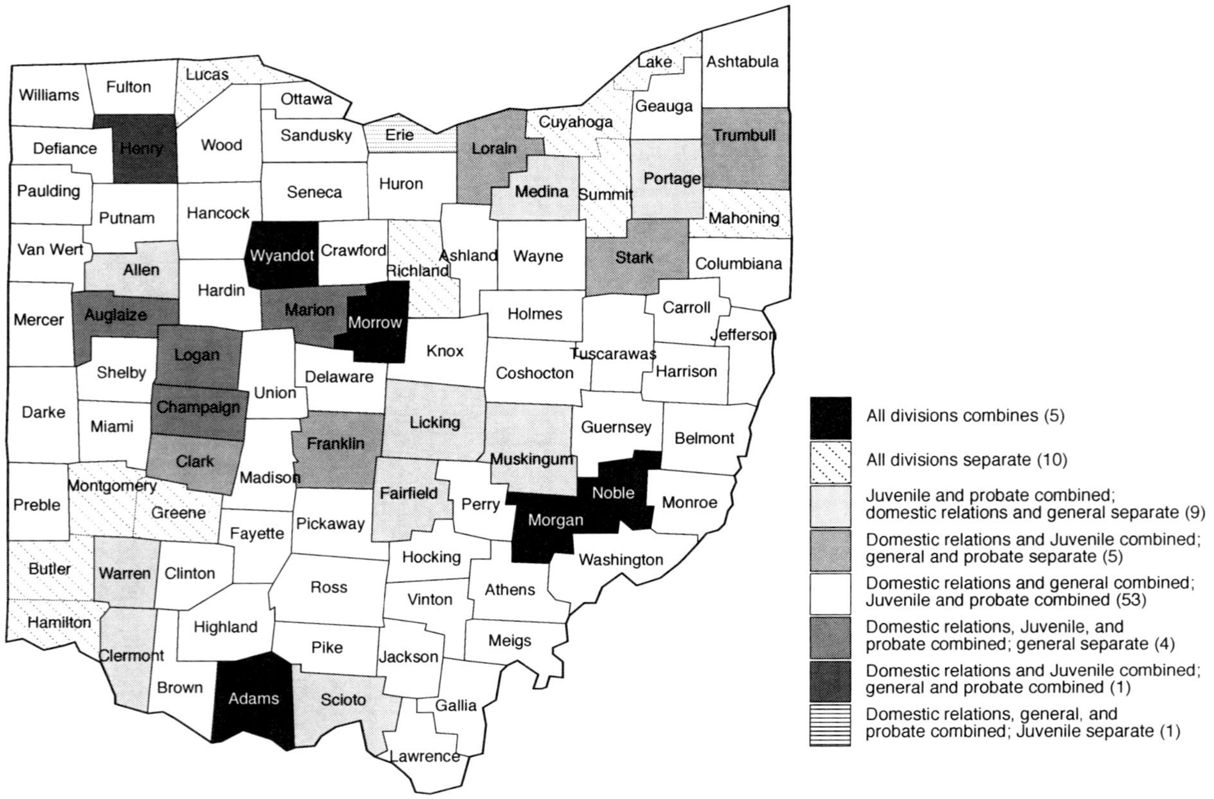

Specific courts of common pleas may be, and often are, divided into separate divisions by the General Assembly, including general, domestic relations, juvenile and probate divisions.

General Division

The general division has original jurisdiction in all criminal felony cases and in all civil cases in which the amount in controversy is more than $15,000. General divisions also have appellate jurisdiction over the decisions of some state administrative agencies.

Domestic Relations Division

Domestic relations courts have jurisdiction over all proceedings involving divorce or dissolution of marriages, annulment, legal separation, spousal support and allocation of parental rights and responsibilities for the care of children.

Juvenile Division

Juvenile courts hear cases involving persons under 18 years of age who are charged with acts that would be crimes if committed by an adult. They also hear cases involving unruly, dependent and neglected children. Juvenile courts have jurisdiction in adult cases involving paternity, child abuse, nonsupport, contributing to the delinquency of minors and the failure to send children to school.

Probate Division

The Ohio Constitution of 1851 provided that probate courts were to be established as separate independent courts with jurisdiction over the probate of wills and supervision of the administration of estates and guardianships. In 1968, under the Modern Courts Amendment of the Ohio Constitution, the probate courts became divisions of the courts of common pleas. Probate courts also have jurisdiction over the issuance of marriage licenses, adoption proceedings, determination of sanity or mental competency and certain eminent domain proceedings. Probate judges can perform marriages and may charge a fee for the service.

Municipal and County Courts

Municipal and county courts are created by the General Assembly as provided in R.C. 1901 and 1907. When municipal courts exercise countywide jurisdiction, no county court is needed. A county court is needed if an area of a county is not served by a municipal court.

The subject-matter jurisdiction of municipal and county courts is nearly identical. Both municipal and county courts have the authority to conduct preliminary hearings in felony cases, and both have jurisdiction over traffic and non-traffic misdemeanors. These courts also have limited civil jurisdiction. Municipal and county courts may hear civil cases in which the amount of money in dispute does not exceed $15,000. Judges sitting in these courts, like probate judges, have the authority to perform marriages.

Municipal court judges are elected to six-year terms on a nonpartisan judicial ballot. A municipal court judge may have jurisdiction in one or more municipalities, across county borders, in adjacent townships, or throughout an entire county. A county court judge is elected to a six-year term on a nonpartisan ballot. All county court judges and 20 municipal court judges are part-time.

Municipal court judges and county court judges must be attorneys with at least six years of experience in the practice of law.

Mayor's Courts

Mayor's courts are not a part of the judicial branch of Ohio government and are not courts of record. Ohio and Louisiana are the only two states that allow the mayors of municipal corporations to preside over a court. A mayor is not required to be a lawyer, but may appoint an attorney who has engaged in the practice of law for three years to hear cases in mayor's court.

In Ohio, in municipalities populated by more than 100 people where there is no municipal court, mayor's courts hear only cases involving violations of local ordinances and state traffic laws. A person convicted in a mayor's court may appeal the conviction to the municipal or county court having jurisdiction within the municipal corporation.

The Supreme Court has adopted rules at the request of the General Assembly which provide for court procedures and basic legal education for mayors. Mayors whose courts hear alcohol- and drug-related traffic offenses have additional educational requirements, and all Mayor's Courts must file statistics quarterly and annually with the Supreme Court.

Figure 4.4: Municipal and County Courts, Basic Information

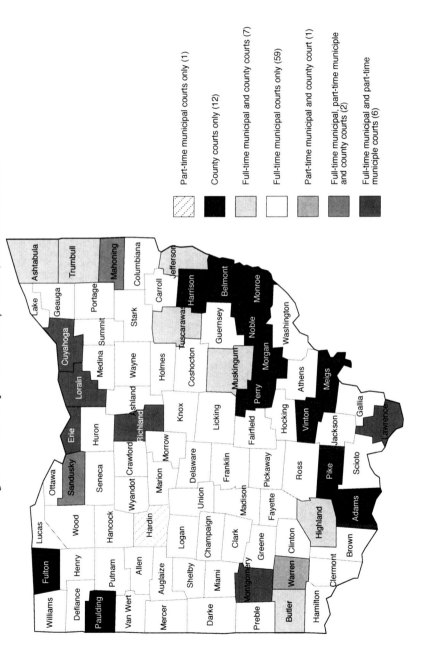

Part-time municipal courts only (1)

County courts only (12)

Full-time municipal and county courts (7)

Full-time municipal courts only (59)

Part-time municipal and county court (1)

Full-time municipal, part-time municiple and county courts (2)

Full-time municipal and part-time municiple courts (6)

Specialized Dockets

In the past several decades, increased attention has been brought across the nation to the usefulness of Specialized Courts or Specialized Dockets, which focus on particular groups of offenders and allows for greater flexibility in handling some cases. These specialized dockets save time and money in the court system and allow for more specialized support to the populations being addressed. The Specialized Dockets Section of the Supreme Court provides technical support to trial courts in analyzing the need for, planning of, and implementation and certification of specialized docket programs (Supreme Court, 2014).

The first specialized court used in the state was a drug court established in Hamilton County and, by 1997, there were over a dozen such courts in use. A study undertaken in 2001 by the University of Cincinnati's Center for Criminal Justice research under a grant from the Ohio Office of Criminal Justice Research found the outcome results of their study to be promising, in that the offenders who participated in the drug court service such as judicial supervision and community-based treatment were less likely to be rearrested than did other offenders who did not use such services (Latressa, 2001).

Rules adopted by The Ohio Supreme Court outline the procedures for a specialized docket program to receive Supreme Court certification. The certification process requires courts operating specialized dockets to submit an application, undergo a site visit, and submit specific program materials to the Specialized Docket Section. The standards seek to create a minimum level of uniform practices for specialized dockets, while still allowing local specialized dockets to innovate and tailor their program to respond to local needs and resources. In addition, specialized dockets that comply with the initial stages of the certification process will be initially certified pending a final review. Specialized docket programs are required to be initially certified by January 1, 2014. The amendments also create a new Commission on Specialized Dockets which will be the body that applies the certification requirements and determines which programs are certified.

The Specialized Dockets presently being used by courts throughout the state include:

- Mental Health Courts
- Drug Courts
- OVI/DUI Courts
- Domestic Violence Courts
- Child Support Enforcement Courts
- Re-entry Courts

- Sex Offender Courts
- Veterans Courts

Specialized dockets are an expanding part of the Court system in Ohio. In 2011, when the Supreme Court first announced proposed rules for formally certifying these courts, there were over 150 operating. As of June 13, 2014, there are now 65 formally certified Ohio Specialized Docket Courts running in 30 different counties, with many others still undergoing the certification process. 29 of these are Drug Courts, 13 focus on Mental Health, 9 on Family dependency or Child Support, with at least one court in one jurisdiction focusing on each of the other topic listed above. Many of these specialized dockets operate out of the Juvenile Division of the Common Pleas Court or the Municipal Court in the County (Supreme Court).

One area where Ohio has taken a leading role in the use of Specialized Dockets is in the use of Veterans' Courts. Although the first such Court was used in New York State, Ohio, whose population of veterans is sixth among the 50 states, increasingly uses veterans' courts to help deserving war veterans who have become criminal defendants. The veterans' court uses a treatment problem-solving model rather than a traditional court model in a manner already used by drug courts and mental health courts in its efforts to assist veterans whose problems can be clearly traced to military service (Ohio State Bar).

A more complete picture of the specialized dockets will be provided in Chapter 7.

Boards and Commissions

The Supreme Court of Ohio relies upon numerous bodies to help meet its constitutional and statutory authority to regulate the practice of law and exercise general superintendence over all courts in the state. Two of these bodies are boards and commissions. Boards are formed to exercise quasi-judicial authority or decision-making authority on behalf of the Court. Commissions are formed to exercise quasi-ministerial authority on behalf of the Court.

Boards and commissions are created by action of the Court and operate under rules or regulations adopted by the Court. Members serve by appointment of the Chief Justice and Justices or by virtue of holding a position within or upon nomination of a group, organization, or association. Boards and commissions are comprised of judges, attorneys, clerks of court, other court personnel, and private citizens from throughout Ohio.

The Court has adopted *Guidelines for the Creation and Operation of Supreme Court Boards, Commissions, Advisory Committees, and Task Forces*. The guidelines specify what constitutes a board, commission, advisory committee, or task force, how they are created, and how members are appointed to these bodies.

Members of the boards and commissions fulfill specifically designated duties and responsibilities. To help guide the activities of the membership, the Court has adopted a *Code of Ethics for Court Appointees* and *Guidelines for Travel by Court Appointees*.

Here is a list of the Boards in place and active in 2014:

- **Board of Bar Examiners:** The Board of Bar Examiners is responsible for developing, administering, and grading the Ohio bar examination. The Board consists of 18 members appointed by the Supreme Court of Ohio. Bar examinations are administered in Columbus in February and July of each year.
- **Board of Commissioners on Character & Fitness:** The Board of Commissioners on Character & Fitness is responsible for ensuring that each applicant for admission to the practice of law possesses the requisite character, fitness, and moral qualifications for admission. The Board consists of 12 members, appointed by the Court, who must be members of the Ohio bar. Pursuant to Gov. Bar R. I, Sections 10–13, the Board's essential functions are to promulgate admission standards and applications, supervise the work of local bar admissions committees, review the character, fitness, and moral qualifications of each applicant for admission, and hear appeals from admission applicants who receive adverse admission recommendations from local bar admission committees.
- **Board of Commissioners on Grievances & Discipline:** The Board of Commissioners on Grievances & Discipline is a 28-member quasi-judicial body appointed by the Supreme Court of Ohio that consists of 17 lawyers, seven active or retired judges, and four non-lawyers. The Board's duties are as follows:
    - Adjudicating formal complaints of misconduct involving judges and lawyers and making recommendations to the Supreme Court on the appropriate sanction
    - Hearing cases involving the mental illness of judges and lawyers and the reinstatement of lawyers suspended from the practice of law
    - Monitoring and assisting bar association certified grievance committees in the regulation of the legal profession
    - Issuing ethics advisory opinions
    - Advising judges and lawyers on ethics compliance

- ○ Conducting educational programs on ethics for judges, lawyers, and judicial candidates
- ○ Receiving and retaining financial disclosure statements filed annually by judges, magistrates, and judicial candidates
- **Board on the Unauthorized Practice of Law:** The Board on the Unauthorized Practice of Law of the Supreme Court of Ohio is established by Rule VII of the Supreme Court Rules for the Government of the Bar of Ohio and consists of 13 members who are appointed to a three-year term by the Supreme Court. The Board conducts hearings, preserves the record, and makes findings and recommendations to the Supreme Court in cases involving the alleged unauthorized practice of law. The Board is also authorized to issue informal nonbinding advisory opinions on matters concerning the unauthorized practice of law.
- **Clients' Security Fund:** The Clients' Security Fund of Ohio was established in 1985 to provide assistance to clients who have been financially harmed by the dishonest conduct of a licensed Ohio attorney. While most lawyers observe high standards of integrity when entrusted with clients' money and property, the dishonest acts of a few can affect the public's image of and confidence in all legal professionals. The Fund's goal is to restore public confidence in the legal profession by reimbursing law clients for losses sustained as a result of the dishonest conduct of their attorney.
- **Judicial College Board of Trustees:** The Judicial College receives advice from and provides support to its oversight body—the Board of Trustees of the Judicial College. The Board of Trustees consists of 10 members plus the Chief Justice, who serves ex officio. The membership consists of seven judges appointed by the various judicial associations, one magistrate appointed by the Ohio Association of Magistrates, and two judges appointed by the Chief Justice.

In addition to Boards listed above, the Court has the following Commissions are in place:

- **Committee on the Appointment of Counsel for Indigent Defendants in Capital Cases:** The Committee on the Appointment of Counsel for Indigent Defendants in Capital Cases administers the requirements of Rule 20 of the Rules of Superintendence for the Courts of Ohio, including the certification of attorneys who are eligible to be appointed to represent indigent capital defendants.
- **Ohio Criminal Sentencing Commission:** In 1990, the General Assembly created the Ohio Criminal Sentencing Commission by statute. The

Commission is chaired by the Chief Justice. It is responsible for conducting a review of Ohio's sentencing statutes and sentencing patterns, and making recommendations regarding necessary statutory changes. The Commission consists of 31 members, 10 of whom are judges appointed by the Chief Justice. A report issued by the Committee to the Governor and the General Assembly in 1993 resulted in Senate Bill 2, the most comprehensive revision of criminal sentencing statutes in over 20 years.

- **Commission on Dispute Resolution**: The purpose of the Commission on Dispute Resolution is to advise the Supreme Court and its staff on all of the following:
  - ○ The promotion of statewide rules and uniform standards concerning the use of dispute resolution in Ohio courts;
  - ○ The development and delivery of dispute resolution education and professional development activities for judges, magistrates, court personnel, attorneys, and court-affiliated dispute resolution professionals;
  - ○ The development and delivery of dispute resolution services for disputes arising among state, county, and local public officials throughout Ohio;
  - ○ The consideration of any other issues the commission deems necessary to assist the Supreme Court and its staff regarding the development and delivery of dispute resolution programs and services.
- **Commission on Specialized Dockets**: The Commission on Specialized Dockets advises the Supreme Court and its staff regarding the promotion of statewide rules and uniform standards concerning specialized dockets in Ohio courts; the development and delivery of specialized docket services to Ohio courts, including training programs for judges and court personnel; and the consideration of any other issues the commission deems necessary to assist the Supreme Court and its staff regarding specialized dockets in Ohio courts.

Other Commissions that provide specialized support to the Supreme Court and the judicial process include:

- Commission on Certification of Attorneys as Specialists
- Commission on Continuing Legal Education
- Commission on the Thomas J. Moyer Ohio Judicial Center
- Commission on Professionalism
- Commission on the Rules of Practice & Procedure
- Commission on the Rules of Superintendence
- Commission on Technology and the Courts

Information on these Boards and Commissions can be found on the Supreme Court website (https://www.supremecourt.ohio.gov/Boards/specDockets/default.asp).

Workload and Processing Statistics

Approximately 2.7 million cases appear before one or another of Ohio's courts, with the overwhelming majority of those (over 2 million) involving the most minor of offenses heard at Municipal and County Courts. Generally speaking, about 500,000–600,000 cases have been heard at the level of the various Common Pleas Courts, with only about 2,000 cases coming before the state Supreme Court each year. These numbers have been generally decreasing each year, a matter generally attributed to an increase in out-of-court settlements, plea bargains, and alternative dispute resolution methods, all of which are less expensive than trials but which are sometimes thought to lessen the justness of the outcomes (Futty, 2014). Figure 4.5, provides the most recent statistics available at the time of writing.

Judicial Selection

As noted above, all judges in Ohio, up to and including those of the Supreme Court, are now elected in non-partisan elections. This was not always the case. Similarly to many states, the original structure of the state's judicial system called for the appointment of judges by the state legislature. The 1803 Constitution provided that the three Judges of the Supreme Court, the President, and the Associate Judges of the Courts of Common Pleas would be appointed by a joint ballot of both Houses of the General Assembly, and would hold their offices for the term of seven years, "if so long they behave well."

During the mid-1800s, there was a national populist movement, and Ohio was not immune to this development. Concerns over the power of the legislature, often seen as beholden to special business interests and not the population, led to a call for a state constitutional convention in 1850, and a number of amendments were adopted. As a result, the Constitution of 1851 created a more democratic system within the state, giving Ohio voters the right to elect the governor, other high-ranking state officials, and judges. Rather than having only two levels of courts within the state, a third level of district courts was added between the Ohio Supreme Court and common pleas courts (Ohio History Central, 2014).

Figure 4.5: Cases and Courts in Ohio

	2003	2004	2005	2006	2007	2008	2009	2010	2011	2012
Supreme Court	2,237	2,178	2,444	2,407	2,459	2,506	2,363	2,293	2,207	2,187
Court of Appeals	10,905	10,713	11,437	11,208	10,512	11,115	10,433	10,277	9,508	9,426
Court of Claims	1,134	1,024	1,138	734	896	1,094	902	1,231	1,337	865
Common Pleas	653,554	649,348	656,473	677,512	673,240	664,138	639,419	613,043	574,900	558,813
General	211,376	216,094	229,352	247,434	261,677	266,547	258,460	244,743	221,181	214,933
Domestic Relations	79,527	80,389	77,888	76,844	74,157	73,087	73,463	73,327	71,499	68,526
Probate	95,338	94,998	93,708	91,621	88,021	88,621	88,178	85,152	85,866	88,798
Juvenile	267,313	257,867	255,525	261,613	249,385	235,883	219,318	209,821	196,354	186,556
Municipal and County	2,700,538	2,417,551	2,469,942	2,525,373	2,518,204	2,534,408	2,322,505	2,203,420	2,121,129	2,136,327
Municipal	2,444,493	2,211,094	2,259,479	2,311,044	2,309,559	2,338,119	2,142,154	2,047,841	1,968,708	1,971,837
County	256,045	206,457	210,463	214,329	208,645	196,289	180,351	155,579	152,421	164,490
All Courts Combined	3,368,368	3,080,814	3,141,434	3,217,234	3,205,311	3,213,261	2,975,622	2,830,264	2,709,081	2,707,618

Source: The Supreme Court of Ohio, Ohio Courts Statistical Summary 2012, http://www.supremecourt.ohio.gov/Publications/annrep/12OCS/summary/trend.pdf

Ohio has continued in selecting its judges through non-partisan elections, although the primaries are partisan, with judicial candidates running in either the Democratic or Republican primaries. This hybrid approach was challenged in state and federal courts by those who believed that the non-partisan elections deprived voters of information about the judicial candidates, but the practice has been recently upheld (Johnson, 2014). Nevertheless, as evidenced by the challenge and as has been the case in other states with elected judiciaries (not to mention the overall tone of American electoral politics) these elections have gotten increasingly expensive and acrimonious, leading to scrutiny of the process by the Supreme Court.

In May 2014, after nearly two years of study and discussion, The Chief Justice of the Ohio Supreme Court proposed a three-point plan for strengthening judicial elections in Ohio. The plan starts with the stated premise that, because the people of Ohio have made clear that they want to elect their judges, the process of judicial elections should be retained. The three proposals in the report, taken together, are intended to elevate judicial elections, more effectively empower voters, and ensure that decisions about who will serve on the bench of the various courts in Ohio will be better-informed made by large numbers of informed voters.

Polls had indicated that, even though Ohioans were satisfied with and wanted to continue a process whereby judges were elected, there remained a significant perception among the populace that judges were unduly influenced by politics, by campaign contributions, and by other factors. In addition, for years it had been noted that voter turnout for judicial races was significantly below that of other elections. Finally, these polls indicated that voters do not have easy access to quality information about the candidates, and as a result the level of knowledge and understanding about the judiciary among the general public is poor.

The Chief Justice's proposal, titled "Ohio Judicial Reform 2014: A Plan to Elevate Judicial Elections," offered three reforms intended to improve judicial elections and strengthen Ohio's system of justice:

1. Move All Judicial Contests to Odd-Numbered Years and Move Judicial Contests to the Top of the Ballot

Research relied upon by the Chief Justice indicated that shows judicial elections in Ohio often take a back seat to high-profile executive and legislative races, with an increasingly small percentage of the electorate participating. On average, even when voters show up at the polls, 25 percent of the time the voters fail to vote for judges further down the ticket. Given that overall voting rates hover at about the 50% of eligible voter level, this judicial roll-off means that, in some cases, judges are being selected by a result of the votes of only one quarter of eligible voters.

To remedy this, the O'Connor plan has proposed that Ohio amend the state Constitution to move all judicial races to odd-numbered years, while at the same time making some modest changes in the Ohio Revised Code to place these races at the top of the ballot.

Moving all judicial elections to odd-numbered years would, it was believed, eliminate the competition of judicial candidates for air time or for public awareness with the races for president or governor. The proposal is intended to recast odd-year elections not as "off-year elections" but instead as the *judicial years*, focused on electing the men and women who serve on the bench in Ohio at every level.

2. Implement a Comprehensive, Robust and Non-partisan Voter Information and Education Plan

The second part of the O'Connor plan focuses on development of a comprehensive voter engagement and information program. The program will provide a website intended to provide voters statewide with a one-stop-shop for information about judicial candidates at every level. The program also will use traditional media, social media, and other methods throughout the year to educate voters about the importance of voting in judicial elections and encouraging participation.

This program is to be launched in 2015 by combining the existing resources of three critical partners: The Ohio State Bar Association, the League of Women Voters of Ohio, and the Ray C. Bliss Institute of Applied Politics at the University of Akron, which will serve as the official home of the state's first comprehensive, ongoing, judicial voter education and engagement program. The goal is to accomplish these objectives without increasing the use of tax dollars.

3. Increase Judicial Qualifications

Increasing the number of years of practice required to run for or be appointed to a judgeship will further elevate judicial elections by giving voters even more experienced candidates to choose from. Currently, an attorney needs only six years of experience before assuming the bench at all levels. The O'Connor plan adopts the recommendation of a bi-partisan panel that examined judicial elections in 2003 and that has been included in at least three recent legislative proposals: longer years of practice requirements for the common pleas bench (8 years), the appellate bench (10 years), and Supreme Court justices (12 years).

Public Defender Services in the State of Ohio

The Office of the Ohio Public Defender is the state agency responsible for providing legal representation and other services to those accused of a crime who cannot afford to hire their own attorney. The United States Constitution and the Ohio Constitution guarantee the right to an attorney, because an attorney is needed to protect an individual's rights and to present the evidence necessary for a fair and reliable determination of guilt or innocence. The Office of the Ohio Public Defender is critical to the fairness of the criminal justice system: the quality of justice the person receives should not be determined by the person's financial status.

Ohio's public defender system was created in 1976 by Chapter 120 of the Ohio Revised Code. Timothy Young is the Director of the Office of the Ohio Public Defender, which is overseen by the nine-member Ohio Public Defender Commission. The Office is divided into Death Penalty, Legal, Juvenile, and Administrative divisions, as well as the Trumbull County Branch Office and the Multi-County Program. The County Reimbursement Program processes payments to reimburse counties for operating their indigent defense systems. These systems include county public defender offices, court-appointed counsel systems, and contracts with not-for-profit organizations (Ohio Public Defender, 2014).

County Indigent Defense Systems

Ohio's indigent defense system consists of County Public Defenders, which includes County offices and also agreements with Non-Profit Corporations, Court-Appointed Counsel, and the Office of the Ohio Public Defender. The defense system used by each county is determined by the local Board of County Commissioners. Together, Ohio county public defenders handled over 254,878 cases in fiscal year 2013.

The following counties do not have a public defender office and, instead, only use court-appointed counsel: Ashland, Champaign, Crawford, Defiance, Delaware, Fairfield, Fulton, Guernsey, Hardin, Henry, Highland, Hocking, Holmes, Jefferson, Lawrence, Licking, Logan, Lorain, Madison, Mahoning, Marion, Mercer, Morgan, Morrow, Muskingum, Noble, Ottawa, Paulding, Perry, Preble, Putnam, Richland, Sandusky, Scioto, Seneca, Vinton, Warren, Williams, and Wyandot.

The Office of the Ohio Public Defender (OPD) offers representation at trial when requested by the courts, as well as at parole and probation revocation hearings for the more than 50,000 people in Ohio's prisons. Given its limited resources, however, the focus of the OPD tends to be on the appeals and post-trial activities of death penalty and other criminal and juvenile delinquency cases.

Other services provided by the OPD include technical assistance, research services, educational programs, investigation and mitigation services, and assistance to court-appointed attorneys throughout the state.

Working with local public defenders, courts, and county commissioners, as well as state leaders and organizations, the Office of the Ohio Public Defender strives to change laws, rules, and practices in order to provide a more effective and efficient indigent defense delivery system.

Pro bono legal support is also provided by volunteer attorneys organized through the Ohio State Legal Services Association (OLSA). The OLSA is a nonprofit, publicly funded, legal services program with nine direct-service offices that provide civil representation to low-income Ohioans in 30 Ohio counties. Federal law defines low income for its eligibility as 125% of the Federal Poverty Level (Ohio Legal Services, 2014).

Key Terms

Appellate Court   Municipal Court
Boards and Commissions   Pro Bono
Court of Appeals   Public Defender
Court of Original Jurisdiction   Specialized Dockets
Drug Courts   Supreme Court
Indigent   Veterans Courts

Resources

Ohio Constitution
    http://www.legislature.state.oh.us/constitution.cfm
Ohio Court News
    www.courtsnewsohio.gov
Ohio Supreme Court
    http://www.supremecourt.ohio.gov/

Review Questions

1. What is the role of the Ohio Constitution in terms of the court system in Ohio?
2. Which courts have original jurisdiction on most criminal cases?
3. What does a specialized docket court do?
4. What is the role of the public defender in the courts?
5. What is a Mayor's court and when is it used?
6. What does a special billet court do and what purpose does it serve?
7. How does the court system in Ohio interact with other courts?

References

Beogher, Stephanie. *Changes to Ohio Court of Claims Structure Take Effect*, Ohio Court News, July 10, 2014. www.courtnewsohio.gov/happening/2014/cocChanges_071014.asp#.U8E9HrHLPCk.

Futty, John. *Trials a Rarity in Ohio*, The Columbus Dispatch , Monday January 13, 2014 http://www.dispatch.com/content/stories/local/2014/01/13/trials-a-rarity-in-ohio-u-s-.html.

Johnson, Alan. *Ohio's partisan system for electing judges OK, court rules*, Columbus Dispatch, June 12, 2014, http://www.dispatch.com/content/stories/local/2014/06/11/Judge-rules-on-Ohios-judge-elections.html.

Latessa, Edward J., et al. *Preliminary Evaluation of Ohio's Drug Court Efforts*, University of Cincinnati Center for Criminal Justice Research, November 2001.

Martinez, Frederico. *Students get up close look at Ohio Supreme Court*, Toledo Blade (April 9, 2014), http://www.toledoblade.com/Courts/2014/04/09/Students-get-up-close-look-at-Ohio-Supreme-Court.html.

Ohio History Central, *Ohio Constitution of 1803 (Transcript)*, http://www.ohiohistorycentral.org/w/Ohio_Constitution_of_1803_%28Transcript%29.

Ohio History Central, *The Ohio Constitutional Convention of 1850–1851*, http://www.ohiohistorycentral.org/w/Ohio_Constitutional_Convention_of_1850-1851?rec=524.

Ohio History Central, *Rutherford v. M'Faddon*, http://www.ohiohistorycentral.org/w/Rutherford_v._M%27Faddon?rec=547.

Ohio Legal Services, www.ohiolegalservices.org/probono.

Ohio Public Defender Services, www.opd.ohio.gov/.

Ohio Secretary of State, The *Constitution of the State of Ohio (1851)(as amended through 2011)*, https://www.sos.state.oh.us/sos/upload/publications/election/Constitution.pdf.

Ohio State Bar Association, *Ohio Veteran's Courts Provide Support,* November 13, 2013, https://www.ohiobar.org/ForPublic/Resources/LawYouCanUse/Pages/Ohio%27s-Veterans%27-Courts-Provide-Support.aspx.

The Supreme Court of Ohio, Press Release, August 19, 2011, *Supreme Court Adopts Specialized Dockets Standards,* http://www.sconet.state.oh.us/PIO/news/2011/ruleAmend_081911.asp.

The Supreme Court of Ohio, *Ohio Judicial System Structure,* www.supreme court.ohio.gov/JudSystem/default.asp.

The Supreme Court of Ohio, *Specialized Docket Section,* http://www.supreme court.ohio.gov/JCS/specDockets/default.asp.

The Supreme Court of Ohio, *Jurisdiction and Authority,* www.supreme court.ohio.gov/SCO/jurisdiction/default.asp.

The Supreme Court of Ohio, *Ohio Courts Statistical Summary 2012,* http://www.supremecourt.ohio.gov/Publications/annrep/12OCS/summary/trend.pdf.

Chapter 5

Criminal Law in Ohio

Learning Objectives

After reading this chapter, students will be able to:

- Explain the purpose and organization of the Ohio Revised Code.
- Describe the different levels of offenses related to murder, assault, robbery, theft, and arson.
- Identify the elements of a crime.
- Analyze the situations in which crime occurs to determine which crime applies.
- Explain how changes are made to the Ohio Revised Code.
- Explain the difference between a felony and a misdemeanor.

Introduction

The Ohio Revised Code (ORC) describes all of the laws and statutes pertaining to illegal behavior and punishments in the state of Ohio. It is organized by provisions, titles, chapters and sections that each describe the details of each particular offense. Title 29 of the Code pertains specifically to criminal behavior.

According to Section 2901.03 of the ORC, "No conduct constitutes a criminal offense against the state unless it is defined as an offense in the Revised Code." This means that no act can be considered illegal unless it is defined as such in the ORC. It also means that a person cannot be arrested for an act unless it is defined as a crime in the ORC. Further, the ORC stipulates that "Every person accused of an offense is presumed innocent until proven guilty beyond a reasonable doubt, and the burden of proof for all elements of the offense is upon the prosecution."[1] Thus, in order to be sentenced for a criminal act, a state prosecutor must prove the act was committed and all elements of that

---

1. Ohio Revised Code, 2901.05.

act were present. Moreover, a person must have committed the act voluntarily and had the specific intention to cause a certain result. They had to have the mental capacity to perform the act and know that their behavior would cause a specific harm.

A person charged with a criminal offense in Ohio will be tried in a court in Ohio to determine their guilt. According to ORC 2901.11, "A person is subject to criminal prosecution and punishment in this state if any of the following occur: The person commits an offense under the laws of this state, any element of which takes place in this state." A person can commit a crime in Ohio and go to another state, but they can be returned to Ohio for a trial and possible punishment. This is also true if a person conspires to commit an offense while in another jurisdiction, or if they bring illegal property into the state.

The laws contained in the ORC are the result of legislative action in the Ohio General Assembly. The elected officials in the Ohio House and Senate have proposed, debated and passed the laws as needed. Each law must define the specific behavior or act that is illegal as well as the associated punishment. There are no ex-post facto laws permitted in Ohio, which would make an offense illegal before a law is passed. A law must be passed that defines a behavior as illegal from a certain implementation date, but not before.

The ORC classifies crimes as either a misdemeanor or felony. A misdemeanor is a less serious offense, such as speeding. These offenses are generally punished by fines with either no time in a local jail or a period of under one year. Other options for punishing a misdemeanor would be community corrections or restitution. A felony is a more serious crime such as murder, rape or kidnapping. If a defendant is charged with a felony, they will likely spend a longer time in a state correctional facility (over one year) or may even be sentenced to death.

Felonies and misdemeanors are also classified by degrees. First-degree felonies are the most serious, while fifth-degree felonies are the least serious. Similarly, first-degree misdemeanors are considered the most serious class, while minor misdemeanors are the least serious. An example of a first-degree felony is rape, and a fifth-degree felony is breaking and entering. An example of a first-degree misdemeanor is unauthorized use of a vehicle, whereas a fifth-degree misdemeanor is disorderly conduct. The possible sentences for misdemeanors and felonies also vary. These are described in Tables 5.1 and 5.2, below.

Crimes

There are many crimes outlined in the Ohio revised code, with multiple levels of seriousness. Some of the more severe offense categories are described here.

Table 5.1: Possible Sentences for Felony Offenses

Degree	Possible Sentence
First-degree felony	3 to 11 years in prison
Second-degree felony	2 to 8 years in prison
Third-degree felony	9 months to 5 years in prison
Fourth-degree felony	6 to 18 months in prison
Fifth-degree felony	6 to 12 months in prison

Source: ORC (2014)

Table 5.2: Possible Sentences for Misdemeanor Offenses

Degree	Possible Jail Time	Possible Fines
First-degree misdemeanor	up to 180 days in jail	up to $1,000 in fines
Second-degree misdemeanor	up to 90 days in jail	up to $750 in fines
Third-degree misdemeanor	up to 60 days in jail	up to $500 in fines
Fourth-degree misdemeanor	up to 30 days in jail	up to $250 in fines
Minor misdemeanor	no jail sentence	up to $150 in fines

Source: ORC (2014)

Murder

According to the Ohio Revised Code (ORC 2903.02), a person commits murder if they cause the death of another person, or if they cause the unlawful termination of another person's pregnancy. A person also commits murder if a death is caused while the offender is committing another act of violence. An example of what might constitute murder occurs when Ron and Michael, who are enjoying a drink in a bar, begin to argue, their voices becoming louder. It doesn't take long before the two men hop off their seats and begin pushing each other. Ron punches Michael in the jaw. Michael falls to the ground, but Ron continues to punch and kick him. Before other bar patrons can pull the two apart, Ron beats Michael so severely that he eventually dies. There was no gun, knife, or other weapon present, nor was the crime planned prior to that evening.

According to the ORC (ORC 2903.01), aggravated murder occurs when a person purposely, with prior calculation and design, causes the death of another person (or terminates another person's pregnancy). If this act occurs while a person is attempting to commit another crime, such as kidnapping, rape, arson, or robbery, or fleeing from a felony offense, it is then considered to be aggravated murder. If the victim is under the age of thirteen or a law enforcement officer, it is also considered to be aggravated murder.

Using the example above, had Ron planned the attack on Michael by inviting him to the bar with the sole intent of beating him until he died, this would be considered to be aggravated murder. In this case, Ron consciously thought out the attack beforehand. Or, if Michael had identified himself as a police officer to Ron before the attack, it would also be categorized as aggravated murder. A murder would also be considered to be aggravated if it occurred as a person was running away from a robbery. In this case, an offender commits a robbery, and is confronted by the building's owner as he leaves. The offender shoots the owner, causing his death. This would be an aggravated murder because it was committed as an offender was fleeing from a first- or second-degree felony offense.

Another type of murder under the Ohio Revised Code (ORC 2903.03) is voluntary manslaughter. In this offense, an offender causes the death of another person while in a sudden fit of rage or passion. The classic example of this is when a person finds their spouse having sexual relations with another, and in a fit of passion, shoots the victim. In this case, the offender was in a sudden fit of rage or passion and therefore not thinking clearly. The critical element is that the offender is provoked by another person to become enraged enough to commit that act. It typically must be more than just teasing or taunting a person to be considered a fit of rage.

Involuntary Manslaughter is defined in the Ohio Revised Code (ORC 2903.04) as causing the death of another person as a result of the offender committing or attempting to commit another crime. The example provided in the ORC is when a person is killed by another as they operate a watercraft (boat) while under the influence of alcohol or drugs. Another example would be if a drunk driver drives into a tree, killing the passenger. In these cases, the deaths were caused by someone who was committing another offense: driving a vehicle while impaired.

A person may be guilty of committing another offense called reckless homicide (found in ORC 2903.041) if it is proven that they recklessly caused the death of another person (or unlawfully terminated a pregnancy). If so, they would be guilty of a third-degree felony. This offense may occur if a person shoots a gun into the air during a fireworks display, accidentally shooting a bystander. Their behavior of shooting a weapon in a crowded area is clearly reckless.

Negligent homicide, according to the Ohio Revised Code (ORC 2903.05) is when a person negligently causes the death of another person or the termination of a pregnancy by means of a deadly weapon. This is considered to be a misdemeanor of the first degree. This could happen if a gun discharges while the owner is cleaning their weapon, killing a person nearby. The gun owner, who did not intend to kill another person, was negligent in ensuring the gun's chamber was empty before cleaning it.

The last type of murder offense in the Ohio Revised Code is aggravated vehicular homicide, which may occur if a death of another person occurs while an offender is operating or participating in the operation of a motor vehicle, motorcycle, locomotive, watercraft, or aircraft. This can be done recklessly (as the result of committing a reckless operation) or negligently (while operating a motor vehicle in a construction zone, speeding or as the result of committing a misdemeanor (ORC 2903.06). An example of this is driving into a crowd of people who have gathered for an event such as a music festival or holiday celebration, and causing the death of attendees.

Assault

According to the Ohio Revised Code, a person commits an assault if they knowingly cause or attempt to cause serious physical harm to another person or to another's unborn baby. An assault is considered to be a misdemeanor of the first degree, however it can be higher if the assault occurs on the grounds of a correctional facility, or if the victim is a school teacher, peace officer, a health care professional, a judge or other court official, among others. A typical assault occurs when one person punches another during an argument at a bar, and the victim is injured but survives. However, if the offense occurs in a school and the victim is a teacher, it would be a more serious offense.

Another more serious offense is a felonious assault, which is a felony of the second degree. In this case, an offender causes serious physical harm to another or to another's unborn (or attempts to cause physical harm) by use of a deadly weapon (such as a gun or knife). If the victim is a police officer, the offense becomes a felony of the first degree. If a person stabs another person, or beats them with a baseball bat, it is considered a felonious assault because a weapon (in this case a bat) was used. In Ohio, if a person with AIDS has sexual relations with another person without their consent, it is also considered to be a felonious assault.

A person may be guilty of an aggravated assault if they cause harm to another or to another's unborn while under the influence of a fit of rage. If this occurs, it is a felony of the fourth degree. If the victim is a peace officer, then it is a felony of the third degree, a more serious crime. An example of this is a fight that ensues after one man discovers another man having relations with his wife. While the man may be injured as a result of the fight, he is alive afterward.

Negligent assault is another category of assaults. Under the Ohio Revised Code, no person shall negligently cause physical harm to another or another's unborn by means of a deadly weapon. This is a misdemeanor of the third degree. A person who shoots another person unintentionally, and that person is injured but not killed, while cleaning a gun may be charged with negligent assault.

A final offense is vehicular assault. This occurs when a person causes serious physical harm to another person or an unborn child while operating a motor vehicle, motorcycle, snowmobile, locomotive, watercraft or aircraft. According to the ORC, reckless vehicular assault occurs when a person operates a vehicle in a construction zone, or while speeding. Or a person may drive a car through a stop sign, causing an accident where a passenger was injured (but not killed). This is either a felony of the third or fourth degree, depending upon the circumstances. The offender may also have their license suspended in addition to other sanctions, including possible time in prison.

Robbery

According to the Ohio Revised Code, a person cannot, in attempting or committing a theft, inflict or threaten to inflict harm on another person. In other words, a person cannot inflict, attempt to inflict, or threaten to inflict physical harm on another person while committing a theft (ORC 2911.02). Thus, it is illegal to threaten someone by saying, "Give me your money or I will beat you." If they do, this behavior may be considered to be the crime of robbery.

Similarly, a person cannot, in attempting or committing a theft offense, or in fleeing after the attempt or offense, either have a weapon or display it, brandish it (show it to others), indicate that the offender possess it or use it to inflict or attempt to inflict serious physical harm on another. This is considered to be aggravated robbery and is a felony of the first degree (ORC 2911.01). It is clear that under this portion of the ORC, a person cannot show a weapon while committing a robbery. If they do, it is an aggravated robbery.

Theft

A theft occurs when a person, with the purpose to deprive the owner of property or services, knowingly obtains or exerts control over either the property or services without the consent of the owner or person authorized to give consent. It may also be beyond the scope of a person's ability to give the consent, which may happen if an individual is older or suffering from mental illness. Consent can also not be obtained through deception, threat or intimidation. If a person is found guilty of this act, they are guilty of a felony of the second degree (ORC 2913.02). An example of this is someone who steals merchandise from a store without payment, or who steals money from a person in a nursing home.

Burglary

In Ohio, a burglary occurs when a person, by force or deception, trespasses in an occupied structure when another person is present with the purpose to commit any criminal offense. This is a second-degree felony (ORC 2911.12). Clearly, a person who breaks into a home when the residents are there in order to steal an item or injure a resident is guilty of burglary. Thus, if Jacob cuts the screen of a window in his neighbor's home while they are sleeping in order to steal money, he could be convicted of burglary.

If the person, upon entering an occupied structure when another person is present, with purpose to commit any criminal offense, inflicts or attempts to inflict harm, or threatens to inflict physical harm on another, or the offender has a deadly weapon, it is then aggravated burglary (ORC 2911.11). This is a more serious offense for which the offender can face a more severe penalty. So, for example, in the above example, if Jacob were carrying a gun as he broke into his neighbor's home, he may be found guilty of aggravated burglary.

If the structure in question is not occupied at the time, but a person breaks into a home and enters it to commit a theft (steal items), it is considered to be breaking and entering, illegal in ORC 2911.13. For example, if Jacob were to break into a shed or barn in an attempt to steal equipment, and no one is in the shed or barn at the time, it would be breaking and entering.

A related offense, criminal trespassing, occurs if a person knowingly enters or remains on the land of another person. This is a misdemeanor of the fourth degree (ORC 2911.21).

Arson

As defined in the Ohio Revised Code, the offense of arson occurs when a person, by means of fire or explosion, knowingly causes physical harm to any property without the other person's consent. This offense is a misdemeanor of the first degree. However, if the value of the property or the value of the harm caused is over $1,000, it is a felony of the fourth degree. Further, if the building burned is a school, statehouse, courthouse or a government building, it is also a fourth-degree felony (ORC 2909.03). This might occur if Anthony tries to burn down an abandoned home in the neighborhood. He might be convicted of arson.

However, if Anthony, after being fired from his job, set fire to the home of former employer, he may be guilty of a more serious crime. This may be considered to be aggravated arson, which is defined under the ORC as knowingly creating a substantial risk of serious physical harm to another person by means of fire or explosion, or to cause physical harm to an occupied structure. This is a felony of either the first degree or second degree (ORC 2909.02).

Summary

The Ohio Revised Code defines all acts or behaviors that are deemed unacceptable in the state. If a person commits those acts, they can be punished with a fine, time in a prison or jail, or even death. Any illegal behavior and the related punishment must be defined as such and described fully. A person accused of committing an offense must be tried in the court system and found guilty before being punished. While there are many more illegal acts than the ones described here, this chapter provided a description of some of the more serious crimes defined in the ORC.

Key Terms

Aggravated Assault

Aggravated Burglary

Aggravated Murder

Aggravated Robbery

Arson

Assault

Breaking and Entering

Burglary

Criminal Trespassing

Degrees of Offenses

Felonious Assault

Felony

Involuntary Manslaughter

Misdemeanor

Murder

Negligent Assault

Negligent Homicide

Ohio Revised Code

Reckless Homicide

Robbery

Theft

Vehicular Assault

Vehicular Homicide

Voluntary Manslaughter

Resources

Ohio Revised Code
  http://codes.ohio.gov/orc/

Review Questions

1. What is the Ohio Revised Code?
2. What is the difference between a misdemeanor and a felony offense?
3. Describe the different forms of murder under the ORC?
4. While at the mall over the weekend, John decides to follow another shopper, Joan, as she leave a store and heads to her car, carrying an armful of packages. Before Joan can open the car trunk, John hits her with a large stick and steals the packages. What offense just occurred?
5. Amanda, a high school senior, was upset after receiving a failing grade on her math test. In order to get revenge on her teacher, she sets fire to the classroom. If you were a prosecutor, with what crime would you charge Amanda?
6. Give an example of a negligent assault. What makes this offense different from an aggravated assault or a felonious assault?

References

Ohio Revised Code. (2014).

Chapter 6

Corrections in Ohio

Learning Objectives

After reading this chapter, students will be able to:

- Describe the organization and structure of prisons in Ohio.
- Explain the characteristics of the prison population in Ohio.
- Describe the programs offered to inmates that allow them to succeed upon leaving the institution.
- Analyze the role of community corrections in the Ohio system of corrections.
- Examine the use of private prisons in Ohio.
- Describe the organization and role of the Department of Rehabilitation and Correction.
- Explain what it takes to be a corrections officer in Ohio.
- Discuss the probation and parole systems in Ohio.

Introduction

If an accused offender is found guilty of serious criminal behavior in Ohio, they may be sentenced to a period of time in a correctional facility. Ohio has numerous prisons and jails located throughout the state, along with a system of community-based corrections, to house convicted offenders. The institutions vary in security level and house inmates who have been convicted of charges ranging from the most serious (murder, rape) to less severe (property offenses). All institutions are overseen by the Ohio Department of Rehabilitation, located in Columbus, and must meet state and federal standards regarding the care and housing of inmates. Ohio has also created a system of probation and parole to maintain control over offenders who are not in a residential setting. These are all described in this chapter. Because of the large amount of information gathered from the Ohio Department of Rehabilitation and Correction, a slightly different citation style will be used to avoid cluttering the text.

Ohio's Correctional Facilities

Prisons in Ohio hold offenders who have been convicted of committing criminal behavior and who have been sentenced to a time of over one year. The prisons in Ohio are differentiated by their security level. There are five security classifications, labeled as Levels 1, 2, 3, 4, and 5. Prisons that are categorized as a Level 5 have the highest security, and Level 1 institutions having the lowest security. The Ohio State Penitentiary in Youngstown is the state's only Level 5 security institution. This prison houses up to 500 dangerous inmates who have committed violent or predatory acts and who are considered to be a potential threat to the security of the facility. Because of this, the security of the institution is considered to be "High Maximum Security."

A Level 4 security prison has less security than a Level 5 prison. The inmates in these facilities are often involved in violent acts, but are not known to lead others into those behaviors. This level of security is known as "Maximum Security." The Southern Ohio Correctional Facility in Lucasville and the Toledo Correctional Institution are two examples of Level 4 facilities.

The facilities that are Level 3 have less security with less direct supervision of inmates. This type of facility is known as "Close Security." Even less security is found in a Level 2 facility, which is more commonly known as "Medium Security." At the lowest level is a Level 1 security institution, where inmates are housed at a correctional camp with a single perimeter fence. These inmates may also be permitted to work outside of the fence with appropriate supervision.

Some prisons are categorized as more than one security level. For example, the Franklin Medical center can hold inmates at both levels 4 and 5 security. The inmates identified as needing different security levels are housed in different wings or areas of the institution.

All new inmates are classified as level 3 security until they have been assessed and placed. New inmates are assessed based on their age, offense, prior record (including past incarcerations), and gang affiliation. Based on these factors, inmates will be sentenced to the most appropriate facility for their status.

Prisons in Ohio are divided into four administrative regions: northwest, northeast, southeast and southwest, primarily for administrative purposes. Each region is monitored by a regional director. Currently, there are 27 institutions distributed throughout the four regions. Table 6.1 indicates the institutions and their inmate population. All of the institutions in Ohio have earned the "Golden Eagle Award" from the American Correctional Association (ACA),

Table 6.1: Ohio Prisons and their Population

Allen/Oakwood Correctional Institution: 1633	Marion Correctional Institution: 2575
Belmont Correctional Institution: 2711	Noble Correctional Institution: 2542
Chillicothe Correctional Institution: 2748	North Central Correctional Complex (Private/Federal): 2705
Correctional Reception Center: 1812	Northeast Pre-Release Center: 557
Dayton Correctional Institution: 935	Ohio Reformatory for Women: 2499
Franklin Medical Center: 527	Ohio State Penitentiary: 424
Grafton Correctional Institution: 2007	Pickaway Correctional Institution: 2016
Hocking Correctional Complex: 0*	Richland Correctional Institution: 2531
Lake Erie Correctional Inst (Private): 1781	Ross Correctional Institution: 2160
Lebanon Correctional Institution: 2470	Southeastern Correctional Complex: 2082
London Correctional Institution: 2289	Southern Ohio Correctional Facility: 1117
Lorain Correctional Institution: 1558	Toledo Correctional Institution: 1012
Madison Correctional Institution: 2486	Trumbull Correctional Institution: 1527
Mansfield Correctional Institution: 2538	Warren Correctional Institution: 1365

* Consolidated with SCC
Source: Ohio Department of Rehabilitation and Correction, 2014 Annual Report; http://www.drc.ohio.gov/web/Reports/Annual/Annual%20Report%202014.pdf.

indicating that Ohio received accreditation from the ACA in all of its institutions, including the prisons, central office, parole services and the parole board.[1]

Ohio Jails

Jails hold inmates who are charged with lower level offenses and typically have a sentence of under one year. They also hold inmates who have not yet been convicted, but who are awaiting trial or some other hearing. In Ohio, jails are operated on the municipal or county level, usually by the sheriff, who

---

1. Ohio Department of Rehabilitation and Correction, Office of the Chief Inspector; http://www.drc.ohio.gov/web/ChiefInspector.htm.

has the responsibility of keeping the inmates safe while they are serving time in the jail. However, the ODRC is responsible for setting and maintaining standards for the state. To do this, the ODRC inspects jails annually to ensure compliance with the standards.

There are different types of jails across the state. Some counties have all of these types, whereas other counties have only one type or even none at all. In those cases, they have arranged with neighboring counties to provide assistance. The types of jails are:

- Full-Service Jails: used to hold adults for a period over 120 hours.
- Five-Day Jails: used to hold adults for a maximum of 120 hours.
- Twelve-Hour Jails: used to detain adults for a maximum of 12 hours.
- Minimum-Security Jails: used to hold adults convicted of a misdemeanor for lower degree felony offense for over 120 hours. These offenders must be identified as posing a minimum security risk to the jail and pose a low escape risk.
- Temporary Holding Facilities: used to hold those who have been arrested for a maximum of six hours as their case is processed or they are awaiting transportation to another facility. This may be a jail cell or an area designated as a temporary holding room.

Ohio's Prison Inmates

From 2011–2012 there was a slight decrease in the number of inmates in Ohio's prisons from 50,964 to 50,876.[2] Women comprised a very small portion of the total number of incarcerated individuals both years, with 3,903 in 2011 and 3,868 in 2012.

In 2014, there were 20,120 offenders sentenced to Ohio's prisons. This number included 17,302 males and 2,818 females. Their offenses ranged from serious crimes to more moderate offenses. About 26% offenders were sent to prison because of a drug related offense (e.g., drug trafficking or drug abuse), and 14% were sentenced for property offenses (theft, arson, receiving stolen property, breaking and entering). About one quarter of inmates were sentenced for committing offenses against persons such as assault or domestic violence,

---

2. E. Ann Carson and Daniela Golinelli, December 2013. "Prisoners in Admissions and Releases, 1991–2012" U.S. Department of Justice, Office of Justice Programs, Bureau of Justice Statistics; http://www.bjs.gov/content/pub/pdf/p12tar9112.pdf.

while 11% were sentenced for burglary. 7% were incarcerated in an institution for a sex offense (e.g., gross sexual imposition, rape, etc.). Other inmates were sentenced for offenses such as motor vehicle, fraud, or firearm offenses, or crimes against justice/public administration or other felonies.[3]

When an inmate is sentenced to a facility in Ohio, they are first processed through one of three reception centers, based on their sex and/or county where they were sentenced. All female inmates must go through intake at The Ohio Reformatory for Women in Marysville, and all male inmates are sent to the intake center based upon their county of commitment. Generally, male inmates from the northern counties appear at the Lorain Correctional Institution, located in Grafton, and the male inmates from the remaining counties are processed at the Correctional Reception Center in Orient, Ohio.

At reception centers, offenders are photographed and fingerprinted. They are also given a physical, along with a dental and eye examination. X-Rays are taken and blood is drawn and tested to identify any health problems. An inmates' educational and intelligence levels are established during the intake process. Interviews are conducted with each offender to collect information on the inmate's family, prior criminal behavior, drug and/or alcohol involvement, military service, employment history, and previous institutional sentences. Each inmate is strip searched to look for contraband, and their property is also searched. They receive a haircut and are given personal hygiene items. They are assigned an Institution Identification number and assigned to a Housing Unit. Each inmate is given a handbook that describes the rules and policies of the institution. Those inmates with a history of mental health problems may be placed in special units.

The characteristics of those entering Ohio's prison system show interesting trends, as shown in the charts below. Table 6.2 below, shows incarceration by race and ethnicity. This shows that there were more males than females sentenced to prison, and more whites than Blacks. There were very few Native Americans and Asians admitted to prison in Ohio in 2014. Table 6.3 indicates that people in their 20s are more likely to be sent to prison in Ohio than any other age group. It is clear from Table 6.4 that males are sentenced more often for third degree felonies, followed by fifth degree felonies. On the other hand, the pattern for females is switched. In total, most inmates in Ohio are serving time for third degree felonies. Tables 6.2 through 6.5, below, indicate that the majority of both male and female inmates are serving time for drug-related offenses.

---

3. Ohio Department of Rehabilitation and Correction, Frequently Asked Questions. http://www.drc.ohio.gov/web/FAQ.htm.

Table 6.2: Commitments to Ohio Prisons by Race and Ethnicity, FY 2014

	Male	Female
Black	6,972	501
White	9,851	2,285
Hispanic	384	22
Native American	23	3
Asian	15	2
Other	57	5
Total	17,302	2,818

Table 6.3: Commitments to Ohio Prisons by Age, FY 2014

Age	Male	Female	Age	Male	Female
16	7	40	44	1,556	247
17	36	2	45–49	1,125	170
18	247	8	50–54	765	103
19	479	35	55–59	370	39
20	620	74	60–64	147	8
21–24	3,008	438	65–69	74	2
25–29	3,472	727	70–74	21	3
30–34	3,243	575	75–79	9	–
35–39	2,119	387	80 and over	4	–

Table 6.4: Commitments to Ohio Prisons by Felony/Sentence Category

Category	Male	Female	Total
Death	2	–	2
Life	269	14	283
1st Degree	1,652	141	1,793
2nd Degree	2,867	338	3,205
3rd Degree	4,915	723	5,638
4th Degree	3,588	604	4,192
5th Degree	4,009	998	5,007
Total	17,302	2,818	20,120

Table 6.5: Commitments to Ohio Prisons by Offense Category

Offense Category	Male	Female	Total
Crimes Against Persons	4,470	475	4,945
Sex	1,409	30	1,439
Burglary	2,011	256	2,267
Misc. Property	2,210	532	2,742
Drugs	4,277	1,001	5,278
Motor Vehicle	321	36	357
Fraud	284	128	412
Firearms	1,130	64	1,194
Crimes Against Public Justice/Administration	1,178	293	1,471
Other	12	3	15
Total	17,302	2,818	20,120

One indicator of the success of Ohio's prisons is the recidivism rate, or the number of inmates who return to prison within three years of their release. In 2014, Ohio's recidivism rate was 27.1 percent, and the previous year it was 28.7 percent. This rate is very low when compared to the national average, which falls between 40–44 percent. The decline in the number of people returning to prison was attributed to the increased use of evidence-based programs, the growth of reintegration units within the prison, enhanced programs to connect offenders with families and resources while incarcerated, a network of community corrections programs and continued work with local communities and reentry coalitions.[4]

Prison Life

All inmates, regardless of their prison location, receive necessary health care. Typical medical services that are available to inmates in each institution include primary care assistance, pharmacy, dental, lab, and telemedicine. Spe-

---

4. Ohio Department of Rehabilitation and Correction, "News Release" March 5, 2014. Available at http://www.drc.ohio.gov/Public/press/press428.htm.

cialized treatment is available at the Franklin Medical Center (FMC). This facility provides inmates with skilled medical and nursing care, long-term care,
an Urgent Care Clinic, mobile magnetic resonance imaging (MRI) and computed tomography (CT) services, and a full-service, in-house laboratory. Specialized services are also available at the Frazier Health Center at the Pickaway
Correctional Institution, including intensive skilled medical and nursing care,
long-term care, and dialysis. Specialty and inpatient hospital care is offered
through comprehensive medical contracts.

Medical care in the institutions is overseen by the Office of Correctional
Health Care and the Bureau of Medical Services. The mission of the Office of
Correctional Health Care is to promote optimal wellness of the inmates by
providing integrated client-centered services. The Bureau of Medical Services
(BOMS) is responsible for the planning, implementation, monitoring, and
evaluation of comprehensive medical services for offenders.

Those inmates who suffer from mental health issues can receive needed
treatment either on an outpatient or inpatient basis. Services can include psy-
chotherapy, treatment groups, psycho-educational programs, psychotropic
medications and prevention services tailored to the offender's treatment plan.
Mental health services are provided through the Bureau of Behavioral Health
Services (BHS). This agency is responsible for evaluating inmates and providing and monitoring mental health services as needed.

BHS also provides treatment for inmates suffering from alcohol abuse or
abuse of other drugs. This includes screening, therapeutic communities, residential treatment programs, intensive program prisons, treatment readiness
programs, intensive outpatient programs, continuous care services, outpatient
programs, individual and group counseling, and other services such as alcohol and other drug education and 12-Step groups.[5]

Religious services are provided to all inmates through the Religious Bureau.
Currently 69% of the inmate population subscribe to one of 50 different religious affiliations.

Inmates in Ohio's prisons can receive visitors from home. Each institution
establishes their own visiting hours and may or may not require reservations
for visitation sessions. DRC permits video visitation using the JPay Kiosks that
have been installed in housing units throughout the institutions, designed to
increase visiting opportunities and reduce burdens on family and friends, especially those traveling long distances. Video visits are available in general pop-

---

5. Ohio Department of Rehabilitation and Correction, 2014 Annual Report; http://
www.drc.ohio.gov/web/Reports/Annual/Annual%20Report%202014.pdf.

ulation housing units seven days a week, in the morning, afternoon and evening at all Level 1, 2, and 3 prisons. Each institution sets a minimum of three hours in the morning, three hours in the afternoon and three hours in the evening where video visits will be available.

Rehabilitation/Treatment Inside Ohio's Prisons

Ohio has made a concerted effort to help inmates succeed by providing many programs and opportunities for offenders to learn skills to succeed upon their release. The goal is for the offender to become a law-abiding citizen and productive member of society upon their release and reentry into the community. The Office of Offender Reentry, part of the ODRC, is responsible for overseeing these programs.

Reentry

ODRC has established a wide range of reentry programs as a way to prepare inmates for release and make the transition from prison life to the community easier. The aim of the reentry plan is to provide offenders with opportunities upon their release to ensure that they will be productive members of their communities and reduce the likelihood that an offender will commit additional crime. This is made evident by their slogan, "Going Home to Stay."

One part of the reentry plan is reintegration units within the prisons themselves. There are currently about 2,500 offenders who are housed in these units that are designed to provide offenders with treatment, community service opportunities and job readiness training that help to prepare offenders for a successful transition into the community.[6] Part of this includes developing partnerships with all stakeholders, including the offender's family members and outside community members so that offenders can be linked with the services they need.

ODRDC also assisting offenders through the reentry process with the Ohio Reentry Resource Center, whose mission is Making Use of Services Can Lead to Empowerment (M.U.S.C.L.E.). They have developed a resource guide that provides a comprehensive list of the resources available in their community to

---

6. Ohio Department of Rehabilitation and Correction, 2014 Annual Report; http://www.drc.ohio.gov/web/Reports/Annual/Annual%20Report%202014.pdf.

assist in finding offenders community resources and information to address their needs as they leave the institution and return home. They are also helpful for family members and others.

Ohio Penal Industries

Ohio Penal Industries (OPI) provides an industrial training program for inmates. OPI is designed to provide vocational skills and a meaningful work experience for the inmate population while producing quality products. Not only do inmates learn a skill, but they are also learning a work ethic that they can take to any place of employment. Some of these products and services include license plates, office furniture, modular furniture, janitorial supplies, asbestos abatement, and vehicle service and repairs.[7] There are currently about 1,500 inmates working for OPI. The revenue for February, 2014, was $3,115,429.06.[8]

Intensive Program Prisons

Ohio has established Intensive Program Prisons (IPPs), which are ninety-day programs for certain inmates that include rigorous specialized treatment services. Those inmates who successfully complete an IPP will have his/her sentence reduced to the amount of time already served and will be released from prison with post-release supervision for an appropriate time.

The IPPs provide inmates a "Second Chance to Change." They have been established based on correctional programs that have been demonstrated to be effective in reducing the likelihood that the offender will re-offend once back in the community. Moreover, those inmates in the IPP programs are assessed prior to the program as a way to determine their individual need and are then assigned to the program that can address those, thus increasing the chance for success.

There are ten programs in the IPP program, each with different goals. For example, for offenders convicted of drunk driving, there is an IPP at the Madison Correctional Institution. Some programs emphasize community service work (at the Southeastern Correctional Institution in Lancaster for male of-

7. Ohio Department of Rehabilitation and Correction, Ohio Penal Industries. http://www.opi.ohio.gov/opi/web/AboutUs.aspx.

8. Ohio Department of Rehabilitation and Correction, Monthly Fact Sheet, July 2014. http://www.drc.ohio.gov/web/Reports/FactSheet/July%202014.pdf.

fenders and the Camp Meridian at the Ohio Reformatory for Women in Marysville for female offenders). Others emphasize academic and vocational education, such as the one at the Grafton Correctional Camp or the Ohio Reformatory for Women in Marysville. Other programs focus on treatment for alcohol and/or drug abuse. One for male offenders can be found at the Belmont Correctional Institution in St. Clairsville, London and at the Pickaway Correctional Institution in Orient. A similar program for women is found at the Ohio Reformatory for Women in Marysville.[9]

Ohio Central School System

Another way ODRC is attempting to help inmates who are returning to their communities is through the Ohio Central School System (OCSS). Chartered in 1973, this organization provides inmates with comprehensive educational opportunities such as a GED, vocational training, or special education. It also gives inmates job training so that they have employment skills and are able to join the workforce. Some of the services provided to inmates include Adult Basic Literacy Education, General Educational Development (GED), Adult High School, Apprenticeship Training, Library Services, Special Education, and Vocational Education.

Even though participation in the program is voluntary, it has been popular among inmates.[10] In recent years, apprenticeship programs have been expanded by OCSS in many institutions. In 2011 only 18 requests for local apprenticeships were received and approved, but in 2012 the number grew to 62. A total of 49 were approved in 2013.[11]

Offender Workforce Development

Offender Workforce Development is also a way in which ODRC helps inmates succeed once released from an institution. The program is designed to provide inmates with a skill that can help them find a job upon their release. Partnerships have been created with the communities for those released of-

9. Ohio Department of Rehabilitation and Correction, Intensive Program Prisons; http://www.drc.ohio.gov/web/ipp.htm.

10. Ohio Department of Rehabilitation and Correction, OCSS; August 9, 2012. http://www.drc.ohio.gov/ocss/ocss_home.htm.

11. Ohio Department of Rehabilitation and Correction, Office of Offender Reentry; http://www.drc.ohio.gov/web/OfficePolicyAndReentry.htm.

fenders who are seeking employment. Staff also provides training, education, and technical assistance to community action organizations, and other state agencies.[12]

Citizen Circles

Another option inmates have to increase their chance of success when they leave a prison in Ohio is by using the services of Citizen Circles. These groups create partnerships that promote positive interaction in the community for offenders upon their release. Citizen Circles address risks that pose avenues for criminal activity by looking for other options or solutions. It is an opportunity for citizens to communicate expectations for successful reentry to the offender and help them recognize the harm that criminal behavior may cause others. Offenders are able to make amends and demonstrate their value and potential to the community.

Offenders and their families develop relationships with members of the community and together develop a plan to help the offender become accepted as a productive citizen and member of the community. The Citizen Circle helps offenders understand being a positive community member demands responsibility and obligation. They do this through focusing on an offender's personal strengths and by looking to the future rather than the past. Offenders must give back through community service and contributions.

These groups concentrated on eight areas:

1. **Employment**: Work and the role of work in the person's life, including education and vocational skills;
2. **Education**: Education and vocational skills desired;
3. **Family/Marital**: Being with family members and the support an offender derives from them;
4. **Associates/Social Interactions**: Positive interaction with community members and non-criminal associates with the opportunity for positive interaction with peers;
5. **Substance Abuse**: Living without reliance on alcohol and/or other drugs;
6. **Community Functioning**: Knowledge and skills for daily living, including safety, an acceptable place to live, health, personal budgeting, leisure activities, and the use of social services;

---

12. Ohio Department of Rehabilitation and Development; Offender Workforce Development; http://www.drc.ohio.gov/web/JOBOFFEN.HTM.

7. **Personal/Emotional Orientation:** Decision-making, coping with stress, and practicing mental health and wellness activities; and
8. **Attitude:** Supporting law-abiding behaviors and involvement with religious activities.

Like other ODRC programs, involvement with a Citizen Circle is voluntarily. The Citizen Circles meet on a regular basis to discuss offender progress, review plans, interview new applicants, admit new members and to discharge both successful and unsuccessful offenders.[13]

Prisoner Community Service

The Office of Prisons supports partnerships with non-profit organizations, government agencies, schools and charitable groups throughout Ohio that give inmates the opportunity to give back to the community while learning a skill. These programs also support the concept of restorative justice by which an offender can make a contribution to society to help repay for their offense. The program, created in 1991, also helps to alleviate the boredom and tension that can occur in prison, creating in a safer environment for both staff and inmates.

Community Service can include training and caring for puppies and dogs for programs that assist individuals in Ohio and elsewhere who are physically and/or visually impaired (through programs called the Pilot Dog Program or the Pilot Puppies Program). Similar programs include the Circle Tail program which trains service dogs; Save our Strays that trains stray dogs for placement in homes; Golden Endings that trains abused and neglected dogs for home placements; Canine Companions that trains service dogs for placement with those suffering from disabilities; and Team Greyhound that trains retired racing dogs for home placements. Inmates can also help Habitat for Humanity build homes for low to moderate income families. Other inmates grow vegetables that are donated to local food banks and shelters. Some inmates make sleep mats for the homeless community, whereas others record books on tape for schools. They also help with a free store for teachers called Crayons to Computers. In other projects, inmates have constructed and installed playgrounds site schools and maintained hiking trails in the Wayne National Forest.[14]

---

13. Ohio Department of Rehabilitation and Correction, Citizen Circles http://www.drc.ohio.gov/web/Citizen/citizencircle.htm.

14. Ohio Department of Rehabilitation and Correction, Prisoner Community Service; http://www.drc.ohio.gov/web/commserv.htm.

Agricultural and Farm Services

The ODRC oversees a Farm Operations program that encompasses 19,000 acres of farm ground at ten prison locations and at two Ohio Penal Industries (OPI) shops. The Farm Operations include dairy, finished beef and feeder cattle, corn, soybean, wheat, oats, rye, sorghum, hay and garden row crops. OPI farms have a relationship with the Ohio Association of Food banks. In 2012, DRC farms supplied approximately 192,056 pounds of produce valued at nearly $100,000.00.

Five Farm sites care for Holstein dairy cattle, which provide over 1.6 million gallons of raw milk for the OPI Beverage Processing Center (BPC), which then pasteurizes and packages it for the ODRC offender population. ODRC Farms also have over 1000 beef cows that produce calves each year. About twenty percent of the calves are kept in the Farms as a way to replace older cows. The others are sent to the OPI Meat Processing Center.

The various farm operations currently employ 68 staff and 225 inmate workers. The different programs are described in Table 6.6, below.

OPI Beverage Processing Center

The Beverage Processing Center (BPC) is located at the Pickaway Correctional Institution. Milk from the Farms is sent there to be processed and used in the other state facilities. The milk produced at the BPC is skim. About 30,000 gallons of milk are processed in the BPC each week. The BPC is a Grade "A" liquid milk processing facility according to the Ohio Department of Agriculture (ODA), which monitors the plant.

OPI Meat Processing Career Center

The Meat Processing Career Center (MPCC) is located at the Pickaway Correctional Institution. It processes and packages meat products and provides ODRC with over 3.2 million pounds of ground and diced meat each year. Offenders who work at the MPCC learn how to butcher meat and about the meat production industry as a whole. They have hands-on training in the field that can help them get a job in the meat processing industry upon their release.[15]

---

15. Ohio Department of Rehabilitation and Correction, Agricultural and Farm Services; http://www.drc.ohio.gov/web/ag_farm.htm.

Table 6.6: Agricultural and Farm Programs in Ohio's Prisons

Allen Correctional Institution (ACI)	505 acres of farm land with a 450 head beef feedlot operation
Grafton Correctional Institution (GCI)	1,130 acres of farm ground for the production of livestock feed commodities supporting the entire DRC herds
Lebanon Correctional Institution (LECI)	LECI has DRC's second largest acreage with 1,746 acres of farm land with a 350-beef-cow herd and a 125-cow dairy
London Correctional Institution (LOCI)	LOCI has DRC's largest acreage with 2,800 acres of farm land supporting the dairy operation consisting of 220 cows, along with the largest beef finishing operation of 800 animals
Marion Correctional Institution (MCI)	995 acres of farm land with a dairy herd consisting of 100 cows and a Holstein steer feedlot
Mansfield Correctional Institution (MANCI)	1,485 acres of farm ground in production through DRC ownership or partnered, with the largest beef cow herd of 350 cows and a beef finishing operation of 500 head
Pickaway Correctional Institution (PCI)	1200 acres of farm land with 900 acres in annual production housing a 200-cow dairy and a Holstein steer feedlot
Chillicothe Correctional Institution (CCI)	1,809 acres of farm land in production through DRC ownership or partnered, with a dairy herd of 125 cows and a beef finishing operation of 550 animals
Southeastern Correctional Complex (SCC)	578 acres of farm ground with a beef cow herd of 200 cows and beef finishing operation consisting of 400 head
Southern Ohio Correctional Facility (SOCF)	640 acres of farm ground for the production of livestock feed commodities supporting the entire DRC herds

Source: Ohio Department of Rehabilitation and Correction, Agricultural and Farm Services; http://www.drc.ohio.gov/web/ag_farm.htm

Permanent Supportive Housing

The ODRC, along with the Corporation for Supportive Housing, has instituted a supportive housing project to help those offenders who are returning to the community find homes. The program, called Returning Home, concentrates on those offenders who have been identified as chronically homeless prior to their incarceration, and are therefore likely to become homeless upon their release from prison. The goal of the program is to prevent inmates from becoming homeless and thereby reducing the chance of recidivism.

Community-Based Corrections

Many convicted felons throughout Ohio are not sentenced to a term in prison after their trial. Instead, they may be sentenced to serve time in a community based correctional facility (CBCF). CBCFs are residential programs that provide programs for offenders in the community rather than in an institution. Convicted felons who have served time in prison can also be placed in a community corrections setting through parole. Parole is a period of supervision prior to full release from the state's correctional system.

Ohio relies on many forms of community corrections. They include restitution, day reporting, community service, and halfway houses.[16] Restitution requires an offender to pay the costs of their crime and reimburse the offender. Day reporting is a program that allows an inmate to return home during the evening but spend the day in the community correction facility. If an offender is sentenced to a period of community service, they must spend time on community projects. Halfway houses are residential programs found within communities that provide offenders who have been released from prison with supervision and treatment services. They also provide inmates with drug and alcohol treatment, job placement, educational programs, or specialized programs for those convicted of sex offenses.

The agency that oversees the community corrections division of the ODRC is the Division of Parole and Community Services. This agency works with local agencies to provide needed community sanctions for offenders. These programs focus on the safety of the public while at the same time providing each offender with opportunities to change the behavior which led to their arrest.

The Bureau of Community Sanctions, within the Division of Parole and Community Services, was created in 1876 to help establish punishments with communities for those adult offenders who would otherwise remain incarcerated. Today, it is the mission of the Bureau to "develop community corrections programs in partnership with state, local and private agencies, for sanctioning and treating adult offenders in the community." This agency provides guidance and oversight to halfway houses, transitional control, electronic monitoring, community-based correctional facilities, community residential centers, and probation agencies. ODRC oversees all programs funded by the

---

16. Ohio Department of Rehabilitation and Correction, Parole and Community Services; http://www.drc.ohio.gov/web/parole.htm.

state to ensure they are complying with minimum standards of operation. BCS also provides technical assistance and training for these programs.[17]

Transitional Control

Another program to help ex-offenders transition into the community is the Transitional Control program. The Parole Board determines what offenders are eligible for this program, and the sentencing judge must give their approval as well. Once admitted to the program, offenders will be transferred to a halfway house where they will complete the last 180 days of their prison term. While in the halfway house, the inmates are supervised by the Adult Parole Authority. If the offender remains employed and otherwise succeeding in the program, they may be placed on electronic monitoring. The goal of the Transitional Control program is to provide offenders with the necessary resources to maintain employment, seek an education or vocational training, or seek treatment so that they may transition to their home community more successfully.

Independent Housing

The Independent Housing Unit was announced in 2004. It provides housing for inmates, along with limited monitoring, case management and community referrals for needed services. In order to participate in the program, offenders must have a viable home placement and be stabilized in the community. They must also have either moderate to low programming needs that can be met in the community.

Private Prisons

In 2011, Ohio became the first state to transfer the operation of its prisons to a private company.[18] This was done by the Governor, John Kasich, as a way to save approximately $6.6 million a year. Corrections Corporation of America purchased Lake Erie Correctional Institution in Lorain County, and took

---

17. Ohio Department of Rehabilitation and Correction, 2014 Annual Report; http://www.drc.ohio.gov/web/Reports/Annual/Annual%20Report%202014.pdf.

18. Julie Carr Smyth, September 2, 2011. "Ohio Becomes First American State to Sell Prison to Private Company" Huffington Post; http://www.huffingtonpost.com/2011/09/02/ohio-prison-sold_n_946862.html.

control of the facility on Dec. 31, 2011. The company agreed to meet the safety policies required by the States.

However, it wasn't long before there were allegations of mistreatment in the private prisons. Inmates at the Lake Erie Correctional Institution, run by CCA, claim that there were unsafe and unsanitary conditions in the institution. When state officials inspected the facility, they found that inmates did not have access to running water or toilets. There were also complaints about prison gangs and assaults, alongside poor food quality and lack of health care. Allegations were made concerning padlocked fire exits, falsification of records, moldy showers, and no guards to monitor medication distribution to inmates.[19] After the report was issued, CCA disciplined 14 employees and reiterated their commitment to providing a secure and safe environment.[20] Additional troubles occurred in 2013 when a riot broke out at the facility. As a result, 39 inmates were transferred to a correctional facility in Mansfield.[21]

More recently, the Director of the ODRC, Gary Mohr, has stated that the state will not seek to privatize any additional prisons, claiming that they did not work.[22] Instead, he plans to focus on rehabilitation and reentry efforts.

Ohio Department of Rehabilitation and Correction

The agency that is responsible for overseeing the prison system in the state of Ohio is the Department of Rehabilitation and Correction (ODRC). Housed in Columbus, the Department's responsibilities are outlined in Ohio Revised

---

19. Aviva Shen, April 15 2013. "Over 18 Months, Nation's First Privately Owned State Prison Has Declined Rapidly." ThinkProgress, http://thinkprogress.org/justice/2013/04/10/1843291/over-18-months-nations-first-privately-owned-state-prison-has-declined-rapidly/; Leigh Owens, October 10, 2012. "Private Prison in Violation of Ohio State Law." Huffington Post; http://www.huffingtonpost.com/2012/10/09/private-prison-violates-state-law_n_1951917.html.

20. Laura A. Bischoff, December 29, 2012. "Auditors Uncover Problems at Private Prisons in Ohio" *Dayton Daily News*; http://www.daytondailynews.com/news/news/state-regional/auditors-uncover-problems-at-private-prisons-in-oh/nTgQ5/.

21. Matt Stroud, January 31, 2013 "Ohio Private Prison Reboots After Weekend Riot" Forbes; http://www.forbes.com/sites/mattstroud/2013/01/31/ohio-private-prison-reboots-after-weekend-riot/.

22. German Lopez, October 5, 2012. "Private Prison Violates State Rules" City Beat; http://citybeat.com/cincinnati/blog-4028-private_prison_violates_state_rules.html; "No More Prisons" January 26, 2014. *The Blade* http://www.theguardianonline.com/news/2012/10/10/ohio-decides-against-privatization-of-more-prisons/#sthash.wW3EzazB.dpuf.

Code section 5120. The ODRC oversees all adult offenders who have been convicted of a felony offense for which the minimum punishment is six months or more.

The Director of the ODRC is appointed by the governor of the state.[23] Currently, the Director of the ODRC is Gary C. Mohr. Mr. Mohr was originally appointed to the position by Governor Kasich in January 2011. He has a strong background in corrections, serving as the deputy director and superintendent of the Ohio Department of Youth Services and the deputy director in DRC's Office of Prisons. Director Mohr also served as the warden at the Ross Correctional Institutional, Chillicothe Correctional Institution, and the Correction Reception Center.[24]

The Director oversees many offices within the ODRC. One of those is the Office of Communication. The mission of this office is to "maintain, both in attitude and action, a cooperative and responsive posture to inform the public, media and other agencies concerning DRC operations, accomplishments, and critical incidents." In general terms, the employees in this office serve to educate the public about the roles and functions of ODRC through brochures, newsletters and reports.[25] They keep people informed of news in the event of a critical incident. They also provide training to outside agencies.[26]

Another critical office within the ODRC is the Office of the Chief Inspector. The people who work in this office review grievances that are filed by inmates and ensure that each problem is addressed as needed. Each institution has an Inspector of Institutional Services who is responsible for overseeing the process for reviewing inmate grievances and ensuring that correct procedures are being followed. Training is provided for all Inspectors at the institutions.[27]

Under the direction of the Office of the Chief Inspector is the Bureau of Agency Policy and Operational Compliance. This office monitors and develops new policies and monitors existing policies regarding health of the inmates and the overall safety of the institutions.[28]

23. Ohio Department of Rehabilitation and Correction, Department Organization; http://www.drc.ohio.gov/web/WHOWEARE.HTM.

24. Ohio Department of Rehabilitation and Correction, Director http://www.drc.ohio.gov/web/director.htm.

25. Ohio Department of Rehabilitation and Correction, Office of Communications; http://www.drc.ohio.gov/Public/publicinformation.htm.

26. Ohio Department of Rehabilitation and Correction, 2014 Annual Report; http://www.drc.ohio.gov/web/Reports/Annual/Annual%20Report%202014.pdf.

27. Ohio Department of Rehabilitation and Correction, 2014 Annual Report; http://www.drc.ohio.gov/web/Reports/Annual/Annual%20Report%202014.pdf.

28. Ohio Department of Rehabilitation and Correction, Office of the Chief Inspector; http://www.drc.ohio.gov/web/ChiefInspector.htm.

The Legal Services Division within the ODRC oversees legal concerns within the ODRC. They assist employees of the ODRC avoid potential litigation, help out with contracts regarding prison services, and consult on issues regarding personnel and operations of the corrections facilities.[29]

The Legislative Office within the ODRC monitors any legislation that has been proposed in the Ohio General Assembly related to the functioning of the ODRC and its inmates. When needed, the employees of the Legislative Office will provide advice to the Director and staff on possible implications of any proposed changes in the law.[30]

The Legislative Liaison provides a clear exchange of information from the ODRC to state legislators and their staff. They also advise the ODRC Director on a possible legislative agenda if any changes are needed. The Liaison will also meet with any top legislators regarding any pending legislative issues, and if needed, assist in preparing relevant testimony that will be presented to committee members. In the case that legislators request information, the Legislative Liaison ensures that the responses are timely and coherent.[31]

The Parole and Community Services office is another office found within the ODRC. The mission of this office is to ensure that adult offenders who are placed in community sanctions are appropriately supervised, and they are held accountable for their actions.[32]

The Office of Prisons was designed to provide institutions that are secure while also safe and humane. They oversee the supervision of inmates in the prisons across Ohio, as well as the Adult Parole Authority field staff. They seek to include rehabilitative services to inmates that will assist offenders in returning successfully to the community. This office also provides support services within the prisons for services including education programs, classification of inmates, critical incident management, recreation, religious services, security, programs for youthful offenders, and the management of disruptive inmate groups.[33] The Office of Prisons is comprised of four regions: northwest, north-

---

29. Ohio Department of Rehabilitation and Correction, Legal Services; http://www.drc.ohio.gov/web/LegalServices.htm.

30. Ohio Department of Rehabilitation and Correction, Legislative; http://www.drc.ohio.gov/web/Legislative.htm.

31. Ohio Department of Rehabilitation and Correction, 2014 Annual Report; http://www.drc.ohio.gov/web/Reports/Annual/Annual%20Report%202014.pdf.

32. Ohio Department of Rehabilitation and Correction, Parole and Community Services; http://www.drc.ohio.gov/web/parole.htm.

33. Ohio Department of Rehabilitation and Correction, Office of Prisons; http://www.drc.ohio.gov/web/OfficeOfPrison.htm.

east, southwest, and southeast, with each region managed by a Regional Director. An Operations Manager in each region is responsible for overseeing the security of the state prisons as well as prison programming, visiting, recreation, placement packets, release planning, and related activities. In addition the Operations Manager oversees the Corrections Training Academy and the Ohio Penal Industries.

Parole and Probation in Ohio

Criminal offenders in Ohio may be sentenced to a term of probation instead of a term inside a prison or jail. When an offender is sentenced to probation, they remain in the community but are assigned to meet regularly with a probation officer (typically once or twice a month). The probation officer will set stipulations for that offender such as maintaining employment or school, completing community service hours, staying drug-free, or avoiding contact with certain individuals. As long as the offender abides by the terms of probation, they remain in the community. If they fail to follow the rules, they may face prison time.

Offenders who have spent time in an institution may be placed on parole upon their release. This is very similar to probation and requires an inmate to meet regularly with a parole officer and meet certain requirements as set by the parole officer. If the offender meets the requirements, they remain out of the institution. However, offenders who fail to meet the stipulated rules may be forced to return to the institution. In July, 2014, there were over 33,000 offenders on parole in Ohio.[34]

In Ohio, the Adult Parole Authority (APA) was created in 1965 to oversee the supervision of adult inmates placed on parole. It is comprised of the Parole Board and Field Services.[35]

The Parole Board helps to determine the release dates of inmates as they leave prison and are placed on parole. The Field Services office helps to supervise those offenders placed on parole and probation. It also provides assistance to all Ohio counties as needed.

---

34. Ohio Department of Rehabilitation and Correction, Adult Parole Authority, Regional Workforce Analysis July 2014. http://www.drc.ohio.gov/web/Reports/APAMonthly/July%202014.pdf.

35. Ohio Department of Rehabilitation and Correction, Adult Parole Authority. http://www.drc.state.oh.us/web/apa.htm.

Corrections Officers

Corrections officers in Ohio receive training through the Corrections Training Academy (CTA). CTA also administers and provides specialized in-service training programs for DRC employees, local law enforcements agencies, and other criminal justice partners.[36]

Training for new employees introduces them to the field of corrections and the Ohio system. The 120 hour curriculum begins with a two day orientation at the prison where they will be working. The remaining hours are completed at the Corrections Training Academy in Orient, Ohio. The curriculum covers topics related to security as well as safety. Ohio's policies regarding reentry and rehabilitation of inmates are also a key component of the training. The courses consist of both lectures and hands on activities. New employees also receive unarmed self-defense certification during the training period and must receive their firearms certification, CPR certification and restraint training. All potential officers must submit to a background investigation and must also present their social security card.

Those staff in the corrections institutions who are considered to be noncustodial must also complete the core curriculum.

In-Service training opportunities are available throughout an employee's career. Correctional officers in Ohio must complete 120 hours of training each year as a way to keep updated on techniques and refresher courses. The Corrections Training Academy offers many different courses that allow officers to stay updated on policies and techniques. They also help to train instructors who can then train others.

Specialized training is available for employees interested in furthering their careers. Training is available for Executive Leadership; Pre-Retirement seminars; Advanced Medical courses; specialized Mental Health training, quarterly Training Officer sessions; Critical Incident Management. Additionally, courses for special teams (Hostage Negotiations; Special Tactics and Response Team; Riflemen Training; Stress Debriefing Teams) are available.[37]

To become a Corrections Officer in Ohio, an applicant must be a U.S. citizen and a resident of Ohio with a high school diploma or GED and a valid driver's license. They must have good communication skills and be able to deal

---

36. Ohio Department of Rehabilitation and Correction, 2014 Annual Report; http://www.drc.ohio.gov/web/Reports/Annual/Annual%20Report%202014.pdf.

37. Ohio Department of Rehabilitation and Correction, Corrections Training Academy; http://www.drc.ohio.gov/web/cta.htm.

well with people. They must be flexible, productive, prompt and show self control. All successful applicants must have a clean financial history and be between 20–37 years old. Applicants cannot have a felony or domestic violence convictions, or any misdemeanor convictions within the last two years. Candidates must be able to drag a dummy and complete an obstacle course where they must traverse 108 steps in 45 seconds while carrying a 20 pound weight. Preference will be given to those applicants who have earned either an associate's degree or bachelor's degree from an accredited university or college. Those with degrees in sociology, criminology, criminal justice, psychology or a related field of study will receive even more preference.

Summary

The corrections system in Ohio is a complex organization designed to hold offenders who have been convicted of criminal behaviors, but also to help them become law abiding and productive members of society once released from the institution. The agency that oversees the prisons is the Ohio Department of Rehabilitation and Correction, which has many offices and agencies to provide a safe and humane environment for inmates alongside treatment programming. Ohio's system of corrections provides inmates with many opportunities to make more healthy choices, and will continue to do so in the years to come.

Key Terms

Agricultural and Farm Services
Citizen Circles
Community-Based Corrections
Five-Day Jail
Full-Service Jail
Independent Housing
Intensive Program Prisons
Jail
Minimum-Security Jail
Offender Workforce Development
Ohio Central School System

Ohio Department of Rehabilitation and Corrections
Ohio Penal Industries
Parole
Permanent Supportive Housing
Prisoner Community Service
Private Prisons
Probation
Recidivism
Reentry
Security Level 1

Security Level 2   Temporary Holding Facility
Security Level 3   Transitions Control
Security Level 4   Twelve-Hour Jail
Security Level 5

Resources

Corrections Center of Northwest Ohio
      http://www.ccnoregionaljail.org/
Ohio Department of Rehabilitation and Correction
      http://www.drc.ohio.gov/
U.S. Department of Justice
      http://www.justice.gov/

Review Questions

1. What are the different types of jails found in Ohio?
2. Describe some characteristics of inmates recently admitted to Ohio's prisons.
3. Outline the various treatment programs available to inmates.
4. Define probation and parole. How are they different?
5. What is the Department of Rehabilitation and Correction and what are some of the offices or agencies included in it?
6. How is the role of community-based corrections facilities different from prisons?
7. Assume you are interested in becoming a corrections officer. What qualifications would you need to have and what would the training include?

Chapter 7

Alternative Courts

Learning Objectives

After reading this chapter, students will be able to:

- Describe the role of alternative courts in Ohio's criminal justice system.
- Explain how alternative courts operate.
- Give some examples of alternative courts in Ohio.
- Analyze the use of alternative courts for drugs, mental health, and veterans.
- Explain the difference between regular courts and alternative courts
- Identify areas in which alternative courts operate.

Introduction

Alternative courts, sometimes referred to as specialized courts or specialized dockets, are courts that have been established in some counties in Ohio to help a particular type of offender. These special dockets rely on a problem-solving approach to assist individual offenders rather than using punishment through traditional court procedures. In the end, these courts help to reduce the caseload in the court system as they remove certain offenders from the traditional court docket and from the prison system, thus saving state resources.

Once an offender is identified as being eligible for an alternative court, they are given the option of participating in the program or having their case heard in a traditional court. Participation in the special court is completely voluntary. If the offender agrees to take part, they will appear in front of a judge where the facts of the case are presented. The judge, along with other court personnel and professionals, will then devise an individualized treatment plan for that offender that is intended to address the underlying cause of their criminal behavior. For example, an offender may be required to participate in a drug treatment program, find a job, or attend an anger management course. The offender must abide by all of the rules established by the judge and the other treatment team members. Those offenders who complete the treatment plan will either see their criminal charges reduced or dropped altogether. Other defendants who do not complete the treatment plan will return to the regular court and face the original criminal charges. If a defendant chooses not to participate in the alternative court, their case will also be heard in a traditional court setting.

By using alternative courts, Ohio saves resources in many ways. One is by streamlining these cases. The court personnel in the alternative courts have all received specialized training so they become experts in a particular area. This means that the judges, attorneys and bailiffs have developed an expertise in that field. They understand the technical terminology, the research relevant to the cases, and past court decisions. The attorneys will not need to spend time during a trial to "teach" the judge and other personnel important concepts with expert testimony. The cases are much more focused and are processed much more quickly.

The state also saves resources by reducing incarceration in traditional correctional facilities. This happens in multiple ways. First, the focus of the court is on treatment of the offender instead of incarceration. In the end, the offender is treated so that they will be less likely to commit another crime. Moreover, at least with regards to mental health courts, it has been found that offenders suffering with severe mental illness are likely to spend more time in a correctional facility than those who do not have mental health issues. Thus, by using a mental health court, Ohio saves money by reducing the chance that the offender will go to prison for the original offense (thereby reducing incarceration in correctional facilities) but also saves money by reducing recidivism (future offenses).

The alternative court approach may also improve the quality of life for the defendant and his or her family and friends. Since the offenders receive treatment for their issues and learn how to stay away from criminal behavior, they have a greater chance of maintaining employment and succeeding in their communities.

The alternative courts are established and maintained on a county level. That means that individual county officials decide what types of alternative courts will be created in their jurisdiction, if any. Many kinds of alternative courts have been developed in Ohio. The first was the Hamilton County Drug Court, created in 1995. Since then, counties have developed over 150 specialized court programs. A common alternative court found in many counties is some form of domestic violence or family court. They deal most often with situations of violence, divorce, or child custody. Other common types of alternative courts are drug courts and mental health courts. A more recent type of alternative court is a valor court, also called a veterans' court.

As a way to provide help and support to the court personnel who operate these courts, the Ohio Supreme Court has developed the Ohio Specialized Dockets Practitioner Network. This agency allows for greater interaction among court personnel who work in these courts. The Ohio Specialized Dockets Network was created as a way to provide peer support and technical assistance to these personnel.

The Network is comprised of three groups of specialized docket professionals, including judges and/or magistrates, program coordinators, and probation officers. Meetings provide opportunities for these personnel to discuss any challenges they are facing in their courtrooms, and to expound on successes they have experienced. They can also provide information on new strategies that they've tried, and if they have been successful or not. This is also an opportunity to identify any possible training needs to the staff of the Supreme Court.

Mental Health Courts

During the 1990s, many mental health facilities closed and individuals suffering from mental illnesses no longer had a place to receive full-time treatment. Instead, local law enforcement agencies, along with jails and prisons, became the new care providers to this population. Many counties created Mental Health Courts in response to the increasing number of criminal cases that involved defendants who were suffering with a mental illness. These defendants often were not aware that they committed offenses, or did not have the intent to commit offenses. They were also more likely to commit crimes that are not violent. At the same time, with proper treatment and care, they could become law-abiding and productive members of their communities.

The process for participation in a mental health court begins when law enforcement arrests a defendant. Upon entering the court system, a defendant will be screened and assessed. Those with identified mental health concerns are offered the opportunity to go through a mental health court in lieu of a tradition court. If they agree, the offender will meet with a judge and a team of mental health experts who identify the specific needs of the offender and relevant treatment options. The team creates an individualized plan for that offender that will help provide focused treatment for that offender. Most often, the team relies on services available in the community for ease of availability and lower costs.

Typically the mental health program is a two-year plan designed around the needs of the defendant. Often, offenders are required to have mental health counseling as an integral part of their treatment plan. They usually are required to meet with a judge (who has received specialized training) on a regular basis to ensure the requirements are being followed. In general, the treatment is in the least restrictive means as possible.

Throughout the process, the defendant will be continually monitored to ensure they are complying with the plan. If the defendant complies, they are rewarded; if they do not, the judge may alter the treatment plan or impose sanctions. If the non-compliance is serious enough or happens frequently, the defendant may be required to go to trial. When the defendants complete the program, the original criminal charges are dismissed. If they make it to the end, a graduation ceremony is held with family, friends, and court officials to congratulate the offender on their success.

Summit County

One Ohio county that has developed a mental health court is Summit County. The admission requirement for participation in the Summit County mental health court includes a diagnosis of schizophrenia, Schizoaffective Disorder, or Bipolar disorder. Moreover, the offender must be charged with a misdemeanor offense. Those who are charged with misdemeanors of the fourth degree will not be accepted into the program unless there are multiple charges with a potential sentence of at least 90 days in jail. If the defendant has been charged with a sex offense, they are unable to participate. If an offender has been charged with a violent crime, the victim must give their consent before the offender is allowed to participate in the Summit County mental health court. The offender must be able to show that they understand the rules of the court, and are willing to comply with them. They must understand that there are consequences for not complying (Akron Municipal Court, 2014).

Preliminary analysis of the success of the court in Akron shows that this type of alternative court is succeeding in reducing the number of mentally ill defendants who commit further crimes and are sent to prison both in the City of Akron and the state of Ohio. Figure 7.1 shows recent trends in the number of beds that were filled with defendants who participated in the program.

Cuyahoga County

Another mental health court was established in Cuyahoga County (Cleveland) in 2003. Called the Mental Health Developmental Disability Court (MHDD), formerly the Mental Health Court Docket, the aim of this court is to help any offender "whose mental illness or intellectual disability contribute to their offense." The mission is to,

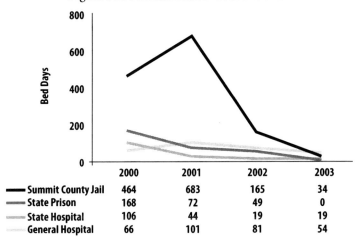

Figure 7.1: Mental Health Court Success

	2000	2001	2002	2003
Summit County Jail	464	683	165	34
State Prison	168	72	49	0
State Hospital	106	44	19	19
General Hospital	66	101	81	54

Source: Akron Municipal Court, Mental Health Court; https://courts.ci.akron.oh.us/programs/
mental_health.htm

promote early identification of defendants with severe mental health/
developmental disabilities in order to promote coordination and co-
operation among law enforcement, jails, community treatment
providers, attorneys and the courts for defendants during the legal
process and achieve outcomes that both protect society and support
the mental health care and disability needs of the defendant.

It is estimated that about 300 offenders in Cuyahoga County suffer from mental illness at any time, and that they spend about twice as much time in jail
(Mental Health Court, 2010).

Those who participate in the Mental Health Court in Cuyahoga County
have been charged with many types of offenses, but are ineligible if they were
charged with capital murder. Offenders are screened during the booking process
to determine their eligibility. Participants are often unemployed, indigent and
homeless. The Pretrial Services Unit (found within in the Adult Probation Department) also helps to determine offenders who are eligible for the Court.

During the arraignment stage, any defendants who may be eligible are assigned to a judge with specialized training as well as provided with a specially
trained attorney who work with community professionals to link the offender
with specialized services. The court provides the offenders with many specialized services. In 2010, 387 cases were assigned to a Mental Health Court docket
in Cuyahoga County (Mental Health Court, 2010).

Drug Courts

Another type of specialized court found in Ohio is the drug court. Defendants who have committed their offenses because of their addiction to drugs or because of drug use may be eligible to participate in a drug court. Offenders who agree to participate are given intensive drug treatment and/or counseling that teach them how to refrain from using illicit drugs in place of being sentenced to a term in prison.

In general terms, offenders who are eligible for participation in the drug court have been charged with low-level, nonviolent offenses. Those offenders who have multiple prior felonies in their backgrounds, or who have prior convictions for drug trafficking or violent offenses, are not permitted to participate. Also excluded are those defendants who have committed a gun-related offense or if the charges against them were of a violent or sexually oriented nature.

Incoming eligible offenders are assessed, and if a history of substance abuse is uncovered, they are given the option to participate in the drug court. If they agree to participate, they must consent to fulfilling the treatment plan designed for them by the court. A typical drug court plan is eighteen months long. Participants are required to meet with court personnel regularly so their progress can be monitored, and upon entering must agree to be tested randomly for drug use. Some offenders are also required to pursue a GED, or even keep and maintain a job. Offenders are rewarded for positive behavior. However, if a participant fails to meet their treatment plan, they can be returned to court to face the original criminal charges against them. Those who successfully complete the drug treatment plan may see their original criminal charges reduced or dismissed.

The concept driving a drug court is to help end the cycle of drug use and crime. If a drug addict no longer has the need to rely on drugs, they will be less likely to commit additional crime to support their drug addiction. The drug courts enhance the treatment that is available to offenders so they become drug-free.

Research on drug courts show that graduates tend to refrain from using drugs as well as the crime associated with drug use. The courts have also been shown to save the state money by reducing prison terms and by reducing recidivism (committing additional offenses and returning to the facility). In the long run, successful graduates are also able to maintain employment and become successful community members and family members.

Summit County

The drug court in Summit County was restructured and renamed the "Turning Point Program" in 2013. This was done to change the focus of the court from being a diversionary program that identifies participants upon their arrest, to a program aimed toward rehabilitating offenders who are already in the system. Now the mission is to provide a "court-supervised Program for substance dependent offenders to enhance public safety, reduce crime, hold offenders accountable, reduce cost to the community and provide an opportunity for offenders to transform into positive, contributing community members."

The Turning Point program has two tracks. The first is for participants who enter the program after being noncompliant with Intervention in Lieu of Conviction (IILC). The second track is for those participants who are on probation. Regardless of the track, all offenders who participate have been identified as having a chemical dependency issue.

The following tables show the number of defendants in the mental health courts in Summit County. Table 7.1 shows the number of potential clients screened. There were more males screened than females, and more Caucasians than Blacks. Table 7.2 is the number of defendants who entered the drug court program. As expected, there were more males than females accepted into the program and who agreed to participate. In Table 7.3 is the number of defendants completing the program. Prior to the reorganization, 70% of the of-

Table 7.1: Summit County Felony Drug Court, Defendants Screened

	Male	Female	Total Screened	African American	Caucasian	Other
January–June 2013	448	165	613	217	393	3
July–December 2013 (Turning Point)	66	31	97	19	77	1

Table 7.2: Summit County Felony Drug Court, Defendants Entering

	Male	Female	Total Screened	African American	Caucasian	Other
January–June 2013	29	16	45	7	38	0
July–December 2013 (Turning Point) Track 1	6	6	12	3	9	0
July–December 2013 (Turning Point) Track 2	24	10	34	4	30	0

fenders satisfied the requirements for graduation. Tables 7.4 and 7.5 indicate the reasons why some defendants were not permitted into the program. They indicate that offenders were not invited into the program for many various reasons, including failure to show up for assessment to a prior history of violent behavior.

Table 7.3: Summit County Felony Drug Court, Defendants Completing

	Successful	Unsuccessful	Success Rate
January–June 2013	69	30	70%
July–December 2013 (Turning Point)	0	1	0%

Table 7.4: Summit County Felony Drug Court, Reason for Ineligibility

On Parole/Post-Release Control or Community Control	49
Trafficking Conviction	68
Trafficking Arrest within Last 10 Years	9
Contempt History	7
Police Deny	11
Current Charge is F-1, F-2 or F-3	46
Prior Felonies	6
Cases Pending	10
Other Court Involvement (Felony or Misdemeanor Pending)	65
History of Violence	15
Rejected by Prosecutor	32
Current Specialty Court Involvement	20
Prior Treatment-Based Diversion	31
Failure to Appear for Drug Court Screening	1
Co-Defendant	68
Rejected by Defendant	7
Companion Charge Disqualifies	129
Drug of Choice Unable to be Screened	2
Tier III Sex Offender or Sexual Predator	1
Rejected by Victim	1

Table 7.5: Summit County Felony Drug Court Turning Point Program,
Reason for Ineligibility

Chemical Dependency Level of Care did not meet minimum requirement	2
Did not meet legal criteria	9
Defendant declined opportunity to participate in Program	10
Judge denied placement based on recommendation of the Treatment Team	16
Assigned Court declined to place defendant into Program	1
Failed to appear for screening process	6

Cuyahoga County

The drug court in Cuyahoga County began accepting participants in 2009 as a way to break the cycle of recidivism that is common in drug users by focusing on an offender's drug addiction. The Drug Court in Cuyahoga County accepts only offenders who have been identified as drug dependent. To date, over 300 individuals have participated in the program and over 110 participants have successfully completed the program and have been able to return home as drug-free individuals. The Cuyahoga County Drug Court works in conjunction with the Greater Cleveland Drug Court. The courts are able to save resources by sharing treatment resources, case managers and graduation ceremonies for those who succeed in the program (Cuyahoga County Drug Court, 2014).

Franklin County

The drug court in Franklin County is called "Treatment is Essential for Success" (TIES). Created in 2004, the court links people who have committed crimes as a result of their drug use to address the root causes of crime. Since it started, about fifty participants have graduated. In Franklin County, offenders could be eligible for participating in the TIES program if they meet the following criteria:

- Committed a Felony 4 or Felony 5 offense
- Charged with a non-violent, non-sexually-oriented offense
- Charge is not gun-related
- May have a Domestic Violence charge (considered on a "case-by-case" basis)
- Offender has no significant history of violent crimes or drug trafficking
- Offender has shown sufficient motivation for treatment/change
- Offender has a primary diagnosis of chemical dependency

The Franklin County TIES Program consists of three twelve-week units, although most participates are able to complete the requirements in under eighteen months. In each unit, the offender must complete different activities to help them stay drug-free. They may have to pay restitution, fines and any court costs, remain drug-free, and maintain a job. If they do so, they will be rewarded; however, if they do not follow the program, they will be sanctioned. As offenders make better choices, they will be required to have less contact with the court. In the last six months, there is a period of traditional probation. If the offender completes this stage, they can participate in a graduation ceremony.

Medina County

Beginning in 2014, Medina County bean an Early Intervention Pre-Trial Program (EIPP) as a way to help offenders who have been charged with low level felonies as a result of their alcohol or drug use. If a defendant is determined to be eligible for EIPP, a hearing is held in which the defendant will enter a plea of either Guilty or No Contest to the charge. The defendant will then be placed into the EIPP. They must agree to follow all the conditions of the year-long program. If the defendant is able to finish the program, the charges against him/her will then be dismissed (Medina County Common Pleas Court Early Intervention Pre-Trial Program, 2013).

The terms and conditions of the Medina County EIPP program are listed below in Table 7.6.

Montgomery County

Montgomery Country established the Women's Therapeutic Court in 2014 to facilitate treatment of women who are charged with committing crimes resulting from a drug addiction or drug abuse. Like drug courts, the WTC uses individualized programs to treat offenders as a way to help the offenders become drug free and reduce the chances of recidivism. The court attempts to treat those with addiction or mental health concerns who have been charged with offenses such as prostitution, sex trafficking, and other women-specific issues (Gokavi, 2014; Montgomery County Common Pleas Court, 2014).

Table 7.6: Terms and Conditions of Medina County EIPP

The defendant agrees to comply with the following terms and conditions:

1. The defendant will appear in court every Wednesday at 2:30 p.m.
2. The defendant will not consume alcohol or any controlled substance. All prescribed drugs must be reported to the program coordinator prior to use.
3. The defendant will tell the truth in all court proceedings, court documents, and treatment sessions.
4. The defendant will agree to complete any diagnostic evaluation required.
5. The defendant will contact Christine Demlow, Program Coordinator at 330-725-9131 every morning, Monday through Friday.
6. The defendant will follow the treatment plan as developed by his/her provider.
7. The defendant will obey all laws, and understand that if he/she engages in any criminal act, he/she may be prosecuted for any new charge and the new charge may be the basis for termination from EIPP.
8. The defendant will not knowingly associate with persons using or possessing controlled substances.
9. The defendant will not live with a convicted felon, unless approved by the program director.
10. The defendant will tell the program coordinator before he/she moves, changes or disconnects his/her telephone number, or changes his/her employment.
11. The defendant will submit to random physiological testing for alcohol and controlled substances as directed, at his/her cost. If the defendant misses a test or refuses to submit to a test, or submits a diluted test, it will count as a positive test.
12. The defendant will submit to a breath alcohol test at any time.
13. The defendant must be employed full-time or in school full-time or will submit a minimum of 7 applications per day.
14. The defendant will attend AA or NA meeting every day, 7 days per week.
15. The defendant will pay all court costs and costs of testing as well as restitution if restitution is ordered. Failure to pay for a test for substance use will be counted as a positive test.
16. The defendant agrees to sign consent for the program coordinator and a representative from the Sheriff's department to search his/her house, car, possessions or person at any time.
17. The defendant shall call required people every day, 7 days a week.
18. The defendant shall get a sponsor and a home group within 3 weeks. Defendant to consult with the program coordinator.

Domestic Relations Courts/ Domestic Violence Courts/ Family Violence Courts

Another type of specialized court established in many counties in Ohio are courts that deal with families, spouse or partners. The names for these courts vary, and can include domestic relations, domestic violence, or family violence courts. These courts provide relief for victims by requiring an offender to complete treatment programs.

Table 7.7 indicates the number of cases heard in domestic relations courts in Ohio. It also shows the kind of cases that appear in these kind of special courts.

Trumbull County

In Trumbull County, the court that handles divorce, dissolution, legal separations, annulments, and civil protection orders necessary because of domestic violence is called the Domestic Relations Division of the Common Pleas Court. This court also hears cases involving cases of determining parental rights and responsibilities, child custody, child support, spousal support or alimony, property division and debt allocation.

Table 7.7: Domestic Relations Courts, Total Cases, 2012

Marriage Terminations with Children	24,023
Marriage Terminations without Children	20,038
Marriage Dissolutions with Children	1,112
Marriage Dissolutions without Children	1,214
Change of Custody	2,759
Enforcement or Modification of Visitation	1,366
Enforcement or Modification of Support	8,579
Domestic Violence	1,562

Source: The Supreme Court of Ohio, Ohio Courts Statistical Report 2012; http://www.supreme court.ohio.gov/Publications/annrep/12OCS/2012OCS.pdf

Brown County

The Domestic Relations Court in Brown County hears cases of divorce, dissolution, separations, civil protection orders, and similar cases. The judges also preside over cases concerning domestic violence cases. They also hear cases involving child custody, parenting issues, spousal support and related matters. The goal of the court is to both protect those individuals involved in the domestic issue, at the same time providing an outlet that does not necessarily lead to the incarceration of a family member.

Medina County

In Medina County, the Domestic Relations Division of the Court of Common Pleas handles all cases revolving around divorce, dissolution, the care and support of children, and the protection of victims of domestic violence. The program also attempts to help families resolve disagreements about finances, property, and children.

In 2004, there were 3,010 cases heard in the Domestic Relations Court in Medina County. Marriage terminations accounted for 755 of these cases, 450 of which involved children. There were also almost 300 cases of domestic violence and 1,489 cases related to the enforcement, modification or termination of child support.

Medina County has also started a mediation program to assist families in resolving their disagreements without violence. There is also a center available for the safe exchange of children in families experiencing divorce or separation, and supervised parenting time for families that have experienced domestic violence.

In 2011, Medina implemented a special docket for Domestic Violence Civil Protection Orders. In this specialized court, all petitions that have been filed requesting a protection order are heard by a Magistrate who only hears Domestic Violence cases. This special court shortens the potential waiting time that victims of domestic violence sometimes experience. Now a victim will not have to wait for a trial magistrate to have the time to hear the petition. There is also a domestic violence advocate who is available to help victims with paperwork, provide crisis intervention, and provide emotional support throughout the hearings.

Trumbull County

Trumbull County created a Family Dependency Treatment Court (FDTC) that has the goal of improving the safety and welfare of children while at the same time assisting in their parents' recovery from alcohol and drug abuse. This is done through comprehensive treatment services and judicial supervision of parents identified as having drug dependency and who are also neglecting or abusing children in the home.

Parents are eligible for FDTC when charges of child abuse, neglect or dependency are filed by the County CSB. Substance abuse by the parents must be identified as an underlying cause for the mistreatment of the children. The information on the parents is given to the FDTC Team, and the Magistrate then approves the admission of clients based on the recommendations of the team members. Parental participation in the program is voluntary. The program consists of graduated phases. As participants complete phases, they will receive rewards from the court. However, if the parents fail to complete the phases, sanctions will be imposed. The program usually lasts about a year.

Montgomery County

Montgomery County created a Felony Non-Support Court (FNS Court) to supervise felons who have been convicted of criminal non-support, who owe support to dependent children, and who have been sentenced to community control sanctions. The Judge may order a defendant to FNS Court after they have been convicted of a felony offense for criminal non-support or as a result of a preliminary hearing by the Probation Department. In order for a defendant to be eligible for FNS Court, they must owe child support for dependent children, agree to community control, be a resident of Ohio and show a willingness to participate in the treatment process (Montgomery County Common Pleas Court, 2014).

Reentry Courts

Another alternative court found in Ohio counties are reentry courts. They are typically designed to assist offenders in making the transition from the correctional facility to their communities with few problems. Offenders usually meet each month with the sentencing judge and a team of professionals to review their progress. Also in that meeting are the hearing officer, parole officer, and any other treatment providers as needed to help that offender succeed. The professionals set goals for the offender which must be met. When the offender completes the program, they receive a certificate. More importantly, they are ready to continue their lives crime-free and not return to prison.

Summit County

The Reentry Court Program in Summit County was established in 2006. It includes the Court of Common Pleas, the Adult Probation Department and a community corrections agency. An offender who wants to join the program is required to submit a letter (or the attorney must file a motion) to the Court in which they express their interest in being chosen for the program. The Court then decides if the offender's request will be permitted. The offender will be screened by a Probation Officer who decides if the offender will be accepted.

If the offender is approved for the year-long program, he or she will be released from custody or transferred to a residential facility operated by the community corrections agency. All offenders are assigned a Reentry Court caseworker who helps them throughout the program by designing an individualized program for that offender. The offender must meet with their caseworker regularly, and must submit to random drug tests. Participants must appear in front of a judge regularly as a way to monitor their progress. When the client successfully completes the program, they will have a graduation ceremony.

In 2013, there were 226 clients in the reentry program in Summit County, with 52 successful graduates. The program had a retention rate of 68% (Court of Common Pleas, 2013).

Veterans' Courts

Yet another type of alternative court in Ohio is the Veterans' Court, or sometimes called Valor Court. The first veterans' court in Ohio opened in the Mansfield Municipal Court in 2009, and the second one was established in Youngstown in 2011. These courts have been designed to address the specific needs of those veterans who suffer from a traumatic brain injury, posttraumatic stress disorder, or other related issues that lead to behavior resulting in criminal charges. The court assists veterans who have been charged with nonviolent misdemeanor offenses, but may also help veterans who have been charged with non-violent felonies. Court personnel provide mental health counseling, alcohol or drug treatment, vocational training, or mentoring as needed. The court also advises veterans about any federal resources that may be of assistance to them.

Like offenders in the other specialty courts, offenders in veterans' courts must take part in a court-supervised treatment plan devised by a team of specialists. This team may include mental health professionals, health care providers, treatment staff, or probation officers, or other professionals as needed. The plan may include counseling, drug treatment or AA, or other related treatments. Those who complete the program will avoid jail or prison time and have their charges dismissed.

Summit County

On September 17, 2013, Summit County Court of Common Pleas, in conjunction with Akron Municipal Court, held the opening ceremony for Valor Court. The purpose of this treatment Court is to address substance abuse and combat-related mental illness in collaboration with the local Veteran's Administration, as well as other community resources, for those veterans honorably released from the military.

The Valor Court in Summit County consists of one Supervisor and two Probation Officers who identify possible applicants early in the court process. Once accepted into Valor Court, all participants report to a Probation Officer each week, in addition to fulfilling other requirements. Participants also must have court appearances twice each month. Since the beginning of the program, there have been 15 offenders screened and 9 offenders accepted (Akron Municipal Court, 2014).

Montgomery County

The Veterans' Court was established in Montgomery County as a way to provide treatment for veterans who have developed drug addiction or mental health issues. Offenders in the program are supervised by the Probation Department as a way to ensure compliance with the requirements of the program. They are also supervised by the "Veterans' Court Team," composed of the Judge assigned to Veterans' Court, Probation Officers, licensed treatment providers, community based employment program personnel, the Veterans' Justice Outreach Coordinator, the Assistant Prosecuting Attorney, and Defense Counsel.

To be eligible for Veteran's Court, an offender must be an Ohio resident and received an honorable discharge from the military. They must agree to plead guilty or no contest to the criminal charges against them. The charges must be a third-, fourth-, or fifth-degree felony. Those who have committed felonies of the first and second degree will be determined on a case-by-case basis. They must be identified as having a chemical abuse problem that caused the criminal behavior. The offender must also agree to community control and be willing to participate in the treatment process.

The offender must complete all phases of the treatment plan. Upon graduation, the offender may be required to remain under community control as a way to ensure continued compliance and success.

If a participant does not comply with requirements, they may receive a warning from the judge, or be demoted to a lower treatment phase. They may be required to have more frequent drug testing or court appearances, with more supervision. If serious enough, the offender may be terminated from the program and be placed in jail (Montgomery County Common Pleas Court, 2014).

Summary

The alternative courts have been established by counties in Ohio as a way to give assistance to a particular group of offenders who are then able to remain out of a correctional facility. These courts help the individual by providing focused services and treatment, allowing them to become productive members of society. However, these courts also help the state save money by reducing the number of offenders housed in residential correctional facilities. They also help the courts by removing certain offenders from a traditional court setting, thus helping to reduce court backlogs. To date, these courts have effectively reached their goals in helping offenders become law-abiding.

Key Terms

Alternative Courts

Domestic Relations/Domestic Violence/Family Violence Courts

Drug Courts

Mental Health Courts

Ohio Specialized Dockets Practitioner Network

Reentry Courts

Special Courts

Veterans' Courts/Valor Courts

Resources

Cuyahoga County Drug Court
http://cp.cuyahogacounty.us/internet/DrugCourt.aspx
Franklin County Drug Court
https://www.fccourts.org/gen/WebFront.nsf/wp/E83AB884D5182D1385
257507005DBE47?opendocument
Mental Health Developmental Disability Court of Cuyahoga County
http://cp.cuyahogacounty.us/internet/MentalHealth.aspx

Review Questions

1. What are Special Courts and why are they useful?
2. Give some examples of Special Courts.
3. Who would be eligible for participation in a special court?
4. How do the different alternative courts differ from one another? How are they the same?
5. What is required of a participant in Cuyahoga County's drug court?
6. What elements are required in the program for someone participating in the mental health court?

References

Akron Municipal Court, Mental Health Court. (2014). Retrieved from https:// courts.ci.akron.oh.us/programs/mental_health.htm.

Court of Common Pleas, General Division, Summit County Ohio (2013). Annual Report For the Year 2013. Retrieved from http://www.summitcpcourt.net/ Annual%20Reports/2013%20ANNUAL%20REPORT%20FINAL%20_%20 2PICS%20NEEDED.pdf.

Cuyahoga County Drug Court, Cuyahoga County Common Pleas Court. (2014). Retrieved from http://cp.cuyahogacounty.us/internet/DrugCourt.aspx.

Gokavi, Mark. (June 17, 2014). "County Kicks Off Women's Therapeutic Court" *Dayton Daily News.* Retrieved from http://www.daytondailynews.com/news/ news/crime-law/county-kicks-off-womens-therapeutic-court/ngMxJ/.

Medina County Common Pleas Court Early Intervention Pre-Trial Program (2013). Retrieved from http://www.co.medina.oh.us/judgecollier/EIPP.pdf.

Mental Health Court, Cuyahoga County Common Pleas Court. (2010). 2010 Annual Report. Retrieved from http://cp.cuyahogacounty.us/Internet/ CourtDocs/web/mh/MHAnRep2010.pdf.

Montgomery County Common Pleas Court. (2014). General Division, Amendments to Local Rules 2.01–3.15. Retrieved from http://www.montcourt.org.

Chapter 8

The Death Penalty in Ohio

Learning Objectives

After reading this chapter, students will be able to:

- Describe the history of the death penalty in the Ohio and across the United States.
- Explain how the "death penalty is different."
- Describe the process of how the death penalty is applied in Ohio.
- Detail the controversy surrounding the death penalty.
- Understand the difficulty in studying the effectiveness of the death penalty.
- Describe how often the death penalty is applied.
- Analyze *Furman*.
- Examine and summarize *Gregg v. Georgia*.
- Explain why appeals take so long in the case of death penalty cases.

Introduction

On January 15, 2014, Dennis McGuire was executed at the State Penitentiary in Marion, Ohio. Using a newly approved two-drug cocktail, Mr. McGuire was said by witnesses to have "gasped" and "snorted," and made "choking sounds" for approximately 10 minutes before falling silent, and subsequently being declared dead (Lyman, 2014). While not the first execution to prove problematic, McGuire's lethal injection once again raised issues with the ultimate penalty for a crime—the death penalty.

Ohio's History with the Death Penalty

Ohio has a long history with the application of the death penalty. Since the state's founding in 1803, offenders have been eligible for the sentence of death (Department of Rehabilitation and Correction, 2014a). Between 1803 and

1885, those who were sentenced to be executed were hanged, often in public, in the counties they were sentenced in. In 1885, the law changed, mandating that all executions in the state be carried out in the State Penitentiary in Columbus, Ohio, the first execution under the new law being carried out that year. In addition to the change that mandated all those condemned to death would be executed in Columbus, there was a change in the method of execution in 1897, when the state adopted electrocution as the method of execution in Ohio (Department of Rehabilitation and Correction, 2014a).

Between the years of 1897 and 1963, 315 people were electrocuted in the state's electric chair, "Old Sparky." This total included three women, the only women who were executed during that period. In 1972 in *Furman v. Georgia* the Supreme Court ruled that the death penalty, as then administered, was unconstitutional.

Also in 1972, Ohio moved the state's Death Row to the Southern Ohio Correctional Facility in Lucasville, Ohio. Shortly thereafter, Ohio presented its newly revised death penalty statute to the Supreme Court, but it was rejected by the court on procedural grounds, in 1978. Those confined on death row, 120 in total, had their sentences commuted from death to life in prison (Department of Rehabilitation and Correction, 2014a).

Though a new death penalty statute was accepted by the Court in 1981, the first execution under the new law did not take place until 1999, when an inmate named Wilford Berry was executed after waiving his appeals. He was executed via lethal injection, which was an option since 1983, when prisoners were given a choice between electrocution and lethal injection as their preferred method of death. Since his execution, there have been a total of eight inmates who waived their right to appeal and have been executed in the state (Department of Rehabilitation and Correction, 2014a).

In recent years, Ohio governors have been willing to use their power of pardon to either grant clemency to inmates on death row, or reduce their sentences to life in prison. Though Ohio's Death Row was moved in 1995, this time to Mansfield Correctional Institution in Mansfield, Ohio, to accommodate larger numbers of inmates, the death penalty remains infrequently used compared to states like Florida and New York. A table of the states that execute prisoners is provided in Table 8.1.

Currently, the troubled executions in Ohio and elsewhere have again raised the discussion of the importance of the death penalty as a method of punishment in Ohio and across the United States. In the sections below, we turn towards both the elements of that debate, as well as Ohio's place in the debate. In order to facilitate this, the cases of *Furman v. Georgia* (1972), the case that made the death penalty unconstitutional, and *Gregg v. Georgia* (1976), which allowed the Court to reinstate the death penalty are examined in detail.

Table 8.1: States With and Without the Death Penalty

STATES WITH THE DEATH PENALTY (32)		
Alabama	Kentucky	Oregon
Arizona	Louisiana	Pennsylvania
Arkansas	Mississippi	South Carolina
California	Missouri	South Dakota
Colorado	Montana	Tennessee
Delaware	Nebraska	Texas
Florida	Nevada	Utah
Georgia	New Hampshire	Virginia
Idaho	North Carolina	Washington
Indiana	Ohio	Wyoming
Kansas	Oklahoma	

STATES WITHOUT THE DEATH PENALTY (18) (Year Abolished in Parentheses)		
Alaska (1957)	Massachusetts (1984)	Rhode Island (1984)^
Connecticut** (2012)	Michigan (1846)	Vermont (1964)
Hawaii (1957)	Minnesota (1911)	West Virginia (1965)
Illinois (2011)	New Jersey (2007)	Wisconsin (1853)
Iowa (1965)	New Mexico* (2009)	
Maine (1887)	New York (2007)#	ALSO
Maryland*** (2013)	North Dakota (1973)	Dist. of Columbia (1981)

* In March 2009, New Mexico voted to abolish the death penalty. However, the repeal was not retroactive, leaving two people on the state's death row.

** In April 2012, Connecticut voted to abolish the death penalty. However, the repeal was not retroactive, leaving 11 people on the state's death row.

*** In May, 2013, Maryland abolished the death penalty. However, the repeal was not retroactive, leaving 5 people on the state's death row.

^ In 1979, the Supreme Court of Rhode Island held that a statute making a death sentence mandatory for someone who killed a fellow prisoner was unconstitutional. The legislature removed the statute in 1984.

In 2004, the New York Court of Appeals held that a portion of the state's death penalty law was unconstitutional. In 2007, they ruled that their prior holding applied to the last remaining person on the state's death row. The legislature has voted down attempts to restore the statute.

Source: http://www.deathpenaltyinfo.org/states-and-without-death-penalty

Furman

In mid-1972, the Supreme Court released a remarkable decision. Not necessarily interesting for its erudition, the result of the decision was monumental in terms of its impact. In *Furman v. Georgia* (1972), the Court ruled that the death penalty, under its current form of administration by the states, was unconstitutional because it violated inmates Eighth Amendment Rights in a way that was tantamount to cruel and unusual punishment.

Though the named case in *Furman* focused on a homicide committed by an African American against a white victim, the case was actually a combination of that case and two others—both of which were rape convictions involving a black suspect and white victim. Those cases were from Georgia and Texas, respectively. In all these, the victims were convicted by juries and sentenced to death under their respective states' death penalty statutes (*Furman v. Georgia*, 1972).

In the decision, the Majority reasoned that if the administration of the death penalty resulted in unequal treatment of individuals because of the race, age, or other factors, that the penalty itself could be considered unconstitutional. In fact, this is what the court found, ruling that,

> It would seem to be incontestable that the death penalty inflicted on one defendant is "unusual" if it discriminates against him by reason of his race, religion, wealth, social position, or class, or if it is imposed under a procedure that gives room for the play of such prejudices (*Furman v. Georgia*, 1972, p. 242).

While the decision in *Furman* was clear in its elimination of the death penalty under the form of the time, it was less clear in several other ways. There were a number of concurring opinions in the cases, making navigation of the legal aspects of implementing a constitutional death penalty difficult. Further, it was unclear whether or not the court had ruled that the death penalty was unconstitutional only under its currently administered form, or whether the practice was *per se* unconstitutional (Acker, Bohm, and Lanier, 2003). Despite these issues, the justices were clear in several aspects required for a constitutional version of the death penalty. First, the punishment cannot cause undue physical or mental anguish. Second, the penalty cannot be arbitrarily imposed. Third, it must meet the requirements of the evolving standards of decency (more on this below). Finally, it must be proportionate to the crime committed.

As mentioned above, the immediate impact on all states that used the death penalty—36 at the time of *Furman*—was enormous. In Ohio, 120 inmates had their sentences commuted to life in prison, and executions were effectively quelled until 1999, though there were inmates sentenced to death after the new statute was approved in 1981. Even with the new statute, however, the death penalty has continued to be controversial both in its principal and its practice.

Continuing Controversies in the Death Penalty

Cruel and Unusual

After *Furman* there have been a number of attempts to demonstrate that the death penalty remains cruel and unusual, despite states' attempts to deal with the issues identified in *Furman*. In *Baze v. Rees* (2008), for instance, a death row inmate in Kentucky alleged that because the death penalty was potentially not painless, that the administration of the death penalty (as it was currently administered) was inherently unconstitutional. The Court was unequivocal in its statement that any pain caused was not enough, in and of itself, to make the death penalty unconstitutional. The Court's majority opinion, written by Chief Justice John Roberts, indicated that

> [s]ome risk of pain is inherent in any method of execution—no matter how humane—if only from the prospect of error in following the required procedure. It is clear, then, that the Constitution does not demand the avoidance of all risk of pain in carrying out executions (*Baze v. Rees*, 2008, p. 8).

This was indicative of the Court's view that, as the death penalty has been consistently ruled constitutional, the necessary burden to overturn it on grounds that it is cruel and unusual is high.

The Court has not been completely consistent in terms of the scope of the death penalty. However, in recent years, it has limited the type of individuals the state can apply the death penalty to, removing juveniles (*Roper v. Simmons*, 2005), as well as those with significant mental handicaps from eligibility for death (*Atkins v. Virginia*, 2002). All of these speak to the Court's slow working out of how the country's "evolving standards of decency" play out in the debate about capital punishment. This is a difficult problem to work out; as the *Baze* Court recognized, "there are no methods of legal execution that are satisfactory to those who oppose the death penalty on moral, religious, or societal grounds," (*Baze v. Rees*, 2008, p. 41) yet many people remain in favor of the death penalty.

Botched Executions

One of the elements that has continually added fuel to the fires of debate about the death penalty, are the so-called botched executions. A botched execution is an execution that does not proceed according to the normal course of action in an execution. Whether or not an execution was botched, however, is not always an easy determination to make. The example given at the beginning of this chapter is a good case in point. While many witnesses to the execution claimed that McGuire suffered, the report developed by the state to examine the execution determined that it was "humane" and that McGuire did not experience pain during the process (Ohio Department of Rehabilitation and Correction, 2014b).

Despite this assertion, the report also indicated that Ohio would (again) change its protocol regarding administering the drugs for lethal injection, suggesting that the protocol used on McGuire was somehow inadequate (Ohio Department of Rehabilitation and Correction, 2014b).

McGuire's execution was by no means the only botched execution in recent memory. Just two weeks prior to Ohio's botched execution, Oklahoma death row inmate Michael Lee Wilson complained of burning as the first drug was injected (CBS News, 2014). More recently, Oklahoma had another botched execution, where Clayton Lockett took over 20 minutes to die, manifesting signs of pain throughout, after an IV was improperly inserted (Oklahoma Department of Public Safety, 2014). Similarly, an execution in Arizona took over 2 hours and required over 15 doses of drugs before the inmate died (Chappell, 2014).

These examples, and others from before the adoption of lethal injection, add to the debate regarding the death penalty, requiring recognition of the potential problems with the process. It is perhaps unsurprising that the drugs used to execute convicted felons are becoming harder to come by, to the point where the protocols for administration are changing regularly to deal with shortages of drugs (Horne, 2014). Relatedly, there are questions about the medical ethics of administering the death penalty for physicians, as the Hippocratic Oath requires that they "do no harm."

The administration of the death penalty is not the only area fueling the debate. There are also significant questions as to whether or not the death penalty is effective.

Effectiveness

One of the difficulties in dealing with Ohio's death penalty, and the death penalty more generally, is the fact that there is no consensus on whether or not it is an effective deterrent (Manski and Pepper, 2012). While there are other justifications for the death penalty—retribution and incapacitation, for instance—the primary rationale tends to be that the death penalty will prevent others from committing similar crimes.

While the surface logic of this makes sense, research has shown that the results of the administration of the death penalty on criminal behavior are much murkier (Manski and Pepper, 2012). Much of the research done on the death penalty as a deterrent has shown either only a very modest effect on subsequent crimes, or, in most cases, no effect at all. Additionally, the argument for the death penalty as a deterrent is complicated by the fact that many people are not aware of when executions happen, limiting their ability to conceptually link the executions to their own actions. Some research suggests that, given the death penalty's low levels of application, that even perfect knowledge of executions would be insufficient to deter a crime from happening.

In addition to these objections, there is one more fundamental. Former Ohio Supreme Court Justice Evelyn Stratton sums it up well. "It's not a deterrent one wit. Nobody thinks, 'I'm not going to kill this person because I might get the death penalty.' They're in the throes of something, and they're not thinking about that" (Demeglio, 2013).

Cost

In addition to questions about whether the death penalty is an effective deterrent, there are important concerns regarding the total cost of administering the death penalty. Though no studies have been conducted regarding Ohio specifically, there is good reason to believe that the process here, as in all other jurisdictions where it has been examined, is extremely expensive compared to a normal criminal trial. In 2007, the American Bar Association reported that the cost of the first person executed in Ohio since the reinstitution of the death penalty cost approximately $1,000,000. Subsequent capital trials have cost a similar amount (ABA, 2007).

This cost is potentially higher in Ohio than in other jurisdictions still maintaining capital punishment. For instance, in Kansas, the average death penalty trial costs nearly $400,000, three times as much as an equivalent non-capital trial (Judicial Council Kansas Legislature, 2014). However, this cost is dwarfed by the estimated costs of a death penalty case in Ohio. Other studies have demonstrated costs beyond financial concerns as well. In a 2013 Colorado study, researchers found that death penalty cases take, on average, *six times longer* than non-capital cases (Marceau and Whitson, 2013). This equated to four calendar years longer simply to reach a conviction. In addition, the study found that even if the defendant in a capital case takes a plea deal for life without parole, it still takes longer than a trial where the maximum sentence was life without parole.

How the Process Works in Ohio

In the case of capital trials, an indictment must be issued by a grand jury containing a statement that an offense has been committed and be signed by the prosecuting attorney. Capital punishment can only be pursued if the defendant is found guilty of aggravated murder, with at least one specification (aggravating circumstance). There are 10 possible aggravating circumstances expressed in the Ohio Revised Code (ORC 2929.04) ranging from the act being associated with terrorism, to the unwanted termination of a pregnancy.

Once the indictment has been issued, the individual accused of a crime is presented before a court or magistrate. During this initial appearance, the defendant will be informed of the charges against him or her, and the right to counsel is reiterated, as are the remaining *Miranda* rights. Additionally, the accused is informed of effects of the various possible pleas—guilty, not guilty, not guilty by reason of insanity, and no contest—as well as the defendant's right to a jury trial.

The next step in the process is arraignment. The indictment is read in open court and, at this point, the defendant enters a plea. The judge must make sure the defendant understands the plea, especially in cases where the defendant chooses to remain unrepresented by council. In cases of capital murder, a defendant must plead separately to each specification, as well as to the crime itself. Once the plea is accepted, the defendant has the right to "knowingly" waive a jury trial. If the jury is waived, the case will be presented to a three-judge panel to determine whether the crime was aggravated murder or something less and impose sentence accordingly. If the defendant is determined to be guilty of aggravated murder, the judges will consider aggravating and mitigating circumstances to determine the appropriate sentence.

In either a jury trial or a trial by the three-judge panel, the defendant has the opportunity to enter pre-trial motions. These include requests for discovery, severance of charges for multiple defendants, or motions to suppress evidence, as well as others. Moreover, if the defendant wishes to demonstrate an alibi, he or she must provide the prosecution with at least seven days notice prior to the trial.

The court of original jurisdiction for capital cases are Ohio's courts of common pleas. The trial phase itself is split into two separate phases. The first phase is the trial itself. If the defendant is being tried by a jury, the state (as well as the defendants counsel) has the right to examine jurors. Jurors can be stricken for a variety of reasons, including if the juror unequivocally states that they would be unable to impose the death penalty for any reasons. Both sides present the case to the jury, have opportunity for cross-examination and present closing arguments. After the closing arguments, the jury retires to decide guilt or innocence. The jury must be unanimous in their decision. If the defendant is found guilty, they proceed to the sentencing phase.

During the sentencing phase, the judge and jury determine the appropriate sentence for the crime committed. In capital cases, where the defendant is found guilty of the crime and one or more specifications attached, the possible sentences are death, life imprisonment without parole, and life in prison with the possibility of parole in 20 or 30 years. In the case of a jury trial, the penalty phase will be held before the jury who decided the case and in the case of a three judge panel, the same judges will preside over both phases.

Once the sentence of death has been passed, there is an automatic appeal that bypasses the Ohio court of appeals and goes immediately to the Ohio Supreme Court. The Court is obligated to hear the appeal, unlike the United States Supreme Court, which can refuse to hear an appeal. The Ohio Supreme Court reviews the judgment for death in a similar manner to other appeals, except that it independently reviews and weighs all the facts and evidence that was a part of the trial, determines whether the aggravating circumstances were sufficiently proven and makes sure the penalty of death was appropriate in terms of issues like proportionality.

The Court has the option to modify, reverse, or affirm the original judgment. The decision of the Court is written, detailing the rationale of the court in the cases where errors in the lower judgment are found. If there is sufficient evidence for conviction, but not death (e.g., the defendant was under 18 at the time of the crime), the trial court will conduct a resentencing hearing. This appeal does not prevent the convicted defendant from appealing to the United States Supreme Court on Constitutional grounds.

A second type of appeal, used after the Ohio Supreme Court has denied the first appeal, is called a "Murnahan" appeal. This type of appeal is used to argue that the defendant had ineffective counsel at the Supreme Court. If the defendant is found to have lacked effective assistance of counsel, the Court must reopen the first appeal.

Once a defendant, now convicted, has exhausted all appeals at the state level, he or she may appeal to the federal court system, arguing that the conviction or sentence was in violation of federal law. This type of appeal is called *habeas corpus*, and is originally filed with the federal district court in Ohio that has jurisdiction. Any claims raised in a *habeas* petition must have been raised in state court prior to filing, and if a defendant (now called petitioner) fails to do so, the district court may deny the appeal. *Habeas corpus* petitions must be filed within one year from the date that the original judgment became file, or that any impediment to filing was removed. This time limit is waived if a new right is recognized by the Supreme Court and the Court applies it retroactively.

Habeas petitions can be summarily dismissed by the district judge, or in the case where the petition has merit, the judge may order a discovery in regards to the issues raised by the petition, and will order the respondent named in the petition time to answer those issues. The judge can also order a new evidentiary hearing (in most cases limited to the issues raised in the *habeas* petition, not the original trial).

If the judge finds against the petitioner, he can appeal the decision to the Sixth Circuit, but only if a district or circuit judge issues a "certificate of appealability" testifying to the substantial showing of the denial of a Constitutional right. Other options available to the judge are to grant a new trial, a new penalty phase, or a new direct appeal.

If, on appeal, the Sixth Circuit determines that the *habeas* petition has merit, it can grant a new appeal in federal district court, an evidentiary hearing by the district court, or a new trial at the state court. If relief is not granted, both parties can seek review of the decision by a petition for a *writ of certiorari* from the United States Supreme Court, which can either grant or denty the petition.

Finally, when all other options are exhausted, the governor can choose to grant clemency, through the issuing of a reprieve, commutation, or a pardon. The governor is assisted in the process by the Adult Parole Authority, and though the clemency is rarely granted, the process for review by the Authority is automatic, once an execution date has been set.

Execution

The execution itself is carried out, as mentioned above, by lethal injection, though given recent issues with executions, it is unclear what the specific injection protocol will be. A variety of individuals can be present at the execution, including the Warden of the correctional institution, officers to assist (the number is decided upon by the warden), the sheriff of the county in which the prisoner was tried, the Director of Rehabilitation and Correction (for the state level), the staff physician for the correctional facility, a clergymember for the prisoner, three individuals named by the prisoner, three individuals representing the victim's family, and representatives for the news media.

Summary

The death penalty is a challenging topic, both because of the emotions it engenders as well as the administrative complications involved. Ohio's death penalty, though largely similar to other states in its administration, is unique in that it has been a leader in introducing new protocols for execution. Moreover, given that Ohio, until very recently, regularly executed prisoners, it stands to reason that the issues generated by discussions of the death penalty—its effectiveness, cost, and the ethics of execution—would be of even more interest to those pursuing a career in criminal justice in Ohio.

Key Terms

Aggravating Factors
Baze v. Rees
Botched Execution
Capital Punishment
Deterrence
Electrocution
Furman v. Georgia
Gregg v. Georgia

Habeas Corpus
Incapacitation
Lethal Injection
Mitigating Factors
Murnahan Appeal
Retribution
Roper v. Simmons

Resources

American Civil Liberties Union of Ohio
    https://www.aclu.org/affiliate/ohio
Death Penalty Information Center
    http://www.deathpenaltyinfo.org/
National Death Penalty Archive
    http://library.albany.edu/speccoll/ndpa.htm
Ohio Department of Rehabilitation and Corrections
    http://www.drc.ohio.gov/

Review Questions

1. What is the primary argument for the death penalty and how well does it comport with the research?
2. Outline the legal process that deals with death penalty cases in Ohio.
3. Describe a Murnahan appeal and under what circumstances it can be used.
4. What was the importance of *Furman* and *Gregg*?
5. What is Ohio's execution protocol? Why don't we know?
6. What are the cost issues associated with the death penalty?
7. Why is the death penalty so expensive?
8. How long does it take a death penalty case to work its way through the court system when compared to other types of cases?

References

Acker, J.R., Bohm, R.M., and Lanier, C.S. (Eds.). (2003). *America's experiment with capital punishment: Reflections on the past, present, and future of the ultimate penal sanction* (2nd ed.). Durham, NC: Carolina Academic Press.

American Bar Association. (2007). *Evaluating fairness and accuracy in state death penalty systems: The Ohio death penalty assessment report*. Retrieved from http://www.americanbar.org/content/dam/aba/migrated/moratorium/assessmentproject/ohio/finalreport.authcheckdam.pdf.

Atkins v. Virginia, 536 U.S. 304 (2002).

Baze v. Rees, 533 U.S. 35 (2008).

CBS News. (January 10, 2014). Condemned man's last words: "I feel my whole body burning." Retrieved from http://www.cbsnews.com/news/okla-man-says-he-can-feel-body-burning-during-execution/.

Chapell, B. (July 23, 2014). Arizona execution of inmate takes nearly 2 hours. *NPR News*. Retrieved from http://www.npr.org/blogs/thetwo-way/2014/07/23/334632862/arizona-execution-of-inmate-takes-nearly-two-hours.

Demeglio, M. (2013). Following her calling: Retired Ohio Supreme Court Justice Evelyn Lundberg Stratton '79 prepares for next chapter in advocacy. *The Law School Magazine*, Winter 2013. Retrieved from http://moritzlaw.osu.edu/news/allrise/2013/02/following-her-calling-retired-ohio-supreme-court-justice-evelyn-lundberg-stratton-79-prepares-for-next-chapter-in-advocacy/.

Furman v. Georgia, 408 U.S. 238 (1972).

Gregg v. Georgia, 428 U.S. 153 (1976).

Horne, J. (2014). Lethal injection drug shortage. Retrieved from http://www.csg.org/pubs/capitolideas/enews/issue65_4.aspx.

Judicial Council Kansas Legislature. (2014). Report of the Judicial Council Death Penalty Advisory Committee. Retrieved from http://www.death penaltyinfo.org/documents/KSCost2014.pdf.

Lyman, R. (January 16, 2014). Ohio execution using untested drug cocktail renews the debate over lethal injection. *The New York Times.* Retrieved from http://nyti.ms/1eOQp6R.

Manski, C.F., and Pepper, J.V. (2012). Deterrence and the death penalty: Partial identification analysis using repeated cross sections. *Journal of Quantitative Criminology, 29,* 123–141.

Marceau, J.F., and Whitson, H.A. (2013). The cost of Colorado's death penalty. *University of Denver Criminal Law Review, 3,* 145–163.

Ohio Department of Rehabilitation and Correction. (2014a). Capital punishment in Ohio. Retrieved from http://www.drc.ohio.gov/public/capital.htm.

Ohio Department of Rehabilitation and Correction. (2014b). Execution review of Dennis McGuire. Retrieved from http://www.dispatch.com/content/downloads/2014/04/Report_on_the_execution_of_Dennis_McGuire.pdf.

Oklahoma Department of Public Safety. (2014). The execution of Clayton D. Lockett. Retrieved from http://www.dps.state.ok.us/Investigation/14-0189SI%20Summary.pdf.

Roper v. Simmons, 543 U.S. 551 (2005).

Chapter 9

Juvenile Justice in Ohio

Learning Objectives

After reading this chapter, students will be able to:

- Describe the history of the juvenile justice system in Ohio.
- Explain the elements of the juvenile justice system.
- Compare the juvenile justice system to the adult justice system in Ohio.
- Explain the idea of Targeted RECLAIM.
- Explain the role of community corrections in relation to the juvenile justice system.

The History of the Juvenile Justice System in Ohio

The Juvenile Justice System in America is founded on the *parens patriae* doctrine and Ohio is no different in this regard (Giannelli & Salvador, 2012). Courts and juvenile facilities were established to "act as a parent," protecting the welfare of the child. Because of the unique situations arising with youth, basic rights of the United States Constitution that were afforded to adults were not necessarily provided to youth. This too was based upon the belief that the court, acting as the "parent," ultimately knew what was in the best interest of the child. Many of the youth served by the system in the late 1800s would not even be considered delinquent by modern standards. Some children were abandoned, neglected, or incorrigible, but since most delinquent children were also destitute, it was thought to be logical to serve all of the children in need together. Children were often held in facilities—reform schools—after being deemed delinquent, dependent or neglected (Giannelli & Salvador, 2012).

Ohio's first reform school of record was opened in Fairfield County in 1858. Initially known as the Ohio Reform School for Boys, it was renamed the Boys Industrial School in 1884. In 1868 the Girls State Reform and Industrial School

opened and was renamed the Girls Industrial School in 1879 (ODYS 25th Anniversary Video). It was located on the west bank of the Scioto River. Whereas
the boys were taught school lessons and industrial trades, the girls programming focused on domestic chores in a homelike cottage setting, though the
girls did attend some classes in the afternoon. Prior to the advent of a formal
Juvenile Court System most youth that would be considered simply "unruly"
today or thought of as low-level criminal cases were held in the Reform Schools.
Children with any serious crimes were still handled by the adult system of
criminal justice (ODYS).

By 1900, over 300 youth were being served in the Industrial Schools, and
in 1902 the first Juvenile Court was established in Cuyahoga County, Ohio
(Pompa, 2000). Although Illinois was the first in the country to establish state
wide law for juvenile courts through the Illinois Juvenile Court Act of 1899,
Ohio had a statewide Juvenile Court System by 1906 (Pompa, 2000). Following the *parens patriae* doctrine, the court was not originally intended to
punish juvenile crime but meant to guide delinquents toward responsible,
productive citizenship.

Ohio adopted the Standard Juvenile Court Act, the national standard in
juvenile court development, in 1937 (Giannelli & Salvador, 2012). In *Cope
v. Campbell* the Supreme Court ruled that juvenile proceedings were "civil
and not criminal" in nature and are "for the purpose of correction and rehabilitation not for punishment." The vision was to "protect the wayward
child from 'evil influences,' and 'save' him from criminal prosecution" (Giannelli
& Salvador, 2012). Yet, due to the assumption that the court would always
know and do what is in the best interest of the welfare of the child basic
rights afforded to adults such as the right to counsel, privilege against self-
incrimination and trial by jury were still inapplicable to juvenile court proceedings.

Critics argued that despite reform schools best intentions, most were mil-
itaristic and overcrowded. Vocational training was more like "slave labor" in practice. By 1940, over 1900 youth were admitted each year to these institutions in
Ohio (ODYS). The focus of the state facilities was no longer on serving all unruly children, but only children considered delinquent. Reform efforts began
in the 1950s under the newly established Ohio Department of Mental Hygiene
and Correction. Youth Camps, Mohican and Zelesky were built to supplement
the reform school system. In the 1960s TICO, Maumee Youth Camp, Cuyahoga
Hills Boys School and Riverview School for Girls were built (ODYS). In keeping with the adult criminal justice system during the 1960s and 1970s, the
trend toward institutionalizing youth grew. The State of Ohio tried to address
the growing number of institutionalized youth with the establishment of the

Ohio Youth Commission (OYC) in 1963. OYC attempted to renew the emphasis on providing youth with sound academics and vocational training.

Despite its best efforts, OYC facilities were grossly overcrowded and plagued with corruption by the early 1980s. Tensions were rising between the judges and the state in regards to how best to handle juveniles. As a result, the Ohio Department of Youth Services (ODYS) was formed via House Bill 440 in November, 1981 (Giannelli & Salvador, 2012). The first Director, Bill Willis, had a presence at the Governor's office and was able to deal with the budget woes that had created significant problems for the Ohio Youth Commission as its buildings had deteriorated and its services were neglected (ODYS). The creation of ODYS created accountability within the department as there were checks and balances built into the system. Local judges sent youth to the institutions and determined how long youth would be held. Prior to ODYS, OYC had sole discretion in how long a youth would be held. Other changes included the rule that misdemeanor offenders were no longer accepted in ODYS facilities. A youth had to be adjudicated delinquent of a felony in order to be committed to ODYS. This was a great stride toward controlling the overcrowding in the institutions. Local jurisdictions received base funding known as the Youth Services Grant to start programming in their local communities to serve youth who previously were sent to ODYS Institutions. Ohio became a leader nationally by not accepting misdemeanants into its facilities. However, ODYS's second director was indicted on several felonies creating yet another controversy for the state agency. At that time Tom Mullen was appointed as interim director. A man of repute, he agreed to stay with ODYS until credibility was restored.

Director Geno Natulucci Persichetti was appointed director in 1987. Under "Director Geno's" leadership the state agency created great partnerships with the juvenile courts. Yet the delinquent population continued to soar and reached an all time high in 1992 with 3,200 youth admitted during that year (ODYS). This time in response to the escalating population, House Bill 152 was passed that created the Reasoned and Equitable Community and Local Alternatives to the Incarceration of Minors (RECLAIM Ohio) Program (Latessa, Lovins & Lux, 2014a). RECLAIM Ohio was implemented throughout the state in January, 1995 (Latessa et al., 2014a). Juvenile courts received an annual allocation of funds for local community based treatment of unruly and delinquent youth. Deductions were taken from each county's allocation based on the number of youth served per day in ODYS Facilities and Community Correction Centers. Thus, counties had an incentive to serve children locally. In 2005, the formula for distribution of funds was updated. The same formula is in use today and takes into consideration every county's average number of felony adjudications, total number of institutional bed day credits in comparison with statewide bed day credits and distributes funds available. The formula is complicated, and some bed days, known as "public safety beds," are not included in the calculation of bed day credits. Commonly referred to as "free beds," all UCR Category One offenses are considered "free" as well as Category Two offenses, with the exception of Aggravated Robbery and Aggravated Burglary (Panzino, 2014).

Both the Youth Services Grant and RECLAIM funds provide a wide variety of programming throughout the state, including but not limited to probation services, mental health counseling, substance abuse services, monitoring and surveillance, diversion, restitution, community service, work detail, sex offender treatment, and residential treatment. More than 80,000 admissions are made to RECLAIM programs annually. Research conducted by Dr. Ed. Latessa and his colleagues (2014a) reported that youth who successfully completed a community based RECLAIM program were less likely to recidivate compared to youth who did not complete a RECLAIM program. RECLAIM Ohio has been successful in reducing commitments to ODYS.

Targeted RECLAIM

In 2009, ODYS challenged the six most populous counties (Cuyahoga, Franklin, Hamilton, Lucas and Montgomery) to reduce commitments even further through Targeted RECLAIM. These same counties were responsible for committing the most children to ODYS. In order to be eligible for Targeted RECLAIM funding juvenile courts had to agree to 1) further reduce and then maintain the number of admissions to ODYS, 2) develop evidenced based programs to serve felony youth that would have historically been committed to ODYS, 3) assess and create case plans for youth using the Ohio Youth Assessment System, 4) submit data and adhere to quality assurance standards (Panzino, 2014). All six counties responded to the call and have further reduced the ODYS population by 70%, while serving youth in the community with evidenced-based programs such as Multi-Systemic Therapy and Functional Family Therapy.

Expansion of Targeted RECLAIM

Building upon the success within the original six Targeted RECLAIM counties, the state expanded funding to nine additional counties: Allen, Ashtabula, Butler, Licking, Lorain, Mahoning, Medina, Stark and Trumbull. Similar success was achieved in those counties. The collective results are displayed in Table 9.1, below.

Table 9.1: Targeted RECLAIM—ODYS Admissions by County

County	FY2009 actual	FY2010 actual	FY2011 Actual	FY2012 actual	FY2013 Actual	% Change Since FY2009	% Change Since FY2011
Cuyahoga	293	208	173	124	96	−62%	
Franklin	212	176	119	97	71	−59%	
Hamilton	147	88	52	27	27	−62%	
Lucas	76	32	33	33	33	−78%	
Montgomery	129	49	38	25	28	−85%	
Summit	132	47	42	29	22	−92%	
6 TR Original county subtotal	989	600	457	335	277	−70%	−35%
Allen			17	8	9		−71%
Ashtabula			46	29	13		−85%
Butler				15	5		−53%
Licking			23	18	18		−39%
Lorain			40	42	34		−48%
Mahoning			26	10	17		−50%
Medina			12	7	4		−67%
Stark			23	12	13		−30%
Trumbull			11	14	7		−36%
9 TR Expansion county subtotal			198	155	120		−53%
TR counties	989	600	655	490	397	−60%	−40%
All OHIO counties	1579	1037	841	633	552	−67%	−38%
NON TR counties	590	437	186	143	155	−78%	−30%

Source: http://www.dys.ohio.gov/dnn/Community/RECLAIMOhio/tabid/131/Default.aspx, author computed decreases.

Between fiscal year 2011 (January 1, 2010–June 30, 2011) and fiscal year 2013, Targeted RECLAIM counties reduced population by 40% whereas counties not involved in Targeted RECLAIM reduced admissions by only 30%.

Community Correction Facilities

In addition to RECLAIM Ohio, twelve Community Corrections Facilities (CCFs) were opened throughout the state of Ohio in the mid 1990s. As a last alternative, facilities are designed to provide local residential treatment to youth found delinquent of a felony charge prior to being committed to the Ohio Department of Youth Services. Cognitive Behavioral Interventions are used in all twelve facilities. Many facilities also offer substance abuse treatment, family and individual counseling and transitional living services. A map of Ohio illustrating the regions served by each facility is displayed as Figure 9.1. A total of 355 beds are funded.

2008 Federal Lawsuit *S.H. v. Stickrath*

Despite the success of the community reform efforts of ODYS, the department's institutions were still plagued with unsafe conditions. In 2008, a federal lawsuit was filed against the Ohio Department of Youth Services in *S.H. v. Stickrath* (Tom Stickrath was the Director at the time). Under the leadership of Director Stickrath, ODYS agreed to a case management plan created by a joint fact finding team. The team found that facilities operated by ODYS used excessive force, excessive isolation and seclusion; arbitrary and excessive discipline; violated residents' right to privacy; did not provide adequate mental health care, medical care, educational services or programming; failed to protect staff and youth from harm; did not adequately train staff and did not provide equal access to placement and services for females. As part of the settlement agreement ODYS agreed to improve clinical, medical and education services for all youth; modify its disciplinary and behavior management system; reduce the use of seclusion, and improve daily programming for youth. ODYS also agreed to shorten timelines of investigations of major incidents, hire additional Juvenile Correction Officers and upgrade and expand officer training.

2012 Sexual Victimization Study

Even with the many gains made after the 2008 lawsuit, a study released by the U.S. Department of Justice revealed that 30.3% of juveniles in Circleville

Figure 9.1: Ohio Department of Youth Services Subsidized Community Correction Facilities

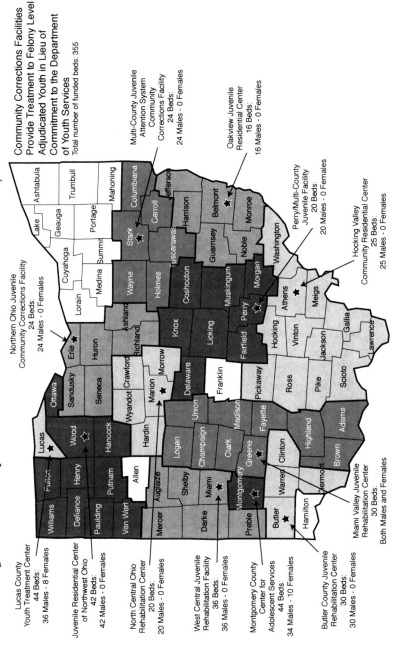

Source: http://www.dys.ohio.gov/DNN/LinkClick.aspx?fileticket=NKQTNku0Gvc=&tabid=130

Juvenile Correctional Facility reported sexual victimization while residing in the facility, likewise Scioto (which is closed today) had 23.2% juveniles report sexual victimization, and in Cuyahoga Hills 19.8% of youth reported sexual victimization (Beck, Cantor, Harge & Smith, 2013). These facilities fell in the top 13 of all facilities in the nation for sexual victimization. The average nationally for sexual victimization in juvenile facilities was 9.5%. Director Harvey Reed took immediate action and an investigatory team quickly learned that among other things many adolescent males were being victimized by female Corrections Officers. Since then, ODYS has become committed to becoming Prison and Rape Elimination Act (PREA) compliant and ensuring that the facilities are safe from sexual abuse. PREA standards are set forth by the federal government and are designed to prevent sexual abuses within facilities.

ODYS Facilities Today

The reform efforts of RECLAIM, Targeted RECLAIM, and caring of children in residential treatment centers such as the Community Correction Facilities identified in Figure 1, has led to a dramatic reduction in the population of the Ohio Department of Youth Services secure facilities. Today, only three facilities remain open: Circleville, Cuyahoga Hills, and Indian River. All three of those facilities only serve boys. Some boys may be placed in an alternative placement at Lighthouse Paint Creek through a contractual agreement with ODYS. All girls committed to ODYS are now placed in alternative placements; none of which are operated by ODYS. Montgomery Center for Adolescent Services screens all females committed to ODYS and serves the general female population through cognitive behavioral interventions. Girls with more significant mental health needs may be placed at Applewood Behavioral Health, Buckeye Ranch for girls or Pomegranate, all located in Ohio.

Table 9.2 above demonstrates the dramatic reduction in commitments over the past two decades. Since 1997 male commitments to ODYS have been reduced by 81% while the female population has been reduced by 91%. Reform efforts in local courts have also resulted in fewer felony adjudications. The rate at which youth adjudicated of felonies have been placed at ODYS has also decreased. In 1997, sixteen percent of all boys and nine percent of all girls adjudicated on felonies were committed to ODYS while in 2013 only nine percent of the boys and three percent of the girls were committed to ODYS. Alternative community options have greatly reduced the burden on the once over-populated system at ODYS institutions while maintaining safety in the community. The reduction in population has also provided a better opportunity to make the facilities safer; by having a lower staff-to-youth ratio better pro-

Table 9.2: State Commitments

1997–2013 Fiscal Year	Male Felony Adjudications	Male Commitments to ODYS	Female Felony Adjudications	Female Commitments to ODYS
2013	4,636	459	578	17
2012	5,074	524	622	39
2011	5,654	687	795	46
2010	6,511	831	880	43
2009	7,103	1,216	901	88
2008	7,999	1,303	1,019	89
2007	8,854	1,518	1,275	104
2006	9,090	1,496	1,255	109
2005	8,752	1,484	1,323	119
2004	9,064	1,703	1,331	162
2003	9,495	1,679	1,361	139
2002	10,069	1,825	1,469	181
2001	9,886	1,927	1,397	190
2000	10,495	2,196	1,495	203
1999	11,656	2,246	1,630	196
1998	13,194	2,328	1,870	195
1997	15,096	2,521	2,026	201

Source: http://www.dys.ohio.gov/DNN/LinkClick.aspx?fileticket=2pDWfSF6CYE%3d&tabid=117&mid=879

gramming and supervision can be provided. In addition, community based options make the community safer. According to recent research conducted by Ryan M. Labrecque and Myrinda Schweitzer youth served through Targeted RECLAIM services were 2.74 times less likely to be incarcerated during a follow up period for a new crime or technical violation than similarly matched youth that were originally sent to ODYS (2014).

Parole

Upon release from a state institution youth are placed on parole with the Ohio Department of Youth Services. There are five regional parole offices located in Akron,

Cleveland, Columbus, Dayton and Toledo. Reentry plans are created by the parole officer with the youth and family that address housing, public assistance, education, treatment, medical, mental health and substance abuse needs. The parole officer works with the local Re-Entry Coalition to help the youth build natural supports in his or her environment so that he or she may be successful.

As mentioned previously, the success of RECLAIM OHIO would not have been possible without partnerships with the local courts. So, let us turn our focus to the practices of the local jurisdictions in the state.

The "Front End of the System": Ohio Multiple Jurisdictions— Basic Case Flow and Court Process

Law Enforcement—Arrests, Diversion

The first point of contact for any juvenile in the juvenile justice system is often the arresting police officer. The functions of the police officer remain largely the same as in the adult system, with the exception of some jurisdictions that have officers that specialize in juvenile issues. Progressive departments have created diversionary programs for low level offenders. Understanding the "first do no harm" principle, many departments understand that once a child is arrested he or she is more likely to recidivate. Recent research from the Annie E. Casey Foundation reports that a youth is 33% more likely to commit a criminal act as an adult if he or she spent even one night in a juvenile detention center (Lubow, 2014). Thus, police have a tough decision to make at a critical moment in a youth's childhood.

Officers must still advise children of their Miranda rights when questioned and arrested. If an officer chooses to take a child into custody, he or she has different choices depending upon their local jurisdiction. Many police departments will allow parents to pick up their child for a low level offense at the police station after holding the child in a non-secure room. Per the Office of Juvenile Justice and Delinquency Prevention most police departments cannot hold a youth beyond six hours. When a child is being held he or she must also be separated by sight and sound from adult criminals.

Despite media portrayals of graphic violence by youth, juvenile arrests have significantly declined since the turn of the century. Tables 9.3, 9.4 and 9.5, below, demonstrate that even with more police agencies reporting data to the UCR, arrests of juveniles in Ohio are trending downwards. UCR Part I Vio-

Table 9.3: Juvenile Arrests in Ohio by Crime Type

Crime Type	Crime against…	2003	2004	2005	2006	2007	2008	2009	2010	2011	2012
Part I Crimes											
Murder/Nonnegligent Manslaughter	Person (Violent)	13	13	17	21	35	21	17	15	20	10
Forcible Rape	Person (Violent)	130	146	154	108	141	104	100	85	70	44
Robbery	Person (Violent)	255	510	583	624	689	804	762	561	553	449
Aggravated Assault	Person (Violent)	652	663	652	657	527	538	409	399	437	411
Burglary-B&E	Property	1,480	2,016	1,776	1,386	1,583	1,811	1,604	1,341	1,196	1,107
Larceny-theft (except MV theft)	Property	5,325	6,692	6,244	5,619	6,396	7,266	6,896	5,799	5,092	4,678
Motor Vehicle Theft	Property	492	870	746	564	502	488	420	274	201	176
Arson	Property	182	205	247	143	158	130	135	93	94	71
Part I Violent Crime		1,050	1,332	1,406	1,410	1,392	1,467	1,288	1,060	1,080	914
Part I Property Crime		7,479	9,783	9,013	7,712	8,639	9,695	9,055	7,507	6,583	6,032
Total Part I Crime		8,520	11,115	10,419	9,122	10,031	11,162	10,343	8,567	7,663	6,946

Data retrieved from Ohio Criminal Justice Services annual reports at http://ocjs.ohio.gov/crime_stats_reports.stm#tog, tables created by author

Table 9.4: Ohio Agency Populations, 2003–2011

	Agencies Reporting	Population
2003	438	8,705,773
2004	366	8,301,623
2005	366	8,301,623
2006	339	7,214,733
2007	590	9,256,969
2008	600	9,660,132
2009	464	9,329,495
2010	639	10,132,806
2011	643	10,142,651

lent juvenile crime decreased by 13% between 2003 and 2012 in the State of Ohio. Likewise, UCR Part I Property juvenile crimes decreased by 18% during the same time period. At the same time, as illustrated in Table 9.4, 205 more agencies were reporting, resulting in a reporting population increase of 16.5%. Thus, while juvenile arrests decreased, the population of and number of reporting jurisdictions increased. Meanwhile, the number of youth incarcerated statewide decreased significantly. Table 9.5 displays even a more dramatic decrease in juvenile arrests for Part II UCR crimes. Part II crimes decreased by 31% from 2003 to 2012. The conclusion from these collective trends is simple, mass incarceration does not improve community safety. As a system, efforts must be continued to rehabilitate offenders in the community.

Court Intake Procedures

Officers do not have to arrest a child to file a charge of delinquency or a status offense with the prosecutor's office. Evidence may be gathered in the field and a report and complaint may be presented to the prosecutor's office for review and filing with the juvenile clerk of court.

Any youth presenting an immediate community safety issue should be arrested by the officer and transported to the local juvenile detention center. Although there are 88 counties in Ohio there are only 38 detention centers, some of which are regional. Each center is either run by an elected judge with administrative duties or a local board. Policy varies among the 38 centers with some guidance being provided by the Ohio Administrative Code in the De-

Table 9.5: Juvenile Arrests by Crime Type, 2003–2012

Crime Type	Crimes against…	2003	2004	2005	2006	2007	2008	2009	2010	2011	2012
Part II Crimes											
Other assaults	Person	4,640	6,627	6,588	6,101	6,996	7,041	6,869	6,543	5,898	5,296
Forgery and counterfeiting	Property	58	82	84	56	53	88	59	33	28	26
Fraud	Property	74	130	103	162	182	210	165	156	119	143
Embezzlement	Property	1	0	4	7	4	4	7	3	0	0
Stolen property (buying, receiving, possessing)	Property	958	1,065	1,136	852	884	755	764	510	533	501
Vandalism	Property	1,777	2,189	2,210	2,164	1,990	1,954	1,931	1,551	1,390	1,258
Weapons (carrying, possessing, etc.)	Society	430	598	656	657	584	731	599	514	447	403
Prostitution and commercialized vice	Society	18	11	11	13	9	5	10	8	11	3
Sex offenses (except forcible rape and prostitution)	Person	253	332	263	236	243	245	252	240	193	206

Table 9.5: Juvenile Arrests by Crime Type, 2003–2012 (cont.)

Crime Type	Crimes against…	2003	2004	2005	2006	2007	2008	2009	2010	2011	2012
Drug abuse violations	Society	2,504	3,477	3,472	3,084	3,394	3,022	2,686	2,642	2,351	2,077
Gambling	Society	4	13	15	22	7	13	12	7	2	3
Offenses against family/children	Person	1,134	1,292	1,055	773	910	730	604	527	452	286
Driving under the influence	Society	248	269	268	238	227	360	197	151	123	71
Liquor laws	Society	2,479	2,764	2,676	2,401	2,839	2,471	2,118	1,950	1,664	1,293
Drunkenness	Society	97	157	103	69	87	72	67	63	24	31
Disorderly conduct	Society	2,653	3,611	3,867	3,712	3,704	3,479	3,272	2,926	2,207	1,920
Vagrancy	Society	2	10	6	19	11	29	23	7	8	3
All other offenses (except traffic)		10,037	11,932	11,386	9,748	10,486	10,248	9,318	7,776	7,482	6,550
Suspicion	Society	26	16	8	2	19	15	8	7	2	2
Curfew/loitering	Society	2,408	2,257	2,455	1,812	1,953	1,597	1,578	1,315	1,005	868
Runaways	Not a crime	1,371	1,506	1,227	884	989	946	678	477	511	621
Total Part II		31,172	38,338	37,593	33,012	35,571	34,015	31,217	27,406	24,450	21,561
Total Part I + Part II		39,692	49,453	48,012	42,134	45,602	45,177	41,560	35,973	32,113	28,507

tention Standards section. That presiding authority, either the judge or the board, ultimately has the decision making power over who will and will not be admitted into the detention center. Requirements such as the minimum age of the offender vary by jurisdiction and local rule. Children may only be placed in detention in Ohio during their "pre-trial" status if the youth is deemed a serious flight risk or the judges determine there are not other less restrictive alternatives to detention that can assure public safety (Children's Defense Fund).

The Ohio Department of Youth Services collects minimal amount of data on detention centers in Ohio since the centers are locally operated. Table 9.6, below, indicates Ohio has a total of 1,941 detention beds in the 38 centers throughout the state. The total average population for 2012 was 1,204 while the average daily population in the centers was 1,194. This is a dramatic decrease from years past when centers were often overcrowded. These overcrowded facilities lead to numerous safety and security risks within the facilities, as discussed above.

The legislative branch of the government influenced juvenile justice in 1974 with the passage of the Juvenile Justice Delinquency Prevention Act that created a federal and state partnership in many juvenile justice matters. These partnerships have had a direct impact on local juvenile detention practices (Hutchinson, 2013). States are mandated to adhere to the core protections of the Act or face financial penalties and lose eligibility for federal funds. There are four core requirements of the Act that have shaped state and local policy. First is the Deinstitutionalization of Status Offenders (DSO). It states, "Juveniles who are charged with or who have committed an offense that would not be criminal if committed by an adult shall not be placed in secure detention or correctional facilities" (Hutchinson, 2013, p. 10).

Despite the direct language of the Act, there exceptions to this requirement. Local jurisdictions may hold an alleged status offender for up to twenty-four hours before and after the initial court appearance. Out-of-state runaways may also be held provided the jurisdiction follows all Interstate Compact Law procedures to return the youth to his or her home state. Also, if a child has violated a valid court order (VCO) a judge may hold him or her (Hutchinson, 2013). This last exception has been met with great controversy and is expected to be eliminated when the law is reauthorized. Critics contend that the rule gives judicial officials a loophole to hold children for excessive lengths of time for non-criminal acts. It is currently before Congress.

The second core protection is "Sight and Sound Separation," a rule that stipulates that juveniles may not be held in *any* institution or holding cell in which he or she may have contact with adult inmates (Hutchinson, 2013). The third core protection was added in 1980 and it prevents juveniles from being detained

Table 9.6: Ohio Juvenile Detention Population Daily Census Snapshot
November 15, 2012 and FY12 Average Daily Population

Facility by County	Total Beds Capacity	Total Population	Number of Females	Number of Males	FY 12 Avg. Daily Pop
Allen	30	29	0	29	26
Ashland	10	9	1	8	8
Ashtabula	20	17	4	13	16
Belmont	19	14	4	10	16
Butler	66	40	10	30	43
Clark	48	32	5	27	31.53
Clermont	36	19	7	12	18
Columbiana	20	18	3	15	18.48
Cuyahoga	180	117	12	105	115
Erie	36	24	5	19	29
Fairfield	48	39	3	36	39
Franklin	132	24	5	19	29
Greene	32	24	3	21	15.48
Hamilton	160	64	6	58	74
Jefferson	22	20	6	14	28
Lake	40	31	3	28	28
Logan	36	11	0	11	12
Lorain	44	37	7	30	49.78
Lucas	125	32	4	28	38.12
Mahoning	40	39	6	33	40
Marion	36	26	8	18	25
Medina	30	23	3	20	18.21
Miami	44	44	11	33	34
Montgomery	144	61	8	53	59.21
Muskingum	48	34	5	29	25
Portage/ Geauga	25	28	6	22	26

Table 9.6: Ohio Juvenile Detention Population Daily Census Snapshot
November 15, 2012 and FY12 Average Daily Population (cont.)

Facility by County	Total Beds Capacity	Total Population	Number of Females	Number of Males	FY 12 Avg. Daily Pop
Richland	25	25	6	19	19
Ross	36	29	3	26	30
Sandusky	36	24	2	22	21.6
Seneca	24	24	7	17	19
Stark	31	13	2	11	10
Summit	100	50	5	45	56.76
Trumbull	36	50	9	41	48
Tuscarawas	20	20	10	10	21
Union	38	31	5	26	24
Warren	24	16	4	12	15.66
Wayne	20	18	1	17	19
Williams	32	33	8	25	29.6
Wood	48	15	4	11	19
OHIO Total	1941	1204	201	1003	1194.43

or confined in any jail or lockup facility for adults. It does not apply to youth transferred or bound over and sentenced to adult prison. It does allow for a youth to be held up to six hours in an adult facility if the youth is separated by sight and sound from adults (this applies to many local police department holding cells and rooms especially when there is a long transport to the nearest juvenile facility).

Lastly, core requirement number four requires states to "address juvenile delinquency prevention efforts and system improvement efforts designed to reduce … the disproportionate number of juvenile members of minority groups who come into contact with the juvenile justice system" (Hutchinson, 2013, p. 17). The Ohio Department of Youth Services uses a Disproportionate Minority Contact (DMC) Reduction Model that includes the following steps: (1) collect data to identify DMC issues, (2) conduct local assessments to determine local issues influencing DMC, (3) identify causes, (4) use evidence informed interventions and (5) evaluate, reassess and improve efforts. Although there are no simple solutions to DMC issues, there is a wealth of research in this area.

Through reform efforts, such as the Juvenile Detention Alternatives Initiative, some counties in Ohio (Lucas, Summit, Montgomery and Franklin) are leading the way nationally in the area of DMC reduction (Lubow, 2014). Thus, one can see the OJJDP Act influences state and local policy, and compliance is monitored by both the federal and state government. Ultimately, the act is intended to protect youth from excessive and/or harmful confinement, especially if the adolescent committed an act that would not be considered criminal if committed by an adult.

Progressive jurisdictions in Ohio have created collaborations between the local law enforcement agencies, court and social service agencies to create alternative non secure drop off locations for youth who are unruly or have committed other low-risk offenses. Some of these centers may focus on a particular issue such as truancy, runaway or sex trafficking. Others are more general and may focus on serving youth delinquent of non-violent Part II UCR charges. Local collaborative groups are instrumental in helping develop effective alternatives to detention. The shift from detention centers and reform schools to community based programming is actually still founded in the *parens patriae* philosophy of making decisions that are in the best interest of the child. Today, we know more from research, which clearly demonstrates confinement is not always in the best interest of the child; in fact it can be detrimental and increase a child's risk to recidivate (Latessa, 2014). Research also indicates that many detention centers had been failing in their efforts during the 20th century. Youth are best served in the least restrictive alternative community based option. Detained youth are 29% more likely to drop out of school, 21% more likely to use illicit drugs and 15% more likely to use alcohol upon release than their peers with similar histories who were not detained (Lubow, 2014). Furthermore, from a cost effectiveness standpoint it is better to use community based options when appropriate. The average cost in five of the most populous counties in Ohio (Franklin, Cuyhahoga, Summit, Montgomery and Lucas) was $86,876 to operate one detention bed annually. Meanwhile, the average annual cost for tuition, room board and books at The Ohio State University for one year was $22,467 and at the state's most expensive private school, Oberlin College was $58,983 (Oprisch, 2013).

Many centers have worked with their local collaborative to develop a Risk Assessment Instrument that is designed to objectively measure immediate risk of safety to the community. This instrument is not designed to measure the likelihood of recidivism. It looks at the immediate offense and determines whether a youth must be confined prior to his or her court hearing. Does the youth pose an imminent risk to the community? If safety of the community is a concern, then the youth must be held. However, alternatives other than detention may be considered for low- to moderate-risk youth. A sample Risk Assessment Instrument is displayed in Figure 9.2, below. The Continuum of Detention Services that is used to determine where a youth should go is shown in Figure 9.3.

Figure 9.2: Sample Risk Assessment

Juvenile's Name:_____ DOB:

Date:_____

Offenses:_____ Gender___ Race_____Age_____

SAMPLE JUVENILE DETENTION INTAKE ASSESSMENT	POINTS	SCORE
A. MANDATORY HOLDS		
Homicide OR Escape from secure custody	11	
OR Felony 1 & 2,new charge or original warrant	11	
OR Violation of CPO / Warrant issued / with harm or threat of harm	11	
OR Violation of CPO with no harm or threat of harm	11	
OR Interstate Cases	11	
OR Illegal Aliens	11	
OR Material Witnesses	11	
OR Firearm - carried OR used during offense or in current possession	11	
OR BB Gun or other "toy" gun USED during the offense and presented to the victim as a real gun / threat	11	
OR Intimate Partner Violence	11	____
B. CURRENT OFFENSE		
Felony 3 & 4, new charge or original warrant	6	
OR Felony 5, new charge or original warrant	4	
OR active warrant, failure to appear on felony 3, 4, 5 offense	6	
OR active warrant, failure to appear on misdemeanor offense (provide notice to appear prior to release)	1	
OR active warrant, failure to appear on same misdemeanor offense for the second or more time	6	
OR active warrant for technical violations (Violation of Probation, MSC, VCO, FTA for a VOP/VCO)	4	____
C. AGGRAVATING FACTORS		
Juvenile resides with victim	3	____
An act of violence (assault, DV, Aggravated Menacing) or sexual offense was present in current offense OR victim sustained an injury and required medical care	3	____
Other weapon besides a firearm (i.e. knife, boxcutter, brass knuckles) used during offense **with an attempt to cause or actually cause serious physical harm** List type:_____	6	____
AND/OR Victim(s) 65 years of age OR older or victim 6 years of age or younger	2	____
D. CURRENT STATUS		
Administrative hold authorized by Detention Administrator or his/her designee, safekeeping	8	____

SERVICES *(circle the all programs the youth is currently*
     Involved in but only score assigned points for the most restrictive program)
     Standard Probation OR Parole (least restrictive)
     Active in YTC or YTC Aftercare/Reentry (RTC), JSOT, Out of Home Placement Disruption
	2
	6	

DETENTION STATUS
     Number of prior admissions into secure detention *w/in 24 mos.*
     1 point for one admission, 2 points for 2 or more admissions, maximum score 2 points.
     Detention Reporting Center OR Home Detention OR Electronic Monitoring
	1 or 2
	
	6
		____
		
		____

E. MITIGATING FACTORS (FACTORS OTHER THAN THOSE LISTED ABOVE)		
Safe Place to release youth and AND offense was not a mandatory hold	-2	____
SCORE GUIDELINES: 0-5 RELEASE, 6-10 COMMUNITY DETN REFERRAL, 11+ SECURE DETENTION. **Automatic Score for Administrative Release (AR)** if youth is charged with Unruly or Status Offense, or Underage Consumption OR if youth is under the age of 12. OTHER OVERRIDE <u>REASON</u> LIST BELOW		TOTAL AR Yes or No? ____ Override Yes or No
Override approved by:_____RAI Completed by:_____		

Source: Kec, 2012

Figure 9.3: Case Flow in Lucas County Juvenile Court

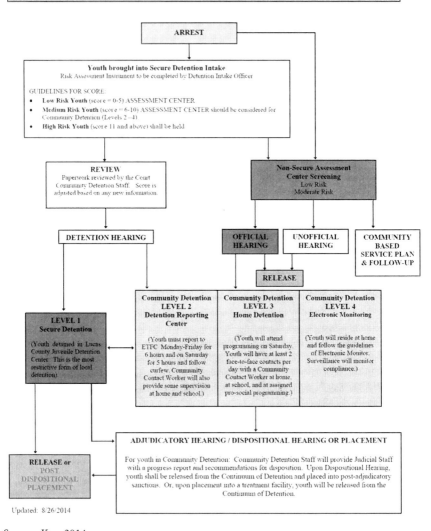

Source: Kec, 2014

Court Process

In 1967, the United States Supreme Court ruled *In Re Gault* that if a juvenile may possibly be confined in a facility that due process rights must be afforded in delinquency proceedings. In addition, juveniles were afforded the right against self-incrimination (right to remain silent—5th Amendment), and 6th Amendment protections, including notice of the charges against them, and the right to counsel. The Supreme Court did not completely nullify the *parens patriae* doctrine, but ruled that juvenile court judges could still seek what is in the best interest of the child while insuring that due process rights were granted (Ventrell, 1998). These increased rights have helped shape Ohio law and local rules in the modern era.

There are eighty-eight counties in the State of Ohio. Some counties have more than one judge handling juvenile matters. Case processing of juvenile matters can vary among communities and sometimes even within the same community among judges. Thus, the description of case processing below will be general. According to the State of Ohio's Supreme Court Annual Report, 92,871 delinquency matters were processed in courts throughout the state in 2012. There were also 16,104 unruly matters and 51,720 traffic offenses processed.

As described earlier in this chapter, cases may come to the court's attention via an arrest by a law enforcement officer. However, an arrest does not have to occur. Complaints may be filed by law enforcement, schools, parents, concerned citizens and the prosecutor's office. Filing procedures vary throughout the state. Some cases may also be diverted at any juncture in the court system. Many cases in the court are handled informally and eventually dismissed. Sometimes during this process a youth voluntarily signs a written agreement which may stipulate that he or she will do things such as pay victim restitution, attend school regularly, seek drug and/or alcohol treatment or mental health counseling. Research demonstrates that for low risk offenders this type of diversion reduces their risk of reoffending; it is in the best interest of the child and community safety (Latessa, 2014). Dismissal may occur only after a youth has completed the items to which he or she agreed. If the youth fails to meet the conditions then the case may still be handled formally.

If the child is arrested and held within a secure detention facility he or she must have a "detention hearing" within twenty-four working hours (48 hours on weekends or 72 hours on 3-day weekends) per the OJJDP Act. The judge or magistrate will review the case to determine if the youth needs to be in a secure facility. In many jurisdictions the youth is also arraigned on his or her charges at this time. Defense representation is not required by Ohio Law at detention hearings. However, critics contend that if a youth's freedom is being restricted he or she should have an attorney at a detention hearing. This issue is still being debated state wide.

Prosecutors often file delinquency complaints on the most serious charges that are considered serious misdemeanors or felonies if committed by an adult.

Different terms are used in the juvenile court setting compared to the adult court, but procedurally the systems are generally similar. An adjudication hearing is set after a complaint is filed. Adjudication hearings are similar to pre-trials and trials within the adult system. If the youth is being held in secure detention, Ohio Law requires that the adjudicatory hearing be set within 15 days. In order to reduce lengths of stay in detention, some jurisdictions hold adjudicatory hearings in even less time. In nearly all cases the judge or magistrate determines, based upon the evidence presented, if the youth is delinquent. Ohio law does allow for some jury trials in serious cases, although they are rare. The standard of evidence that a judicial official must use when considering if the youth committed the alleged act is "beyond a reasonable doubt." The "reasonable doubt standard" was ruled applicable in juvenile court delinquency findings by the U.S. Supreme court in the 1970 case *In Re Winship.* If a youth may possibly be committed to a locked facility as a result of his or her disposition the court must find him delinquent "beyond a reasonable doubt" (Whitehead & Lab, 2009).

The prosecutor may, in the most serious cases, file a motion to transfer jurisdiction to the adult court. Some of the most egregious crimes are "mandatory transfers." The prosecutor has no discretion and the case must be sent to adult court. In other cases, the prosecutor must demonstrate that the youth is no longer amenable to treatment and rehabilitation in the juvenile system. Should the judge find that the youth is not amenable to treatment than he or she will be certified and jurisdiction of the case will be transferred to the adult court.

Should the youth be "found delinquent" of a felony or misdemeanor in the juvenile court (the term "guilty" is not used in juvenile court), a dispositional report is often completed by probation staff prior to disposition (sentencing). Probation staff will recommend a rehabilitative plan that addresses the risks and needs of the child and his or her family. The basic flow of a case through juvenile court is found in Figure 4, but remember this flow may vary from jurisdiction to jurisdiction and even among jurists within the jurisdiction.

Probation

Just as every court jurisdiction may handle juvenile cases differently, there are no two juvenile probation departments in the State of Ohio that are managed the same way. The Administrative Juvenile Judge in the jurisdiction is responsible for the oversight of Probation Services. It is recommended, but not required, by the Ohio Department of Youth Services that an objective risk, needs,

and responsivity assessment be conducted on every youth to determine probation case planning. The University of Cincinnati has developed, normed, and
validated a tool known as the Ohio Youth Assessment System (OYAS), which is
used by many jurisdictions to drive probation case planning, management, and
services (Latessa, Lovins & Lux, 2014b). The assessment measures the risk that
the youth will reoffend, the youth's need for services and how responsive (responsivity) the youth will be to the services. Seven criminogenic domain areas
are evaluated through a series of questions to determine a risk score. The risk
score helps the probation officer to determine what level of programming is
most appropriate for the youth. The domain areas considered are: (1) Juvenile
Justice History, (2) Family and Living Arrangements, (3) Peers and Social Support Network, (4) Education and Employment, (5) Prosocial Skills, (6) Substance
Use, Mental Health and Personality and (7) Attitudes, Values and Beliefs.

Research demonstrates that low risk youth should receive minimal intervention (Latessa et al., 2014b). Over programming a low-risk child can actually increase recidivism (Latessa et al., 2014b). Likewise moderate-risk
youth are best served via community based programming and reoffended
less than their counterparts who were institutionalized. In many cases, even
high risk youth could adequately be served in the community without jeop-
ardizing community safety. However, placement in an ODYS facility or residential treatment option is appropriate for high-risk youth (Latessa et al.,
2014b).

Probation departments have a myriad of programming to address the developmental needs of adolescents, some of which are paid for with RECLAIM
and Targeted RECLAIM funds. Below is a very basic description of the types
of services probation staff use.

> **Community Service:** Youth are typically required to volunteer hours at a
> non-profit agency. Some courts have formal programs in which court staff
> supervise volunteer hours.
>
> **Restitution:** After an assessment of loss to the victim is conducted, the
> court orders a youth to either pay restitution to the victim via the Clerk
> of Courts office. Some courts offer work crews in which a youth can "earn"
> restitution money to be paid to the victim.
>
> **Mediation Services:** Mediators trained by the Supreme Court of Ohio fa-
> cilitate an unbiased mediation in which the victim and youthful offender
> reach an agreement to restore harm done to the victim.
>
> **Case Facilitation:** Facilitated meeting may be held between the youth and
> parent and sometimes school to reach an agreement on the youth's be-
> havioral issues and what the youth will do to correct behaviors at home or
> at school.

Restorative Circles: Community members hold a session with community members, extended family, agency workers, the youth and the victim in a neutral setting to determine how the offender can be held accountable and restore harm to the victim while maintaining community safety.

Mentoring Programs: Youth are matched one on one with a mentor who will provide guidance and teach the youth pro-social skills. There are many variations of mentoring models, some paid and some are unpaid. It is important that the model be evidence informed.

Mental Health and Substance Abuse Services: Community Mental Health and Substance Abuse providers provide assessments, individual and family counseling, outpatient group therapy, residential treatment. Public agencies are overseen by local Mental Health and Recovery Services Boards.

Multi-Systemic Therapy (MST): MST is strives to change how youth with a mental health diagnosis function in their natural settings including home school and the neighborhood. Caseworkers work with the family in the home to and teach ways that promote positive social behavior while decreasing anti-social behavior.

Functional Family Therapy (FFT): FFT engages youth and their families to decrease negativity such as hopelessness and blaming through individualized behavior change interventions. FFT uses cognitive methods and provides systematic skill training in family communication, parenting, conflict management and problem-solving skills.

Wraparound Services: Wraparound is not treatment but a process in which the family, including the youth, are given primary importance in developing services and supports that will be used to support pro-social behavior. Extended family, caring providers, faith-based services, teachers and anyone else who may be a natural support to the youth are included in the process.

Domestic Violence Programming: Most domestic violence (DV) cases filed in the juvenile court are NOT intimate partner violence but are youth perpetrated incidents against a parental figure or sometimes a sibling. There is a wide range of behaviors that are filed as DV. Programming has been developed to address the varying levels of severity in DV cases, some of which are simple situations of family dysfunction, verbal arguments and chaos whereas others involve chronic violent DV offenders. DV groups teach youth and parents skills to manage behavioral issues in the home.

Sex Offender Treatment: Many adolescent sex offenders have often been victims of sex abuse and can be treated best for their reactive offending in community-based settings. Intensive treatment options include cognitive behavioral treatment, wrap-around services, specialty court involvement and have demonstrated that 94% of youth in a sample size can be safely maintained in the community (Lovins, 2014).

Electronic Monitoring/GPS Systems: Typically used as an alternative to secure detention, youths whereabouts are monitored via an electronic monitor tethered to his/her ankle or a global positioning unit.

Cognitive Behavior Services: Cognitive Behavioral Programming is considered one of the most effective interventions available. Many evidenced based models teach youth how to identify negative thoughts and feelings and deal with those feelings in a pro-social way rather than in a harmful, destructive way, thereby reducing delinquent behaviors.

Social and Life Skills: Pro-social life skills that will help youth be successful are modeled and practiced with youth by an adult, mentor, probation officer or group leader.

Educational Support: Educational specialists or case managers assist a youth in his or her transition back into the classroom and assist school staff with effective behavioral interventions for the adolescent.

Specialty Dockets: There are many types of specialty dockets and specialty courts throughout Ohio that require a high level of accountability on the youth's part. Youth and their parents must appear before the Judge either weekly or bi-weekly to report on progress made on their treatment plans. Drug Courts, Treatment Courts, Domestic Violence Courts and Mental Health Courts are some of the types of specialized dockets in Ohio.

Requirements for termination from probation can also vary among jurisdictions, but typically youth must cooperate with the probation case plan and demonstrate progress toward his or her goals. The partnership between the state and local authorities is key in providing meaningful interventions for each child that will prevent further penetration into the system.

Conclusion

The juvenile justice system in Ohio is complex. However, the counties and state have learned that by forming partnerships and working together collaboratively the best interest of the child, family, and community can be protected. It is important to use evidence informed models and develop case plans that meet each youth's needs while maintaining community safety. Trends toward de-incarceration have reduced recidivism while increased public safety. Ongoing research of what works, and what does not, will lead the next decade of reform efforts as the juvenile justice community becomes more adept at habilitating adolescents.

Key Terms

Adjudication

Community Corrections Facilities

Cope v. Campbell

Deinstitutionalization

Delinquent

Detention

Disproportionate Minority Contact

Diversion

In re Galt

Juvenile Justice Delinquency Prevention Act

Ohio Department of Youth Services

Parens Patriae

Parole

RECLAIM Ohio

S.H. v. Stickrath

Status Offense

Targeted RECLAIM

Youth Camps

Resources

Annie E. Casey Foundation
   http://aecf.org

Burns Institute for Juvenile Justice Fairness and Racial Equity
   http://www.burnsinstitute.org/

Center for Juvenile Justice Reform
   http://cjjr.georgetown.edu/index.html

Coalition for Juvenile Justice
   http://www.juvjustice.org/

MacArthur Foundation
   http://www.macfound.org/tags/justice/

Models for Change
   http://www.modelsforchange.net/index.html

National Council of Juvenile and Family Court Judges
   http://www.ncjfcj.org/

Ohio Department of Youth Services
   http://www.dys.ohio.gov

Ohio School Resource Officers Association
   http://www.osroa.org/links/general.html

Office of Criminal Justice Services
   http://www.ocjs.ohio.gov/

Office of Juvenile Justice and Delinquency Prevention
   http://www.ojjdp.gov/

Robert Wood Johnson Foundation, RECLAIMING FUTURES
    http://reclaimingfutures.org/
The Supreme Court of Ohio
    http://www.supremecourt.ohio.gov/

Review Questions

1. Discuss how Supreme Court Rulings have influenced Ohio Juvenile Law.
2. Examine the data tables in this chapter. What can you conclude from analyzing the data?
3. How have RECLAIM and Targeted RECLAIM changed juvenile justice in Ohio?
4. Describe how the juvenile justice system is different from the adult system. What elements are similar?

References

Ames, M. (2012). *Ohio Juvenile Detention Population — Daily Census Snapshot — November 15, 2012 and FY12 Average Daily Population.* Columbus, OH: Ohio Department of Youth Services.

Baker, Chris (2014). *Ohio Department of Youth Services, Subsidized Community Correction Facilities Map.* Columbus, OH: Ohio Department of Youth Services.

Beck, A., Cantor, D., Harge, J. & Smith, T. (2013). *Sexual Victimization in Juvenile Facilities Reported by Youth, 2012, National Survey of Youth in Custody.* Washington D.C.: Bureau of Justice Statistics, U.S. Department of Justice.

Case Flow Diagram. (n.d.). Retrieved August 17, 2014, from http://www.ojjdp.gov/ojstatbb/structure_process/case.html.

Ellis, M. (2014). *Juvenile Arrest Data — 2012.* Columbus, OH: Office of Criminal Justice Services.

Evaluating Juvenile Justice in Ohio. (2011). In (Second ed.). Cleveland, OH: American Civil Liberties Union.

Functional Family Therapy: Clinical Model. (n.d.). Retrieved July 10, 2014, from http://www.functionalfamilytherapy.com/about-fft/clinical-model/.

Giannelli, P. C. & Salvador, P. Y. (2012). *Ohio Juvenile Law.* Eagan, MN: Thomson Reuters.

Hutchinson, L. (2013). *Ohio Governor's Council on Juvenile Justice State Advisory Group Strategic Planning Training.* Columbus, OH: U.S. Department of Justice, Office of Juvenile Justice and Delinquency Prevention.

Juvenile Detention Reform in Ohio: Fact Sheet, (2010). Columbus, Ohio, Children's Defense Fund.

Kec, K. (2012). Juvenile Detention Intake Assessment. Toledo, Ohio.

Kec, K. (2014). Case Flow Through Levels of Detention Diagram. Toledo, Ohio.

Labrecque, R. & Schweitzer, M. (2014). Outcome Study of Ohio's Targeted RECLAIM Programs.

Latessa, E., Lovins, B., & Lux, J. (2014a). Evaluation of Ohio's RECLAIM Programs.

Latessa, E., Lovins, B., & Lux, J. (2014b). The Validity and Reliability of the Ohio Youth Assessment System (OYAS): A Summary of Four Studies.

Lovins, L. (2014). An Outcome Evaluation of the Management of Juvenile Sex Offenders in Lucas County, Ohio: Brief Summary.

Lubow, B. (2014). *Ohio Communities for Kids Summit: Detention Alternatives.* Columbus, OH: Ohio Department of Youth Services.

MST: An Overview. (n.d.) Retrieved July 10, 2014, from http://www.mst services.com/overview_a.pdf.

National Wraparound Initiative: Wraparound Basics. (n.d.) Retrieved July 10, 2014 from http://www.nwi.pdx.edu/wraparoundbasics.shtml.

Office of Criminal Justice Services Juvenile Arrest Data (2003–2011). Retrieved March 4, 2014, from http://www.ocjs.ohio.gov/.

Ohio Department of Youth Services 25th Anniversary Video. (n.d.). Retrieved January 27, 2014, from http://www.dys.ohio.gov/dnn/AgencyInformation/GeneralInformation/ODYSHistoryVideo/tabid/141/Default.aspx

Oprisch, B. (2013). Ohio Juvenile Detention Alternatives Initiative: Progress 2009–2013. Columbus, OH: Ohio Department of Youth Services.

Panzino, T. (2014). *RECLAIM Ohio and TARGETED RECLAIM.* Columbus, OH: Ohio Department of Youth Services.

Panzino, T. (2014). *Targeted Reclaim Data, FY 2009–2013.* Columbus, OH: Ohio Department of Youth Services.

Pompa, D. (2000). Lucas County Juvenile Court Annual Report, 1999. Toledo, OH.

S.H. v. Stickrath. United States District Court, Southern District of Ohio, Eastern Division, (2008). Retrieved August 14, 2014, from http://www.dys.ohio.gov/dnn/AgencyInformation/SettlementAgreement/tabid/81/Default.aspx.

Statewide Felony Adjudications and Commitments. (1997–2013). Retrieved July 30, 2014 from http://www.dys.ohio.gov/DNN/LinkClick.aspx?file ticket=2pDWfSF6CYE%3d&tabid=117&mid=879.

Ventrell, M. (1998). Evolution of the Dependency Component of the Juvenile Court. *National Council of Juvenile and Family Court Judges Juvenile and Family Court Journal*, *49*(4), 17–38.

Whitehead, J. & Lab, S. (2009) *Juvenile justice: An Introduction* (6th ed.). LexisNexis Group.

Chapter 10

Victims of Crime

Learning Objectives

After reading this chapter, student will be able to:

- Describe the rights that victims of crime have in the state of Ohio.
- Explain the different agencies and programs designed to aid victims of crime in Ohio.
- Give examples of how victims are part of the legal process, and at what stages they can engage.
- Describe the purpose of a victim's statement.
- Explain how victims can receive restitution and in what cases victims are ineligible
- Explain the role of the Victims' Rights Amendment in Ohio.

Introduction

Victims of crime often feel helpless and disoriented after they experience an act of violence. They have not only suffered from physical harm or lost property, but have also suffered from traumatic emotional distress that can last for years. These emotions can be intensified by the frustration of the sometimes slow adjudicatory process. Most victims do not comprehend the seemingly endless legal motions and hearings that seem only to delay the trial process and punishment of the offender. Officials in Ohio have developed many programs to aid those people who become the innocent victim of a crime. From the time that a crime is reported to law enforcement until an offender is released from an institution, there are multiple programs available to assist victims coping with the after-effects of criminal behavior perpetrated against them. This chapter describes the programs that are currently available to provide services to victims of crime in Ohio and help them recover from the after-effects of their victimization.

188   10 · VICTIMS OF CRIME

Constitutional Amendment

Victims of crime in Ohio are afforded certain rights by virtue of their victimization. Some of their rights are outlined in a Constitutional Amendment that was passed by both houses of the Ohio General Assembly in the summer of 1994, known as the Crime Victims' Amendment. Once passed in the General Assembly, the proposed amendment was ratified by the voters in the state. This happened in November, 1994, when 77% of the voters showed their approval of the change to the state Constitution. This made Ohio one of thirty-two states that have added an amendment to their state's legal structure that specifically outline the rights provided to crime victims.

The Crime Victims' Amendment is found in Article I, Section 10a of the Ohio Constitution. It reads as follows:

> Victims of criminal offenses shall be accorded fairness, dignity, and respect in the criminal justice process, and, as the General Assembly shall define and provide by law, shall be accorded rights to reasonable and appropriate notice, information, access, and protection and to a meaningful role in the criminal justice process. This section does not confer upon any person a right to appeal or modify any decision in a criminal proceeding, does not abridge any other right guaranteed by the Constitution of the United States or this Constitution, and does not create any cause of action for compensation or damages against the State, any political subdivision of the State, any officer, employee, or agent of the State or of any political subdivision, or any officer of the court (National Center for Victims of Crime, 2012).

Victims' Rights in the Ohio Revised Code

Crime victims are also afforded additional rights through the Ohio Revised Code (ORC). The specific privileges that are guaranteed to victims are described in ORC 2930 (see Table 10.1). These rights are provided to those who are the victim of any felony (both property and violent crimes) or are the victim of a violent misdemeanor. These rights also apply to victims of a juvenile offender.

According to the ORC, crime victims should be given reasonable notice, information, access, and protection in the criminal justice process, along with a meaningful role in it. This statement has several significant implications, beginning with the right of victims to be informed about the status of their case.

Table 10.1: Victims' Rights in Ohio Revised Code

2930.01: Definitions
2930.02: Victim's Representative
2930.03: Methods of Giving Notice
2930.04: Information Provided to Victim by Law Enforcement Agency
2930.05: Notice of Arrest or Detention of Offender
2930.06: Prosecutor to Confer with Victim—Court to Give Notice of Proceedings to Victim
2930.061: Notice of Charges to Department of Developmental Disabilities
2930.062: Notification of Victim's Injuries
2930.07: Protection of Victim's Identification Information
2930.08: Notification of Substantial Delay in Prosecution
2930.09: Victim's Presence at Trial
2930.10: Minimizing Contact Between Victim and Defendant—Separate Waiting Areas
2930.11: Returning or Retaining Victim's Property
2930.12: Notice of the Defendant's Acquittal or Conviction
2930.13: Victim Impact Statement
2930.14: Victim's Statement
2930.15: Notice of Appeal
2930.16: Notice of Incarceration and Release Date
2930.17: Statement of Victim Prior to Judicial Release or Early Release
2930.18: No Employee Discipline for Court Attendance Necessary to Protect Rights of Victim
2930.19: Prosecutor to Protect Rights of Victims

Source: ORC

As described in the ORC (2930.04), the law enforcement agency investigating the crime is required to give the victim an explanation of their rights. They also need to inform the victim of any assistance that may be available such as medical, counseling, or other emergency services. Information about compensation and possible protection orders is also imperative. Finally, the victim must be provided with the name and telephone number of the law enforcement officer investigating the case and the prosecutor assigned to oversee the case.

According to ORC 2930.05, the law enforcement agency with jurisdiction over the case must give the victim notice of the offender's arrest or detention of the defendant, and details as to whether the offender is eligible for pretrial release. If an offender who has been released on bail either attempts to commit, or actually commits, additional acts of violence against the victim, the victim can ask for a reconsideration of the bail.

The prosecutor, under ORC 2930.06, must meet with the victim to discuss the possibility of pretrial diversion for the offender. Additionally, the prosecutor must confer with the victim before amending or dismissing an indictment, information or complaint against the defendant. After the trial has started, a prosecutor must give the victim the name of the specific crime charged, the file number of the case, a statement outlining the procedural steps in a criminal prosecution, a summary of the victim's rights, procedures if the victim is threatened. The victim should also be given the name and number of a contact person in the prosecutor's office if that victim should need any additional information or has any questions. According to ORC 2930.08, if there is a substantial delay in the prosecution of the case caused by a motion or request, the victim should be notified. If the victim objects to the delay, the court will be notified and the victim's objections will be taken into consideration.

According to the ORC, crime victims in Ohio have the right to provide the prosecutor with written notification of their injuries, and if those change throughout the duration of the case. Moreover, a victim may be present during any stage of the proceedings. The court must make reasonable efforts to minimize the contact between the victim and members of the victim's family. However, the prosecutor may file a motion with the court asking the court specify that the victim or any witnesses not be forced to give testimony that may disclose the victims address, place of employment or other identifying information. To the extent possible, all property taken from the victim to be used as evidence must be returned promptly to the victim.

Upon completion of the trial, the prosecutor shall give the victim notice of the defendant's acquittal or conviction. If the offender appeals his or her conviction, the prosecutors shall notify the victim of the basis for the appeal, and the time and place of any proceedings. Moreover, if a defendant is released from a facility or moved to another facility, the victim must be made aware of that as well. If the offender is scheduled to be released early, the victim has the right to make a statement about the effects of the crime in front of the parole board.

Under section 2930.13 of the ORC, every victim has the right to deliver a Victim Impact Statement to the court. This is a victim's account of the impact that the crime has had on them and their families. Given at the sentencing phase of the trial, this is a way to inform the sentencing judge or jury of the effects of the crime. Beyond that, these statements serve other purposes as well. They serve to promote justice and create a perception of fairness. The statements also have a therapeutic effect on the victims, helping them to recover from the crimes. The statement may also help to educate the defendant about the consequences of his or her crime (Cassell, 2009).

If the offender has already been convicted and is participating in a parole hearing in front of the Ohio Parole Board, the victim has the option of giving a written or oral statement regarding the impact of the crime on themselves or their families. In this statement, the offender can detail the physical, psychological or emotional harm caused by the case, the extent to which restitution may be needed to pay for the harm caused by the crime, and/or a recommendation for an appropriate sanction.

Throughout this process, those victims who are minors or who are otherwise incapacitated, incompetent, or deceased, can choose another person to act as their representative in hearings and proceedings. This can also occur if the victim simply chooses to designate another person to represent them. The representative can be a member of a victim's family but does not need to be. The victim's representative will then exercise the rights of the victim.

Ohio Attorney General: Crime Victim Services Section

The rights assigned to victims are outlined in the Ohio Constitution and Ohio Revised Code, but are fulfilled or carried out by the Ohio Attorney General's Office, specifically the Crime Victim Services Section. This office provides funding and services to aid crime victims, training for professionals who assist them, grants for victim service providers, and crime prevention programs for communities. Many of the services available to victims by this office are included in a publication called *Ohio Crime Victims Rights*, formerly called *Picking up the Pieces* (Ohio's Crime Victims' Rights).

Outreach Initiative

Through their Outreach Initiative, the Attorney General has attempted to increase the number of Ohioans who receive information about the crime victim's services they provide. This includes critical material such as instructions on how to apply to the Crime Victims Compensation Program. In addition, the Initiative provides training and resources to every county in the State to ensure that victims receive the services as outlined in the Constitution and ORC. The Initiative also works to strengthen the existing partnerships with they have with law enforcement personnel, prosecutors, and grant award recipients, as well as to create new relationships with other groups that may have contact with crime victims or provide a service to them (Ohio Attorney General's Office, 2014).

Victim Compensation Programs

The Ohio Attorney General's office, through the Crime Victims Services Section, has established a Crime Victims' fund that provides monetary compensation to victims for any economic losses that resulted because of the offense. Through the program, victims of violent crimes and their families may receive payments to help pay for certain out-of-pocket expenses related to the physical or emotional damages from the incident. If the crime resulted in the death of the victim, the dependents of that victim may receive money.

A victim or their families can receive compensation for many expenses related to the crime. The money can help a victim pay for medical services or the costs associated with the care or recovery of the victim. It can also help pay for counseling services (up to $2,500 a person), or for transportation fees or mileage costs for medical appointments or to attend court hearings. In some cases, the loss of wages due to missing work, or the costs related to protection orders that separate the victim from the offender will be covered. The fund may also cover a person's wages lost as a result of attending funeral or court proceedings. Sometime, the crime scene cleanup/repair for safety will be covered, evidence replacement, or funeral expenses.

In order to qualify for compensation, the victim must have been harmed as the result of a crime that caused a substantial threat of personal injury or death. This includes assault, sexual assault, domestic violence, homicide, menacing and stalking. Some motor vehicle crimes are also considered to be "eligible offenses." These include operating a vehicle while impaired, fleeing a felony, vehicular assault or homicide, or a hit and run. The crime must be reported to the police within 72 hours of the incident, and the claim must be made to the attorney general's office within two years of the event.

Another requirement for compensation is that the victim shall not have committed a criminal act that caused or contributed to their injuries. Additionally, the victim must have incurred expenses that are not fully covered by collateral sources such as insurance, Social Security, Medicare/Medicaid, or workman's compensation. If the victim is underaged, the application must be filed by his or her 20th birthday or within two years of the date a complaint, indictment, or information is filed against the alleged offender, whichever is later.

If an Ohio resident becomes the victim of a crime while outside of Ohio, that victim may still receive compensation. However, a claim must first be filed in the state where the original offense occurred. At the same time, a non-resident who becomes the victim of a crime while in Ohio may apply for compensation from the attorney general.

Some victims may not be eligible for compensation. Offenders and accomplices are prohibited from receiving money. Moreover, a person who committed a violent felony or drug trafficking offense within the ten years prior to the crime that caused the injury or during the time the claim was pending, is prohibited from receiving money. A person who was convicted of a child endangering or a domestic violence offense within ten years prior to the crime that caused the injury or during the time the claim was pending is also not eligible for compensation. Moreover, compensation will not be provided for pain and suffering, stolen, damaged, or lost property (Ohio Attorney General).

Not all victims who apply for the state compensation receive it. Each case is reviewed carefully by personnel in the attorney general's office to determine if the victim is eligible. When their investigation is completed, a representative from the attorney general's office will file a Finding of Fact and Recommendation with the Ohio Court of Claims. Personnel in the Court of Claims will then determine whether or not an award will be granted. Table 10.2 shows the number of claims paid by type of crime, as well as the total amount paid by crime category. It is clear that the crime for which most claims are made is as-

Table 10.2: Payment Statistics by Crime Category

Type of Crime	Number of Claims Paid	Total Amount Paid by Category
Assault	3,361	$3,713,625
Homicide	558	$2,995,112
Sexual Assault	292	$205,003
Child Abuse	487	$373,297
DWI/DUI	39	$113,402
Other Vehicular Crimes	241	$809,285
Stalking	166	$114,249
Robbery	493	$488,764
Terrorism	0	0
Kidnapping	14	$14,027
Arson	0	0
Total	5,651	$8,826,764

Source: Office of Victim Compensation, Victims of Crime Act, State Compensation Program; 2013 Ohio State Wide Compensation Report; http://ojp.gov/ovc/grants/sbsmap/ovccp13oh1.htm

Table 10.3: Total Expenses Paid by Service

Medical/Dental	$2,616,146
Mental Health	$279,458
Economic Support	$4,226,296
Funeral/Burial	$1,186,006
Crime Scene Cleanup	$25,286
Forensic Sexual Assault Exams	$2,932,384
Other	$493,572

Source: Office of Victim Compensation, Victims of Crime Act, State Compensation Program; 2013 Ohio State Wide Compensation Report; http://ojp.gov/ovc/grants/sbsmap/ovccp13oh1.htm

sault, which also has the highest payout. In second place was homicide for both number of claims made and the total amount paid.

The maximum amount a person can claim is $7,500. Since the program began in 1976, the Crime Victims Compensation Fund has paid out $300 million to thousands of Ohioans. The fund is overseen by the attorney general's office and funded through federal grants, criminal fines, and license fees, and not through citizen taxes. Table 10.3 shows the money granted to victims by expense category. According to this, the highest amount of money was given to victims for economic support. The second highest was Forensic Sexual Assault Exams, followed by medical/dental costs.

Victim Notification Laws

The Attorney General oversees another important service for victims in Ohio called Victim Information and Notification Everyday (or VINE). This is a free, anonymous computer program that provides victims of crime with information about their case. The goal is to notify the victim about the status of the offender throughout the entire criminal justice system. VINE is operated by the Ohio Attorney General's office in conjunction with the Buckeye State Sheriff's Association, the Ohio Prosecuting Attorneys Association, the Ohio Department of Rehabilitation and Correction, and the Ohio Department of Youth Services.

Victims can choose whether to register with the VINE program. Once registered, a victim will receive comprehensive information on the offender's status, any changes in that status. They will also be informed of any upcoming hearings (including things like parole hearings, clemency hearings), results of the hearings, any escapes or attempted escapes, or if the offender is transferred to another prison in Ohio or moved to another state (Ohio Department of Rehabilitation and Correction, 2011a). If relevant, VINE provides a victim with a scheduled execution date for the offender. This information is available to victims 24 hours a day, 365 days a year. A victim may call the tollfree VINE hotline to access this information, which is available in both English and Spanish. Callers may also register with VINE to receive telephone notification of any changes in the custody status if the offender. A live operator is available 24 hours a day to assist callers in accessing information or registering for VINE.

The notification program was expanded in 2013 when the Ohio General Assembly passed a new law entitled Roberta's Law. This regulation expanded victim notification regarding the release or transfer of an offender under custody. If an offender was convicted of aggravated murder, murder, a first-, second- or third-degree violent crime or was sentenced to life in prison, the victim will be automatically notified of significant changes or events. If a victim does not wish to be notified of an inmate's release or transfer, they can opt out of the program.

Some of the important events an offender may be informed of include the date an offender is to be released from prison; any upcoming hearings such as parole and clemency hearings; the offender's involvement in early release programs; any escapes from custody; the offender's death, shall it occur; the offender's scheduled execution date (in death penalty cases); an offender's return to a county for a local hearing; the offender's transfer to another state.

Ohio Department of Rehabilitation and Correction

Additional services and programs designed to help victims are found within the Ohio Department of Rehabilitation and Correction. Many of the programs are delivered by the Office of Victim Services, as described below.

Office of Victim Services

The Ohio Department of Rehabilitation and Corrections is comprised of the Division of Parole and Community Services, which in turn is comprised of four bureaus, one of which is the Office of Victim Services (OVS). They provide assistance to victims and advocate for them throughout the entire justice process.

OVS can be traced back to 1980 when the Ohio Parole Board began notifying victims of upcoming parole hearings. The Board members quickly recognized the importance of having input from the victims of crime in the decision-making process. Then in 1987, the General Assembly passed Senate Bill 6 that allowed crime victims the right to submit a statement to the Parole Board describing their experiences when the offender came up for parole. The Department of Rehabilitation and Correction further expanded the rights of victims in 1994 when they established new policies to provide victim services throughout the Department. The General Assembly then passed Senate Bill 2 in July of 1996. This bill, also called the "truth in sentencing" bill, mandated that victims be given information from the time an offender is arrested through the trial and sentencing phases and even beyond. Also in Senate Bill 2 was a plan to establish the Office of Victim Services within the Department of Rehabilitation and Correction.

The mission of the OVS is "to work in partnerships to make a positive difference in the lives of crime victims, by affording them meaningful participation throughout the Ohio corrections process" (Ohio Department of Rehabilitation and Correction, 2011a & b). Alongside of this is their Vision Statement, which reads, "Crime victims are informed, involved and understand their rights throughout the corrections process and that all victims are treated with dignity and afforded comprehensive, effective and culturally competent services" (Ohio Department of Rehabilitation and Correction, 2011a).

Currently, OVS is comprised of three sections: administration, regional victim advocates, and notification. It is the responsibility of the regional victim advocates' to assist victims and their families in understanding their rights in throughout the trial and sentencing processes. These victim advocates, which are located throughout the state, serve as liaisons between the victim and the criminal justice system, as they help the victim through the process.

Even after the offender is sentenced to a facility, OVS provides victims with many services. This includes notifying the victim of the status of the offender, Victim Conference Day, Full Board Hearings, Victim-Offender Dialogue, Crisis Intervention, and Education. They address the concerns of victims regarding inmates and offenders, provide information regarding the status of inmates or parolees, provide support for surviving family members. They also have programs to educate the community and make referrals to other state and local services within the community as needed.

Since its inception, OVS has played an important role in providing development, training and monitoring of the Victim Awareness Program that exist throughout the state of Ohio (Department of Rehabilitation and Correction, 2011b). The services they provide to victims include those described in Figure 10.1.

Figure 10.1: Services Provided to Victims by the OVS

- Crisis intervention and advocacy throughout the corrections process.
- Assisting victims with concerns related to inmates and parolees under our jurisdiction.
- Information regarding status of inmates in prison or under supervision of the Department's Adult Parole Authority.
- Community education about policies and procedures of the Department of Rehabilitation and Correction.
- Referrals to other state and community services.
- Petitions the Parole Board for Full Board hearings as appropriate.
- Monitors network of Victim Coordinators located in each prison and Adult Parole Authority district office throughout the state, serving as liaisons for the Office of Victim Services.
- Provides education to Department staff to increase awareness of victims' issues.
- Assists Parole Board and Adult Parole Authority's parole and probation staff in identifying victims' issues and provides input into decision-making process as appropriate.
- Facilitates meetings of the Department of Rehabilitation and Correction's Ohio Council on Victims Justice.

Source: Ohio Department of Rehabilitation and Correction, "Office of Victim Services" available at http://www.drc.ohio.gov/web/VICTIM.HTM.

Parole Board Victim Notification Section

Victims of inmates who are incarcerated in one of Ohio's prisons may register with the Victim Notification Section of the Parole Board. If they choose to do this, a victim will be notified by officials before any hearings to consider the possible release of the inmate. When a hearing occurs, a victim can choose to write to the Board or personally voice their concerns in an interview with members of the Parole Board. A "victims' conference day" is held once a month for this purpose.

Conference Day

Another way that the OVS attempts to help crime victims is through their monthly Conference Day. This is a time during which members of the Ohio Parole Board reserves time to meet with crime victims, their families and survivors to discuss their feelings about an offender's upcoming parole hearings. In this discussion, the victim or survivors are able to share relevant information with the Board members that they can consider at the hearing with the inmate. Victims are also given the option of participating in the Conference Day via phone. Offenders are not permitted to participate in the Conference Day hearings. Very often, as a way to explain the impact of the crime to parole board members, many families bring photographs, letters, and video or audio tapes to share with the Board (Ohio Department of Rehabilitation and Correction, 2011c).

Victim Awareness Program

The Victim Awareness Program is a restorative justice program offered by OVS that requires offenders to acknowledge and be responsible for the harm they caused through their criminal behavior. The program was initiated in the London Correctional Institution in 1995 and then later expanded to other facilities in the state. It is also available for those offenders on parole or in halfway houses and other community based correctional facilities. This program gives offenders the opportunity to think about their offenses from the victim's point of view. Through this reflection, the offender will be able to understand how their actions affected the victim, their families and their friends. It also permits offenders to take responsibility for their criminal actions. This is important to provide the chance for offenders to see things from a different point of view.

Through written exercises, group discussions and activities, offenders learn to understand the repercussions of their crimes. When appropriate, victim impact panels bring the offender face to face with a person who has been directly affected by the crime. Victims or the survivors volunteer to tell offenders about their experiences (Ohio Department of Rehabilitation and Correction, 2011c). This means that the victims can play a role in the justice process.

The premise behind the program is that the majority of offenders are not incarcerated for violent offenses. Thus, it is argued that the programs encourage offenders to accept responsibility for their actions. They help the tendency of offenders to blame others, and thus increase their ability to accept responsibility for their actions. This is because many offenders were not fully aware of the impact their crime had on victims (Department of Rehabilitation and Correction, 2011b).

The program was updated and revised in 2009 to include a section on the media that provides offenders with a better understanding of the impact the media has on issues surrounding crime victims. Another new aspect is Forgiveness/Making Amends in which offenders develop an understanding of the concept of forgiveness from the victim's point of view (Department of Rehabilitation and Correction, 2011b). The program in Ohio also includes a gender-specific curriculum for female offenders. This covers female domestic violence and female sex offenders.

Additionally, ODRC implemented a new 13-week program intended for high-risk offenders who are scheduled for release into the community. The goal of the new program is to increase offenders' awareness of how crime affects victims and the community. If offenders do not begin to empathize with the victim they will not be able to begin the process of mending the harm done. Throughout the program offenders are encouraged to accept responsibility for their crimes.

The program covers:

- Community Justice
- Cultural Barriers
- Media Issues
- Property Crime and Identity Theft
- Substance Abuse
- Drunk Driving
- Domestic Violence and Stalking
- Family Violence
- Sexual Assault
- Homicide
- Forgiveness and Making Amends
- Reentry

The frequency of meetings vary, depending on the institution. The classes are held primarily once a week and last approximately an hour and a half or two hours. Courses are taught in a group setting, and offenders are encouraged to participate. In Ohio, victim impact speakers are invited to participate. These speakers provide offenders with more information as to how their crimes have forever affected the lives of their victims. The speakers can be direct victims of crime in addition to their surviving family members (i.e., parents of murdered children). Speakers describe how their lives were changed by the crime.

Studies of these programs have proven that both male and female offenders participating in the program develop a better understanding of how their crime affected more than just the direct victim. The offenders also demonstrated a noticeable change in taking responsibility for their actions. Male offenders recognized the seriousness of both physical and non-physical abuse. The men also acknowledged how hurtful it can be for victims when the trust they had in their abuser is taken advantage of. Female offenders demonstrated an increase in their knowledge of how drug and alcohol abuse increases the likelihood of child abuse or neglect.

Apology Letters

In some cases, offenders will write apology letters to their victims as a way to show their accountability for the offense, remorse, or as a way to acknowledge the pain caused by the actions. Most of the time, the letters are not sent directly to the victims. The victim must first agree to accept a letter from the offender. If an offender writes a letter, it will be reviewed by the ODRC. Sometimes the letters are not sent but are stored in ODRC until a later date (Ohio Department of Rehabilitation and Correction, 2011e).

Witnessing Executions

In some cases, victims' families have the right to witness an offender's execution, and the OVS will assist those victims through this process. According to Administrative Regulation 5120-9-54 and DRC Policy, up to three people can be chosen by the victim's family to witness an execution. In the period before the execution, OVS will maintain contact with the victim to notify them of different proceedings and hearings. Just prior to the execution, the witnesses will be taken to the death house by a representative from OVS (Ohio Department for Rehabilitation and Correction, 2011f). Afterwards, they are then again escorted out of the prison and taken to an area where they will be safe.

Ohio Council on Victims Justice

The Ohio Council on Victims Justice is an organization whose role it is to improve the programs designed to assist victims of crime that are provided by the DRC. The group makes suggestions for changes to existing programs, or even new programs that could be implemented to help victims. They often have contact with victims, making them liaisons between the Department and the victims.

The Council also helps to educate the public about response to victims by meeting with professional associations and discussing victim issues. They also serve as a source of information for the on correctional issues relevant to victims. Members of the council represent victims, victim service coalitions, law enforcement, prosecutors, judges, and other stakeholders (Ohio Department of Rehabilitation and Correction, 2014).

Victim Coordinators—
Institutions and Parole Offices

Every correctional institution and parole office in Ohio has a staff member who has been assigned to serve as the "victim coordinator." These staff members respond to victim issues and concerns at the local level and serve as liaisons to the Office of Victim Services.

Juvenile Offenders

Some services are available specifically for the victims of juvenile offenders through the OVS and the Ohio Department of Youth Services (DYS). A victim of juvenile crime will receive (Ohio Department of Rehabilitation and Correction):

- Notification of the specific rights of victims of juvenile under Ohio law, including the right to designate a victim representative;
- A Victim Impact Statement to be completed by the victim or designated representative to identify the impact of the crime upon the victim; and
- A Victim Notification Form (VNF), which may be completed by the victim and returned to OVS to secure the following provisions and considerations:
  - Information, referral services and advocacy on behalf of the victims throughout the juvenile corrections process;
  - An opportunity to meet in person, or to speak by telephone with a representative of the Release Authority;
  - Information regarding the status of a youth committed to DYS institution or under parole supervision;
  - Notification of upcoming reviews, releases, discharges, and revocation decisions;
  - Information regarding policies and procedures of the Department of Youth Services, including the operation of the Release Authority and the Office of Victim Services;
  - Referrals to appropriate federal, state, or local community resources, including victim service agencies;
  - Notification of a letter of apology available to the victim, if such a letter was written by the youthful offender;
  - Opportunity to meet with the offender, if requested by the victim, to participate in a victim offender mediation process; and

◦ Opportunity for the victim of crime to participate in a victim impact panel and to speak directly to incarcerated youth regarding the impact the crime had on the victim.

Justice League of Ohio

In addition to state agencies, private groups also help to ensure the rights of crime victims. One of these groups, The Justice League of Ohio, is an organization that was founded on the idea that crime victims deserve and require legal representation that will protect their legal rights throughout criminal justice proceedings. The groups is the only crime victims' rights legal center in the state that provides free legal representation in criminal court to citizens victimized. The group also provides free training on victims' rights to hospitals, victim advocates, law enforcement, prosecutors, courts, and the community (Justice League of Ohio).

Summary

For many years, officials in Ohio have recognized that the impact of a crime on a victim can be long-lasting and can include economic, medical and psychological effects. In order to help victims recover from the crimes, officials have created many programs designed to provide a variety of services to victims. They range from providing money to help cover the costs of medical treatment to allowing the victim to express the extent of the harm in a courtroom. In some programs, victims can even interact with offenders as a way to provide a sense of justice. In the end, the available programs help the victim mend and regain their sense of security once again.

Key Terms

Apology Letters
Conference Day
Crime Victims Services Section
Justice League of Ohio
Office of Victim Services
Ohio Council on Victims Justice
Outreach Initiative

Victim Awareness Program
Victim Compensation
Victim Coordinators
Victim Impact Statement
Victim Notification
Victim Rights and Restitution Act
VINE

Resources

Ohio Attorney General's Office — Services for Victims
  http://www.ohioattorneygeneral.gov/Individuals-and-Families/Victims
Ohio Department of Rehabilitation and Correction Office of Victims Services
  http://www.drc.ohio.gov/web/victim.htm
Ohio Victim Witness Association
  http://www.ovwa.org/
Restorative Justice Online
  http://restorativejustice.org/

Review Questions

1. Describe the rights promised to victims in the Ohio Constitution and the Ohio Revised Code.
2. Who is eligible for compensation from the crime victims fund, and for what purposes can the money be used?
3. What is the purpose behind the Conference Day and Victim Awareness Programs?
4. How do the Attorney General's Office and the ODRC help victims of crime recover from their victimization?
5. How does the Justice League of Ohio help victims?
6. Describe how victims of juvenile offenses are assisted.

References

Cassell, P. G., (2009). "In Defense of Victim Impact Statements." *Ohio State Journal of Criminal Law*, Vol 6, 611–648.
Justice League of Ohio; Retrieved from http://www.thejusticeleagueohio.org/.
National Center for Victims of Crime. (2012). "Ohio" Retrieved from http://www.victimsofcrime.org/our-programs/public-policy/amendments/ohio.
Ohio Attorney General, "Ohio Victims of Crime Compensation Program." Retrieved from http://www.zamoralaw.com/documents/Victims-Compensation-Application-(PDF).pdf.
Ohio Attorney General's Office. (2014). "Crime Victim Services Section Outreach Initiative." Retrieved from http://www.ohioattorneygeneral.gov/

Individuals-and-Families/Victims/Crime-Victim-Services-Section-2014-Outreach-Initia.

Ohio Crime Victim's Rights. Retrieved from http://www.ohioattorneygeneral.gov/getattachment/6a036767-97bc-41d5-bff9-81b8ee3e5dbd/Picking-Up-the-Pieces-A-Guide-to-Helping-Crime-Vic.aspx.

Ohio Department of Rehabilitation and Correction, Office of Victim Services. (2011a). "Victim Notification." Retrieved from http://www.drc.ohio.gov/web/OVSNotification.pdf.

Ohio Department of Rehabilitation and Correction. (2011b). "Victim Awareness Program," pg. 3. Retrieved from http://www.publicsafety.ohio.gov/links/ocjs_VictimAwarenessStudy2011.pdf.

Ohio Department of Rehabilitation and Correction, Office of Victim Services. (2011c). "Victim Conference Day." Retrieved from http://www.drc.ohio.gov/web/OVSconference.pdf.

Ohio Department of Rehabilitation and Correction, Office of Victim Services. (2011d). "Victim Awareness Program." Retrieved from http://www.drc.ohio.gov/web/OVSawareness.pdf.

Ohio Department of Rehabilitation and Correction, Office of Victim Services. (2011e). "Apology Letters." Retrieved from http://www.drc.ohio.gov/web/OVSapology.pdf.

Ohio Department of Rehabilitation and Correction, Office of Victim Services. (2011f). "Witnessing Executions in Ohio." Retrieved from http://www.drc.ohio.gov/web/OVSExecution.pdf.

Ohio Department of Rehabilitation and Correction. (2014). "Victim Services." Retrieved from http://www.drc.state.oh.us/web/victlist.htm.

Ohio Department of Youth Services. "Victim Services." Retrieved from http://www.dys.ohio.gov/dnn/InsideDYS/DYSDivisions/VictimServices/tabid/132.

Index